GREAT PEOPLE

of the

20th

CENTURY

TIME

THE WEEKLY NEWSMAGAZINE

MANAGING EDITOR	Walter Isaacson
PRESIDENT	E. Bruce Hallett
VICE PRESIDENT	Kenneth Godshall
SPECIAL PROJECTS EDITOR	Barrett Seaman

GREAT PEOPLE OF THE 20TH CENTURY

EDITOR	Kelly Knauer
ART DIRECTOR	Anthony Kosner
RESEARCH DIRECTOR	Leah Gordon
PICTURE EDITOR	Rose Keyser
ESSAY	Lance Morrow
COPY DESK	Bruce Christopher Carr
	Bob Braine
RESEARCH ASSOCIATES	Anne Hopkins, Valerie J. Marchant
RESEARCH ASSISTANT	Rudi Papiri

TIME INC. NEW BUSINESS DEVELOPMENT

DIRECTOR	David Gitow
ASSOCIATE DIRECTOR	Stuart Hotchkiss
ASSISTANT DIRECTOR	Peter Shapiro
FULFILLMENT DIRECTOR	Mary Warner McGrade
DEVELOPMENT MANAGERS	Robert Fox, Michael Holahan,
	John Sandklev, Alicia Wilcox
EDITORIAL OPERATIONS MANAGER	John Calvano
PRODUCTION MANAGER	Donna Mianb-Ferrara
FINANCIAL MANAGER	Tricia Griffin
ASSOCIATE DEVELOPMENT MANAGERS	Ken Katzman, Daniel Melore
	Allison Weiss, Dawn Weland
ASSISTANT DEVELOPMENT MANAGER	Charlotte Siddiqui
MARKETING ASSISTANT	Lyndsay Jenks

GREAT PEOPLE
of the
20th
CENTURY

BY THE EDITORS OF

TIME

CONTENTS

"I wish to preach, not the doctrine of ignoble ease, but the doctrine of the strenuous life."

—Theodore Roosevelt

THE LEADERS   4

"… one's opponent … must be weaned from error by patience and sympathy."

—Mohandas Gandhi

THE ACTIVISTS   48

"I saw a fleet of fishing boats … I flew down … and yelled at them, asking if I was on the right road to Ireland."

—Charles Lindbergh

THE PIONEERS   86

*"A car for the masses ...
one in every family ...
Nothing will do as much
to make good roads as
a car in every family."*

—Henry Ford

THE INNOVATORS 108

*"... a spirit is manifest in
the laws of the Universe ...
in the face of which ... we
must feel humble."*

—Albert Einstein

THE SCIENTISTS 130

*"God is really [an] artist.
He invented the giraffe, the
elephant and the cat. He
has no real style. He just
keeps trying other things."*

—Pablo Picasso

THE CREATORS 152

FOREWORD

READERS OF A BOOK THAT DARES TO NAME THE "GREAT PEOPLE OF THE CENTURY" deserve to know the editors' definition of greatness. In weighing the candidates for this volume, TIME's editors employed the same criteria used in designating the magazine's annual Man or Woman of the Year: choosing those individuals who have made the greatest impact on history—for good or evil. Thus Adolf Hitler (Man of the Year 1938) and Joseph Stalin (1939 and 1943), though they are among the deadliest mass murderers of history, are included. Three further points about the selections should be made.

First, considerations of race, creed, gender and nationality were not employed as criteria in the selection process. Nor did we attempt to "balance" the list of profiles along such lines. As a result, the book includes significantly more men than women—a reflection less of our judgment than of the prevailing social climate for most of the century.

Second, because TIME was not published until 1923, the early years of the century are slightly under-represented in these pages. The book's first profile, Theodore Roosevelt, is drawn from a TIME cover story that appeared in 1958, marking the centennial of T.R.'s birth.

Third, important figures whose major work was completed in the 19th century but who lived into the 20th century (Leo Tolstoy and Thomas Edison, for instance) were not considered for the book.

Every reader of these pages will find favorite people missing—no Ronald Reagan? no Anwar Sadat? no Katharine Hepburn? But the book's length was finite—and the editors miss them too!

GODS AND DEMIGODS IN AN EXPANDING UNIVERSE

By Lance Morrow

T HE HISTORY OF THE WORLD," THOMAS CARLYLE wrote in 1841, "is but the biography of great men." That was the 19th century's majestic self-importance speaking—individualist, commanding, and grandiloquent: man in charge of destiny. Carlyle invented the Great Man approach to history. At the end of the 20th century, looking back a hundred years, we are inclined to see that destiny has many components—impressive, headlong, sometimes scary and unpredictable.

We amend Carlyle to say: "The history of the world is the richly complicated story of men and women and accidents and ideas—of astonishing inventions (the flying machine, the automobile assembly line, radio, air conditioning, television, the computer, the spacecraft, the communications satellite, and so on); of ideology (Marxism-Leninism, for example) and religious faith and its political manifestations (in Islam, say), of racial, ethnic and tribal hatreds (Nazi Germany, the Middle East, Bosnia, Rwanda); of diseases (the flu epidemic of 1918-19 that killed 20 million people worldwide, or polio, or AIDS), of brilliant progress and evil regressions.

"It is the story not only of a few Great Men and Women, but of masses of ordinary men and women. In the 20th century, those masses—in their migrations, to America and elsewhere, and in the sheer restless pressure of their numbers (in China, for instance, or in India and Africa)—have driven the human narrative as powerfully as any statesmen or dictators have."

Yet the lives of the great still have an exemplary fascination in them. Their stories are our version of the gossip-filled and wonder-working and sometimes doom-laden careers of the gods and goddesses in Homer. They fly through the upper air of their dazzling power and publicity, they plot against one another on Olympus, and they descend to intercede in the affairs of ordinary mortals. They may take the form of a swan or somesuch, in order to—what?—pleasure themselves? Or inject into ordinary life the seed of the supernatural?

This book, containing the stories of some of the 20th century's gods and goddesses—great men and women in their struggles with an age incomparably bright and incomparably dark—is a sort of Homeric inventory of recent time. The book traces, through its 80-some full-length lives, both the immense changes that have occurred in the century but also the change in our conception of greatness itself.

Carlyle's formulation implied a model of greatness with certain implicit characteristics. Carlyle meant Great Leaders, and Great Leaders, in his 19th century universe, almost inevitably suggested maleness and the context of great powers lumbering across history with military force. The silhouettes of Frederick the Great and Napoleon and Wellington, or of statesmen like Metternich and Disraeli, loomed over his idea of the sort of people who write "the history of the world."

The 20th century is the story of an expanding universe of

A richly complicated story of accidents and inventions

history. Forces destructive or wonderful—and now and then both of those at once—have driven it. The lowest impulses of human nature (an instinct toward death and annihilation) have coexisted with the most glorious creative human urges—genocide and space travel, Hiroshima and Salk vaccine.

The Carlyle Great Man formula serves best in discussing, say, Churchill and F.D.R. and Hitler and Stalin. For the first half-century or so of TIME's career, the magazine instinctively interpreted events in Carlyle's terms. But the Great Man approach is inadequate to make a full exploration of the expanding universe, to appreciate what amounts to a new physics of history. And TIME has changed accordingly.

In any case, the Great Man idea needs to be enlarged to become, obviously, the Great Person idea, and after that, rethought to comprehend a more diverse idea of greatness, one that will take account not only of the great monster (Hitler) but also of the comic genius (Chaplin) who satirized him; will understand Mao Zedong, but also Carl Jung, Jacques Cousteau, Walt Disney, the Beatles, and Bill Gates.

DEMOCRACY AND TECHNOLOGY HAVE FORMED A partnership in recent years, each driving and nourishing the other. Much of the world—even those parts under the tyranny of dictators or poverty—has been touched by a global democracy of communications. If the possibilities of history are expanding, it is because of this potent force, a lift-off of much human enterprise from the agricultural and industrial to the electronic and informational. Communications satellites hover over the world and human affairs as far-darting Apollo and Pallas Athena once hung brightly in the air above the Trojan and Greek armies.

In August 1945 over the Japanese city of Hiroshima, the apocalyptic possibility of virtual global destruction by nuclear war was born. Today we are exploring the happier possibilities of a collective global destiny. The fax machine, CNN, the Internet, the ubiquitous international telephone, have all obliterated the traditional physics of time and space on the planet. The sense that distance equals one's rate of speed times time has been replaced with the principle of the instantaneous. Such communications have enabled the global interpenetrations of business, or farflung product assembly and distribution across continents.

For all that the arena has changed, the characteristics of greatness remain mostly the same as they were in Homer's time. It is a good idea to approach greatness modestly, by acknowledging that it is a mystery, as leadership ultimately is.

Beyond that, greatness in a human being is, first of all, a vital sign. Greatness is almost always vivid—either clearer and more luminous than the ordinary, or, in its appalling forms, darker and more terrible.

We think of greatness as the embodiment, in one person, of what the human creature is capable of—a kind of pioneering demonstration, whereby the rest of us may learn the map of our own possibilities for good or evil. Hitler's career established a sort of base line of evil in the 20th century—not entirely because of the sheer numbers of people he destroyed (Stalin, for example, probably destroyed millions more) but because of the satanic and hyperrational advertence of the Nazi enterprise, perpetrated, ominously, by the people of Bach and Beethoven and Goethe.

Franklin Roosevelt, on the other hand, defined a new base line of buoyant optimism and sanity in the face, first, of his personal affliction (paralyzing polio), then national economic calamity (the Great Depression) and then of international evil (the Axis). F.D.R. turned government into a high political art and, to some, elevated it to a kind of sanctity, a principle of salvation. That lofty trajectory later crashed to earth, in the aftermath of the Great Society and Vietnam and a painful accompanying understanding of the limits of government.

It is often said, in a traditional way (meaning in the realm of statecraft, war, national destiny and so on) that the times call forth the leaders, people who rise to the occasion of the crisis. The 20th century contains many cases to prove the theory—Churchill inspiriting England in the early days of World War II, for example.

Yet in that same arena, one can think of far more instances when no greatness arose to meet the challenge, when the crisis went on and on, unresolved. Very little in history is inevitable—and certainly greatness is not. Where is the greatness, for example, that might lead the Irish out of the everlasting "troubles"?

It has also been said that genius is the collision of a mind with its proper object. Greatness is the inspired and no doubt lucky introduction of a personality to its proper work in the world. In the 1820s, when the British Cabinet summoned the Duke of Wellington and asked him who was the ablest general to take Rangoon, the unhesitating reply was "Lord Combermere." "But we have always understood that your Grace thought Lord Combermere a fool," the Cabinet protested. "So he is a fool, and a damned fool," said Wellington. "But he can take Rangoon." Rangoon, the Duke of Wellington meant, was Lord Combermere's proper, destined object.

Greatness is changeable. Great men and women look very

In our time the lowest impulses of human nature have

different from different points in time. Take Harry Truman, for example. When the giant Franklin Roosevelt died in 1945, just at the end of World War II, his obscure Vice President stepped into those enormous historical shoes with a sense of his own inadequacy; the American people and the rest of the world shared Truman's view of Truman. Here to lead the U.S., the Allies and the Free World, almost everyone agreed, came an ordinary ex-haberdasher from Independence, Missouri, a Democratic Party hack, a man without even a college degree, and, it seemed, no more eloquence than the average Rotarian at a weekly luncheon meeting in Kansas City. Hopeless.

Truman served out the rest of Roosevelt's fourth term and then was elected in his own right in 1948 in the most famous electoral upset of the century. Truman gained ground and stature over the years of his presidency, and then in the early '50s, he seemed to lose it again, and in the midst of the Korean War, his popularity sank to the lowest level (23%) of any post-World War II President.

Today, Harry Truman is generally counted among the great or near-great Presidents of the century. The lesson of his story is especially important to remember in an era still governed, so to speak, by the metaphysics of Marshall McLuhan and Andy Warhol, wherein everyone is supposedly entitled to be famous for 15 minutes, and then is ritually slain and exiled to Outer Obscurity. In either direction (obscurity-to-greatness or greatness-to-obscurity), the judgments of history work by a dynamic of subjective ruthlessness. And today those judgments are interestingly complicated by global access to instant communications.

John Kennedy's case shows how the enduring images of greatness and the stock exchange of world opinion may change. The gods-and-goddesses analogy applies with almost gaudy aptness to the offspring of old Joe Kennedy and to their careers in politics and publicity. John Kennedy's foreshortened tour in the White House was hard to judge by objective standards. He accomplished some things and failed at some; his record was mixed and above all incomplete. Then his assassination elevated him to god of Camelot, golden American dreamboat and martyr. In the years since Dallas, 1963, however, the image has undergone a hundred revisionist reworkings—a tarnishing process, in most cases—but an amazing quantity of fairly filthy gossip has not dislodged him from the house of the gods.

Richard Nixon's passage through the multiple stages of his political life and afterlife illustrates the strange spin-and-morphing cycles of historical evaluation. Nixon seemed to many Americans the dark and devious prince of American

postwar-Cold War politics—"Tricky Dick." And yet in the years after his resignation and exile to San Clemente, California, he transformed his persona into that of international elder statesman, a back-door adviser to Presidents (even to Democrats), an improbable Yoda.

Evanescent images: publicity and hype can create a sort of historical holograph of greatness—virtual greatness rather than the thing itself. But in the longer run, we insist that greatness makes something happen. It is active, not passive. Even Gandhi's passive resistance, after all, represented a massively organized assault upon the British Empire, just as Nelson Mandela's long incarceration toppled apartheid.

An expanded idea of leadership and greatness reflects the vast expansion in this century of the ambitions and capabilities of the human mind itself. This expansion has liberated new forces of history—notably the dynamics of information and multiplicity.

THE 20TH CENTURY MIGHT HAVE ADOPTED AS ITS SLOgan a statement that the French anarchist Pierre-Joseph Proudhon made in the 19th: "The fecundity of the unexpected far exceeds the prudence of statesmen." The biggest mistake of futurists, it is said, is that they always envision the future by simply extrapolating and extending what is happening in the present; a 17th century futurist of navigation, for example, would predict bigger and bigger ships with bigger and bigger sails. The most interesting minds have always been those capable of intelligent farming in Proudhon's rich soil of the unknown, the surprising and the hitherto unimagined.

Hence the range of characters in this book, not only the giant leaders whose images rest upon the landscape of the century's history like those enigmatic stone heads on Easter Island, but also daring solitaries, like Lindbergh and Earhart, and navigators of myth and mind (Jung and Freud); and James Joyce, the Magellan of unconscious language; and Pablo Picasso, the Michaelangelo of unconscious image; and intergalactic thinkers like Albert Einstein and Stephen Hawking; and a baseball player, Jackie Robinson, who became one of the pioneers of racial integration in America.

A characteristic of greatness is its drama: it is human nature to find greatness (even horrible greatness, perhaps especially horrible greatness, tinged, as greatness sometimes is, by obsession) to be both fascinating and entertaining. The following inventory of the 20th century's most vivid figures is a dramatic measure of how, and how far, the human universe has expanded in the past 100 years. ∎

coexisted with the most glorious creative human urges

THE LE

As the century dawned, the long period of Pax Britannica still held sway: Queen Victoria died in 1901. The old order, running on sheer inertia, was shattered in World War I, which unleashed forces that would shape the century: the struggle against colonialism, the rise of revolutionary Marxism, the intense nationalism too easily corrupted into totalitarianism. The uneasy peace that followed the first great war bred monsters; an even greater war was required to silence them. And the second war gave way to a new, unnerving cold war that kept the peace only through an insane nuclear ransom: the threat of mutual assured destruction. Meanwhile, the vacuum left by the collapse of empires was filled by the voices of millions, clamoring to enjoy prosperity and dignity—now! ■

ADERS

V.I. Lenin, 1919

ROOSEVELT

Bully for you, **Theodore Roosevelt!** *You wrangled the U.S. into a new era*

DOWN THE WILDERNESS TRAIL IN NEW YORK State's Adirondack Mountains a rattletrap buckboard jolted through the night, skidding out of ruts, creaking and clattering through the silence of the forest. The night was black and misty, the horses barely under control. The passenger sat tensed, eyes screwed up behind steel-rimmed spectacles, mouth clenched like a steel clamp, his thoughts projected far out across a new century big with change. "Too fast?" the driver shouted. Theodore Roosevelt, Vice President of the U.S. and due before dawn to become President of the U.S., rattled back like a Gatling gun: "Go ahead … Go on … Go on."

Around the man in the buckboard in the dark night hung the gathering storm of change. It was Sept. 14, 1901. Eight days before, in Buffalo, the old century's President, William McKinley, had been shot by an anarchist. Now he lay dying. The needs of the hour summoned Roosevelt back from a mountain-climbing trip with the urgency of the wire from McKinley's bedside: COME AT ONCE. That day at Buffalo, Theodore Roosevelt took the oath of office as 26th President of the U.S. That day the new century was born.

A nation adrift. Everywhere the new President was beset by signs of liberty sliding out of control. The endless sweep of the frontier had recently been shut off; the trend was on to the tenement. Capital, levering itself out of the chaos of cutthroat competition, was forming monoliths of monopoly. Labor was adolescent, agitated, angry. Government was minimal at best; at worst it could be bought. As the new President saw it, the nation was lurching out of certainty into uncertainty, from faith to doubt, from classlessness to class, from dedication to don't care, in a downgrading of the land of promise into a factory in which the gates of opportunity might snap shut.

Theodore Roosevelt, peering out into the new century with the eye of the new century, was determined that those gates would remain open. "I preach the gospel of hope," he said. And Roosevelt, aware that the ineluctable reduction of distances was thrusting the U.S. and the outside world together, was also aware that the U.S. had little time in which to revive and redefine its humanity-spanning dream—and get its defenses in order—before foreign autocracy closed in. "We enjoy exceptional advantages," he said, "and we are menaced by exceptional dangers … all signs indicate that we shall either fail greatly or succeed greatly."

That Republican Roosevelt did not fail greatly and did succeed greatly is the compelling but little recognized fact behind the U.S.'s social health and world strength in this century. At

March 3, 1958

1858 Born in New York City
1901 McKinley shot; T.R. becomes President
1905 Wins Nobel Peace Prize
1912 Fails in third-party presidential run
1919 Dies at 60

home he introduced a new kind of peacetime power—the power of the U.S. government—to slap down robber barons and labor agitators and to conserve the freedoms of U.S. business and U.S. labor as American institutions. Abroad he introduced another new kind of power—deterrence, as symbolized by the U.S. armed forces—to promote American self-interest in world peace and world order. Said Roosevelt, one of the most successful peacekeepers in American history: "I have always been fond of the West African proverb 'Speak softly and carry a big stick; you will go far.' "

He went far. Roosevelt was the youngest President the U.S. ever had—in office at 42, out of office at 50. He was also, despite a succession of afflictions, the most vigorous President the U.S. ever had. An advocate of what he called "the strenuous life," he turned the White House years into a bully spectacle of romps and pillow fights with his sons, presidential judo battles with imported Japanese wrestlers, boxing matches with his aides, mass scrambles across Washington's Rock Creek with Cabinet members. The man's very countenance was strenuous. The presidential grimace—the glint behind the spectacles, the mustache, the teeth, the granite jaw, the machine-gun voice—rallied his dispirited countrymen behind his challenging concepts of freedom through order and duty and pride.

Roosevelt also had a wide-ranging, cultivated mind. He read Ronsard's verses while rowing the River of Doubt in Brazil; he wrote a biography of Missouri's Senator Thomas Hart Benton while running a couple of cattle ranches in North Dakota Territory; he identified 64 different bird species while strolling though England's New Forest before World War I. Rudyard Kipling's quintessential "man in the arena," he was an engaged intellectual, constantly courting controversy and reveling in it.

Eccentric orbit. Theodore Roosevelt was born on East 50th Street in Manhattan in 1858. His father was a merchant-banker of Dutch descent and a Lincoln Republican; his mother was a Georgia-bred secessionist. Young Teddy was a sickly, delicate boy who suffered from asthma. But he was determined to grow strong, so he organized a gymnasium in his town house—and grew strong. After years of private tutoring, he graduated Phi Beta Kappa from Harvard, where he courted and later married a Chestnut Hill belle named Alice Lee. He suffered all the torments of a young man with power hunger and high ideals who lacks any access to power. He wanted to help make government better, he claimed, but he didn't know exactly how.

Through the next 17 years Roosevelt groped toward power along what one friend called "an eccentric orbit." Shrugging off the wealthy, well-born friends who warned him that pol-

itics was "low," he was elected and re-elected as a Republican to three rambunctious years in the lower house of the New York State legislature. In the winter of 1884 his wife Alice died in childbirth, and he headed west to the solace of the silent spaces of the north Dakota Territory. There he rode the range beneath springtime stars and winter snow dust, got sworn in as a deputy by Sherriff "Hell-Roaring" Bill Jones and generally gathered in the feel of what he called "the masterful, overbearing spirit of the West."

Go east, young man. Revitalized, he headed back to the power centers of the East. He was nominated as G.O.P. reform candidate for mayor of New York City—and lost. He went to London and married a childhood playmate named Edith Kermit Carow. After settling down in Washington for six years as Civil Service Commissioner, he put in two years as police board chairman of New York City, booting out corrupt cops and promoting the worthy, and making headlines by prowling the slums with the crusading journalist Jacob Riis.

In April 1897 Roosevelt ("T.R." to most Americans) was appointed Assistant Secretary of the Navy by President McKinley. Spanish troops were pouring across the Atlantic to wipe out freedom fighters in Cuba. More ominously, Germany and Japan were building fleets to challenge Britain's empire and tilt the world balance of power. When war with Spain came in 1898, it was Roosevelt's early-warning order—issued when his superior took the afternoon off—that made possible Admiral Dewey's great victory at Manila Bay.

But T.R. craved action for himself. He helped raise, train, lead and inspire the blue-shirted, slouch-hatted Rough Riders—the 1st U.S. Volunteer Cavalry—a wonderful T.R. concoction of sinewy ranch hands and fuzzy-cheeked Ivy Leaguers, jaunty Southwesterners and ex-badmen. T.R. went into Cuba as second-in-command of the Rough Riders; when leader Colonel

AT EASE: Captured in an unusual pose—sitting still—1918

Leonard Wood was promoted, Roosevelt took over. On horseback at the head of his men, decked out in a sombrero and blue polka-dot handkerchief, T.R. caught the nation's imagination by leading the Rough Riders on his slamming, successful charge against the Spanish defenses outside Santiago.

Only six weeks after the Rough Riders landed back in the U.S., T.R. got the G.O.P. nomination for New York State Gov-

DECISIVE MOMENTS

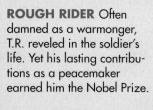

ROUGH RIDER Often damned as a warmonger, T.R. reveled in the soldier's life. Yet his lasting contributions as a peacemaker earned him the Nobel Prize.

COWPOKE T.R. went west after his first wife died, and his frontier days made him an ardent conservationist.

LEADER An energetic T.R. drags an overmatched Uncle Sam in his wake. The caption for this 1910 cartoon: "Do you follow me, Sam?"

ernor; six weeks after that he was elected. He served with distinction, but he was a nationwide hero, and his party called him to be its vice-presidential candidate in 1900. Ten months after he and McKinley were elected, he was President.

At 42, Theodore Roosevelt stood at the pinnacle of the power he had long sought. His initial efforts were aimed at capital and labor. To safeguard the right of free competition, he brought the first successful antitrust suit by an American President that dissolved a corporate monopoly, in the Northern Securities case. To safeguard the rights of working people, he arranged the first mediation between management and labor by an American President, in the anthracite coal strike. Moving on to international affairs, he sent the U.S.S. *Nashville* to Panama to support a rebellion against Panama's colonial overlord, Colombia. His long-term goal, of course, was to obtain possession for the U.S. of a canal zone in Panama, dig the canal, and in that way safeguard the defenses of both coasts of the U.S. His plan succeeded.

In March 1905 he was inaugurated President in his own right. Now T.R. hurled forth one antitrust suit after another that led to indictments, including a heavy blow at John D. Rockefeller Sr.'s mammoth Standard Oil Co. He maneuvered through congressional bear traps to pass the U.S.'s first pure-food bill, began federal inspection of slaughterhouses, even won the right for the Interstate Commerce Commission to set railroad rates. Alerted by his years in the West to the value of America's natural lands, he doubled the number of national parks, established 51 wildlife refuges and revitalized the Forest Service. T.R. was thus the great working pioneer of the 20th century's whole new trend toward federal action to watch over large sectors of public welfare.

He continued to confront the question of America's place in a shrinking world. When the Russo-Japanese War exploded in 1904, he volunteered to negotiate a peace. His tactful diplomacy led to peace—and to a Nobel Peace Prize. In one of the most visionary acts of his presidency, he sent the U.S. fleet—painted white—steaming around the world. He thus showed both Japan and Europe that the U.S. was a great world power, able to defend its interests and deter war anywhere. And he showed the people of America that from now on the U.S. was to be part of the world.

Raging Bull. When Roosevelt left the White House, the nation was on course for the century. From that point, his life was a series of steps going down, of huge energy pounding at fate for an outlet, of idealism frustrated by the lack of the mechanisms of power. Angry at his designated successor, William Howard Taft, he split the G.O.P. in 1912, launched his epic Bull Moose campaign—and handed the White House to Woodrow Wilson. He set off to explore the River of Doubt in Brazil, went big-game hunting and chronicled his exploits.

When the U.S. entered World War I, Roosevelt asked Woodrow Wilson for permission to raise a volunteer division and rush over to help the Allies. Still drawn by T.R.'s magic, 250,000 Americans volunteered, but Wilson declined. T.R. was forced to watch his four sons, Theodore Jr., Kermit, Archibald and Quentin, head off to war in his stead. When Quentin, a pilot aged 21, was shot down and killed, his grievously afflicted father wrote this tribute to his son: "Only those are fit to live who do not fear to die, and none are fit to die who have shrunk from the joys of life and the duty of life. Both life and death are part of the same Great Adventure."

At 5 o'clock on the morning of Jan. 6, 1919, Theodore Roosevelt's great adventure came to an end. Yet even as he was dying, his country was throbbing with new vitality and new hope. His last words to the American people were sent to a benefit rally in New York City. Said T.R.: "I cannot be with you, and so all I can do is wish you Godspeed." ∎

FATHER The nation was charmed by the lively goings-on as the young President raised his six children in the White House. In this 1906 picture, Alice ("Blue Gown") Roosevelt Longworth is second from right; she remained a beloved fixture in the nation's capital until her death in 1980.

HUNTER Roosevelt on safari in Kenya in 1909. Restless out of office, he roamed the world in search of exotic new experiences.

WILSON

At battle's end, Woodrow Wilson

was alone, isolated in his idealism

WAS WOODROW WILSON A GREAT President? In vision, certainly. In accomplishment, less certainly. For Wilson's great virtue—and his great fault—was that he yearned, personally and godlike, to sculpt the world. Not for him the notion that honest men may differ honestly, that democracy's ends must to be accomplished by trimming and adjusting, that politics, even world politics, was the art of the possible. His ambition was to fling a vision in the face of mankind and challenge it to respond. If the world did not quite work like that, that was the world's fault. Wilson answered only to his conscience, and his conscience answered only to God. Unfortunately, history is what actually can be accomplished. Still, if Wilson's unyielding pride ultimately destroyed him and he failed, at the least he gave men a vision that mankind still yearns to achieve.

Wilson drew his strict faith and his devotion to the power

of words from his father, a highly literate Presbyterian preacher. In the family's wanderings from Wilson's birthplace in Staunton, Virginia, throughout the South, Father Wilson would conduct morning prayers and read aloud from Dickens and Scott in the evening. Young Woodrow graduated from Princeton, studied law, briefly practiced. But mostly he wrote. At 28 he had published many articles, as well as his first book, *Congressional Government.* On the strength of these he won his academic jobs—at Bryn Mawr, then Wesleyan and finally at Princeton. There he quickly became popular with students for the wit and pith of his lectures, and he wrote prodigiously (some 12 scholarly volumes, countless published articles). In 1902, at 45, he was unanimously elected Princeton's president.

From Princeton to power. Characteristically, he set out to reshape the university, spent seven years at it, then blew up a minor issue into a matter of principle that he presented to Princeton on a well-publicized take-it-or-leave-it basis. In reality, he was already dickering with New Jersey Democratic bosses for nomination as Governor. Once in office, he soon was busy stumping the country proposing himself for President. He almost did not make it. The favorite for the Democratic nomination was House Speaker Champ Clark of Missouri. It took 46 ballots before the delegates swung to Wilson. In the election, the G.O.P. was split between William Howard Taft and the rebellious Progressives of Theodore Roosevelt. So Wilson won, with only 42% of the popular vote. In his first term, he got a tariff reduction passed, fortuitously with a constitutional amendment that authorized the first graduated income tax. He won approval of the Federal Reserve Act, which created the present banking system. Then there was the Clayton Antitrust Act, which has been called the Magna Carta of labor, since it recognized that a labor union was not to be considered an illegal combination in restraint of trade.

Personally, he was an enigma. From a podium he could move people deeply, and with his own family and a handful of intimates he could be charming and totally without stiffness. He liked to dance jigs, sing music-hall melodies, recite nonsense rhymes, tell dialect stories. He sincerely loved the common man in the abstract; it was actual contact that he shrank from. "No man would ... ever familiarly slap me on the back in a hail-fellow-well-met way. I should hate it," Wilson said.

He was passionately devoted to his first wife Ellen Axson, a Georgia girl he married at 28, and their three daughters. When she died 18 months after his Inauguration, he wailed, "Oh, my God, what am I to do?" Seven months later, he met Edith Galt, the handsome 42-year-old widow of a prosperous Washington jeweler. They were married nine months later, and thenceforth Wilson consulted her on every subject, even having her sit in on his highest councils.

The most anxious consultations involved foreign affairs, for which Wilson was admittedly ill-prepared. But the war in Europe left him no choice. He felt armed by his conviction that he was born to save the world from itself, but he found that task harder than it seemed. At first Wilson merely proclaimed U.S. neutrality. Even when German U-boats sank a U.S. tanker, followed by the sinking of the *Lusitania* without warning, he was content to protest. He squeaked through the 1916 election

CRUSADER: Wilson in Dover, England, 1919. Many Europeans loved him, but not France's Georges Clemenceau: "President Wilson and his 14 Points bore me," said he. "Even God Almighty has only 10."

largely on his domestic record and his party's cry—"He kept us out of war!"—defeating Charles Evans Hughes by the grace of some 4,000 votes, which gave him California.

Then he tried a plea for "Peace Without Victory," for he knew the only peace that could be lasting was one in which the vanquished nations were not left impoverished and embittered. Neither side responded. However, when the Germans resumed unlimited submarine warfare, Wilson asked Congress to declare war. It was to be "a war without rancor and without selfish object, without revenge." "The world," he said, "must be made safe for democracy." Wilson appointed able men to mobilize the economy and command the armed forces, never interfering with either. His real heart was in the peace, and he produced his 14 Points, a blueprint for a peaceful world that included a League of Nations.

Over there. Wilson insisted on going to the postwar conference at Versailles himself. Was he not peace's leading apostle? European crowds cheered him wildly, but their leaders were harder to sway. He finally won approval for his League of Nations, but the effort exhausted him. He returned to find mounting resistance to the treaty and to him: a group of Senators led by Massachusetts' Henry Cabot Lodge refused to accept the treaty as a package, as Wilson demanded.

Frustrated, Wilson typically decided to appeal over

November 12, 1923

1856 Born in Virginia
1901 Becomes president of Princeton
1912 Elected President in a close race
1919 Issues 14 Points, then collapses on a national speaking tour
1924 Dies at 67

the Senators' heads to the country. He set out upon a tour that took him through 30 cities in 24 days. But after speaking at Pueblo, Colorado, he collapsed with a slight stroke. A week later, a second and more severe stroke paralyzed his left side. For the next few weeks he was near death. Nobody was permitted to see him except his wife Edith, who would carry messages to his bedroom and then emerge with an answer. The press began to talk of the "Presidentess."

For seven months Wilson was an almost total recluse in the White House, but slowly his mind cleared—even though his physical state remained precarious—and his old stubbornness came back. When he was presented with Lodge's version of the League Covenant, even Edith suggested he agree to the compromise. He flatly refused. "Let Lodge compromise," he croaked. The treaty was rejected, and in the election of 1920, so were the Democrats.

Wilson moved with his wife to a quiet house on S Street in the capital. There, standing on his porch and tottering on his cane, he made his last defiant speech: "I have seen fools resist providence before, and I have seen their destruction, as it will come upon these again—utter destruction and contempt. That we shall prevail is as sure as God reigns." Three months later, at age 67, Woodrow Wilson was dead. ∎

LENIN

Messianic Marxist **V.I. Lenin** *faced a rebel's greatest challenge: success*

THE LIFE OF AN EXILED REVOLUTIONARY had its horrors: the constant fear of betrayal, the nagging suspicion of even close comrades. Nostalgia for the vast spaces of Mother Russia plunged some into deep melancholy, drove others to suicide. Vladimir Ulyanov—known as Lenin to his comrades—suffered blinding headaches and recurrent insomnia. What kept him going was a missionary fervor, a quasi-religious intoxication, not with God but with man—and with man not as Lenin knew him, but as he could be once he had been forcibly re-created. For the new man could only be forged under pressure. Lenin loved music, but he claimed he hated listening to it: "It makes you want to … stroke the heads of people who could create such beauty while living in this vile hell. But you mustn't stroke anyone's head—you'll get your hand bitten off. You have to hit them on the head, without mercy."

Lenin would keep hitting people on the head, until—in a succession of events that stemmed more from the exhaustion of the czarist regime than from the popularity of Lenin's agenda—he and his fellow communists were absolute rulers of Russia. The balding exile would preside over the first successful Marxist revolution in history, setting the stage for the ideological and geopolitical struggles that would define the 20th century. Transformed into an icon after death, demonized first by the Nazis and then by Europe and the U.S., his heritage bitterly squabbled over by followers in Russia and China, Lenin cast a long shadow that would dominate the century.

Rebel's journey. Vladimir Ilyich Ulyanov was born in the small, sleepy city of Simbirsk, deep in the Russian heartland. Son of a highly cultured schoolteacher, Vladimir and his older brother Alexander enjoyed an idyllic childhood. They swam in the Volga, hunted for mushrooms in the woods, played games invented by Vladimir with rules that he changed according to his whim. It was a habit he never lost. But unknown even to Vladimir, Alexander joined a revolutionary

April 24, 1964

1870 Born in Simbirsk, Russia
1897 Exiled to Siberia
1917 With German aid, returns to Russia to lead the revolution
1921 Crushes the revolt of the sailors
1924 Dies at 53

movement called the People's Will, and at 20 was hanged for taking part in a failed plot to assassinate the Czar. Young Vladimir vowed, "I'll make them pay for this!" Payment was to be long deferred.

Payment meant revolt against the Czar, and 19th century Europe offered young Vladimir many forms of revolution to shop among: France's utopian socialists; the British Chartists, who demanded universal suffrage and representation; the syndicalists and anarchists, who wanted to abolish the state immediately and have men live in blessed freedom. Vladimir was most influenced by the Russian revolutionary tradition stemming from the anarchists. He accepted the statement of the anarchist intriguer Nechaev: "Everything that promotes the success of the revolution is moral; everything that hinders it is immoral."

In 1888 Ulyanov—soon to be known as Lenin—discovered the works of Karl Marx. Marx predicted that the collapse of capitalism was inevitable in an advanced industrial society, and he shaped his theories to this prophecy; Lenin would apply them to a backward peasant country. Marx was inclined to sit back and let the revolution come; Lenin taught that it had to be helped along with the aid of a corps of professional revolutionaries. He owed nearly as much to Machiavelli as to Marx.

After earning a law degree, Lenin went to Switzerland to meet the exiled Georgi Plekhanov, the éminence grise of Russian Marxism; then to meetings with other radicals in Paris and Berlin; then, on his return home, to arrest, trial, jail and exile in Siberia. When he emerged from Siberia in 1900, he once again joined forces with Plekhanov and his small Social Democrat party. With other Marxists he founded a party newspaper, *Iskra* (Spark), and attended the second meeting of the party in Brussels and London in 1903.

Lenin was determined the party should remain small, highly disciplined and "as conspiratorial as possible." His more open-minded opponents wanted to take in any and all supporters, find partners and make coalitions. Lenin got his way. With their majority, the Leninists took the name of Bolshevik, after *bol-*

WORKERS OF THE WORLD, UNITE! Two years in power, Lenin leads a 1919 May Day rally in Moscow

way carriage, like a container for a deadly bacillus, and sneaked him into Russia.

And so, on April 16, 1917, after almost 20 years in exile, Lenin finally arrived by train to a tumultuous welcome at the Finland Station in Petrograd (St. Petersburg). Climbing onto an armored car, he called for revolution. Rioting broke out in July but quickly fizzled out. The Bolsheviks (who grew fourfold, to hundreds of thousands, in 1917) were banned and Lenin went into hiding in Finland.

"Little Robespierre." In October Lenin returned to Petrograd and called for an immediate revolt. Kerensky, now in command, called in troops to maintain order in the capital. But the government forces would not fight. Led by Lenin and almost without opposition, the Bolsheviks in November seized government buildings, electric plants, the post office and finally the Winter Palace, where Kerensky's Cabinet had taken refuge. The ministers were forced to resign at gunpoint.

Meanwhile, in the first democratic vote in Russian history, a Constituent Assembly was elected. Voters had rejected the Bolsheviks, but Lenin simply sent troops to disperse the new assembly. Thereafter the "Little Robespierre," as Trotsky once called him, launched his own Terror. The Czar and his family were executed, the systematic liquidation of the aristocracy and the bourgeoisie begun. For muscle, Lenin formed the Cheka (secret police), whose dread grip would last for decades.

shoi, big. The small group was called Mensheviks (minority).

Plekhanov tended to side with the Mensheviks, and so did a brilliant newcomer named Lev Bronstein, who signed his pamphlets "Trotsky." Lenin fought ruthlessly for control of the movement, but when the Russian workers rose up in the largely spontaneous revolt of 1905, Trotsky was a leader in St. Petersburg's first soviet of workers and temporarily seized power in its name. The Czar's soldiers crushed the revolt and Trotsky was jailed and later sent to Siberia. Lenin remained in exile in Switzerland, plotting. In 1912 he finally forced the Mensheviks to form a separate party.

The disasters of war and its invincible stupidity finally brought down the czarist regime. It was replaced by a provisional government under the liberal-minded Prince Lvov, and then by socialist revolutionary Aleksander Kerensky. Lenin, living in Zurich, worked feverishly to get back to Russia; the government refused. Lenin, who had received $10 million from the Germans to further the revolution, again turned to Berlin. The Germans finally provided him with a closed rail-

Not even Soviet historians are sure how Lenin's regime managed to survive the next few years: the invasion by Allied armies, the civil war, the total economic chaos. The prophet of revolt had made literally no plans for governing. He told his Bolshevik high command, "Try to nationalize the banks, and then see what to do next. We'll learn from experience."

In 1921 the sailors of Kronstadt, who had helped bring about the revolution, rose up against the Lenin regime, crying, "Enough shooting of our brothers!" The old revolutionary crushed the revolt. By some estimates, 5 million died in the first few years of his rule. A crashing economy soon forced him to trim his Marxist sails: in 1921 he instituted the New Economic Policy, a right turn toward partial capitalism that gave Russia a brief respite from monetary woes—though politically the regime remained dictatorial. This reform was to be among Lenin's last official acts, for in 1922 he suffered a series of strokes that left him paralyzed and almost speechless. He died in 1924 at only 53 years old, exhausted from a lifetime of perfecting men by hitting them on the head.　■

HITLER

Nurturing his vengeance, **Adolf Hitler**

sowed hatred and harvested sorrow

PRIL 1945: MILLIONS OF PEOPLE AROUND the world had hoped implacably for the death of a single man. Yet no end his enemies could devise for him could be as cruel as must have been Adolf Hitler's 11th-hour thoughts on the completeness of his failure. He was cornered at last, his realm reduced to an underground bunker in Berlin. Around him the Third Reich—designed by the would-be architecture student to last 1,000 years—sank to embers as flames fused over its gutted cities. His total war against non-German mankind was ending in total defeat. The historic crash of what had been Europe's most formidable state was audible in the shrieks of dying men and the point-blank artillery fire against its buckling buildings.

All that was certain to remain after 1,000 years was the almost incredible story of the fanatical man who rose by preaching hatred to make himself absolute master of most of Europe, and to change the history of the world more decisively than any other 20th century figures but Lenin and Mao. Seldom in human history, never in modern times, had a man so insignificantly monstrous become the head of a great nation. It was impossible to dismiss him simply as a mountebank, a paper hanger, a failed artist. The suffering and desolation that he wrought were beyond human power to comprehend. The bodies of his victims were heaped across Europe from Stalingrad to London. In his concentration camps—previews of hell—incinerators raged night and day to burn the bodies of those he had condemned to death. The ruin in terms of human lives was immense. It had required a coalition of the whole world to destroy the power his political inspiration had contrived.

April 14, 1941

1889 Born in Austria
1914 Serves as a corporal in World War I
1924 Jailed, he writes *Mein Kampf*
1933 Named Chancellor of Germany
1939 Invades Poland
1945 Dies in Berlin

Forging of a Führer. How had it happened? If it was necessary to exterminate Hitler and his works, it was equally necessary to try and understand him. Clearly so absurd a character, so warped and inadequate a mind—despite its cold-blooded political discernment— could not in so short a time have worked such universal havoc if it had not embodied forces of evil in the world far greater than itself.

The beginnings of the future scourge of mankind were bucolic, even idyllic. Hitler was born in 1889 at Braunau in Austria-Hungary, among the blue foot- hills of the Tyrolean redoubt. The son of an Austrian petty customs official, he was raised a spoiled child by a doting mother, Klara. His father Alois, nominally a Roman Catholic, placed his faith in the whip. When the sixth of his eight children misbehaved, he was beaten unmercifully. Alois died when Adolf was 13, a lively and artistic youth racked by the need for recognition—and the appetite for vengeance.

By Adolf Hitler's lights, there was much to avenge. Consistently failing even the most elementary studies, he grew up a half-educated young man, untrained for any trade or profession, seemingly doomed to failure. The Vienna Academy of Fine Arts twice refused to admit the apprentice painter. Very well, then, he would become an architect. But he was unqualified for further study. The rejections were aggravated by

SIEG HEIL!
Only Mao Zedong would rival Adolf Hitler in the use of dramatic rallies and potent iconography to arouse the masses. Hitler's rallies—like this outdoor extravaganza at Bückeburg in 1934—were staged by the magus of Nazi symbolism, Dr. Joseph Goebbels

the death of Hitler's beloved mother. The young man with no vices—he neither drank nor smoked nor pursued women—drifted in the city, living in flophouses, supporting himself by illustrating street scenes. His self-education was wide but shallow. Vienna was charming and cosmopolitan, peopled with brilliant artists and thinkers: Sigmund Freud, Arnold Schoenberg, Oskar Kokoschka. But Hitler dismissed modern art as "decadent." And he came to loathe Vienna for what he called its Semitism. Encountering Jews for the first time, he was swayed by the publications of Vienna's violently anti-Semitic mayor, Doktor Karl Lueger. Soon Hitler's researches revealed to him that the Jew is the enemy of all mankind, but by special malice, the particular enemy of the Germans.

In 1912 he moved from racially impure Vienna to more homogeneous Munich. To this man of no trade and few interests, World War I was a welcome event that gave him some purpose in life. For the first time, he distinguished himself: Corporal Hitler took part in 48 engagements, won the German Iron Cross, was wounded once and gassed once; he was in a hospital when the Armistice was declared in November 1918.

An orator is born. Hitler's political career began in 1919 when he became Member No. 7 of the midget German Labor Party. Soon he found one of the critical tools that would bring him to power: his voice. One night a visitor said some friendly words about Jews. Without thinking twice, Hitler burst forth in speech. He had become an orator. Soon he became the party's leader, changed its name to the Nation-

NOTORIETY Hitler, war hero General Ludendorff and comrades after the failed putsch in a Munich beer hall in 1923. The incident gave the Nazis the oxygen of publicity.

REFLECTION As a coddled prisoner in the Landsberg prison after the failed Beer Hall Putsch in 1923, Hitler worked on *Mein Kampf*. The terrible arithmetic of racial supremacy, the war and the Holocaust was prefigured on every page.

TRIUMPH With Britain's Neville Chamberlain, who ceded Czechoslovak lands to Germany in 1938, believing "appeasement" would satisfy the Führer. The Czechs were not invited to the conference.

REVENGE A gleeful Hitler celebrates his victory over France as he arrives at Compiègne, just outside Paris, for the signing of the French surrender.

GLORY Hitler's galvanic oratory was central to his hold over the German people. He claimed that "the mass, the people, is for me a woman," ready to be seduced.

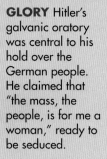

al Socialist German Labor Party—Nazi for short—and wrote its anti-Semitic, antidemocratic, authoritarian program.

The party's first mass meeting took place in Munich in February 1920. The young party Führer (leader) intended to participate in a right-wing attempt to seize power a month later, but for this abortive putsch Hitler arrived too late. An even less successful Nazi attempt—the famed Munich Beer Hall Putsch of 1923—provided the party with dead martyrs and landed Herr Hitler in jail. His incarceration at Landsberg prison (in a cozy cell, thanks to sympathetic jailers) gave him time to write the first volume of *Mein Kampf* (My Struggle). Seldom has a plotter set forth his purposes in plainer language or more explicit detail. The book included the plans for

Hitler's aggression against Germany and the rest of the world, his intense hatred of Jews, his radical triumphalism.

Hitler had been sentenced to jail for five years; he was out in nine months. His prestige had increased. One by one the perverse paladins of the Nazi inner circle gathered around him: Hermann Göring, eventual head of the air force, the Luftwaffe; Dr. Joseph Goebbels, the chief propagandist; Joachim von Ribbentrop, who became Hitler's main diplomat; Captain Ernst Röhm, the organizer of the Nazis' street army, the Brown Shirts.

Outlawed in many German districts, the National Socialist Party nevertheless climbed steadily in membership. Time-honored methods of patronage were combined with rowdy terrorism and lurid propaganda. The picture of a mystic, abstemious, charismatic Führer was assiduously cultivated. Slowly the party extended its connections among financiers, industrialists and government men. For Hitler had learned one lesson from the Beer Hall Putsch: legal, not violent, revolution was the strategy for Germany.

Triumph of the will. The situation that gave rise to this demagogic, desperate movement was the craving of large sections of the politically immature German people for strong, masterful leadership. Democracy in Germany was conceived in the womb of military defeat in World War I. The Weimar government's signature on the Versailles Treaty was a brand of shame that had never been lived down in German minds.

In the wake of the war, Russia had been taken over by Lenin's Marxist revolution. Hitler offered Germany protection against Marxism and fought communism with its own weapons. In place of the dictatorship of the proletariat, the Nazis offered the dictatorship of the party. In place of Bolshevism's scapegoat, the bourgeoisie, the Nazis offered the Jew. In place of internationalism, the Nazis offered fanatical German nationalism. In place of unemployment, the Nazis offered an economy geared to war production, with jobs for all.

The scheme worked, and the Nazis advanced through the ballot. In 1928 they won 12 seats in the Reichstag; in 1930 they won 107, and in 1932, 230. In January 1933, senescent President Paul von Hindenburg appointed Hitler Chancellor. In June 1934, Hitler carried through the Blood Purge and became absolute Führer of the Nazi Party. In August he became absolute head of the German state. The Nazis had triumphed.

THE LEGACY: U.S. Senator Alben Barkley surveys the remains of Hitler's victims at the Buchenwald camp in 1945

What Hitler did to Germany in the next few years was applauded wildly and ecstatically by most Germans. He lifted the nation from postwar defeatism. Under the swastika Germany was unified. His was no ordinary dictatorship, but rather one of great energy. The miles of magnificent highways built, schemes for cheap cars for all, grandiose plans for rebuilding German cities, made its citizens burst with pride.

But what Hitler did to the German people in those years left civilized men and women aghast. Civil rights and liberties disappeared. Opposition to the Nazi regime became tantamount to suicide. Free speech and free assembly were anachronisms. The reputations of the once vaunted German centers of learning vanished. Books were burned at propaganda rallies. Germany's Jews were tortured physically, robbed of homes and property, denied a chance to earn a living, chased off the streets. Germany became a nation of uniforms, goose-stepping to Hitler's tune, where boys of 10 were taught to throw hand grenades and women were regarded as breeding machines.

Hitler's battle to win Germany was complete. Now the ter-

rible battle to win the world began. In 1935 the Saar returned to Germany. In 1936 Germany reoccupied the Rhineland and signed a pact with equally imperialist Japan. In March 1938 Hitler seized Austria. In September he enticed Britain's aging, idealistic Prime Minister Neville Chamberlain to Munich. There the Sudetenland of Czechoslovakia was ceded to Germany as the price of "peace for our time." With memories of World War I still running deep, the leaders of Western Europe pursued the policy of appeasement with pride, committed to negotiating with Hitler rather than fighting him.

In March 1939 Hitler occupied the rest of Czechoslovakia. In April he made territorial demands on Poland, and Britain threatened war. On Aug. 23 Hitler's Nazi Germany and Stalin's Marxist-Leninist Russia—bitter enemies—agreed to sign a nonaggression pact. With his eastern flank now secure, Hitler launched a blitzkrieg—lightning attack—on Poland one week later, launching Europe into war. A series of incredible victories followed: German troops crushed Poland; rolled over Norway, the Balkans, the Netherlands; and surged through the "impenetrable" Maginot line to conquer France. Only Britain, under its new leader Winston Churchill, held Hitler at bay.

The turning point. In the spring of 1941 TIME said, "If the campaigns Hitler launches this spring are as successful as those he launched a year ago, he will ... soon be master of at least half the world." TIME misjudged the man's hubris; it expected him to move only against Greece. But intoxicated with victory, Hitler violated the pact with Stalin and invaded Russia in June 1941. Now the war had two fronts. And when the Japanese attack on Pearl Harbor drew the U.S. into the conflict the following December, Hitler finally met a situation he could not master. Four years after that fateful spring of 1941, he killed himself in his bunker.

But in those remaining years of world war, Hitler's evil policies brought death to millions, despair to millions more. His "New Order"—a system based on terror, forced labor and concentration camps—ravished occupied Europe. His long hatred of the Jews became institutionalized as the "final solution," a deliberate policy of liquidation that ended in the Holocaust, the brutal murder of 6 million European Jews.

When Hitler's armies entered Paris in June 1940, the Führer was taken on a triumphal tour of the City of Light. He paused at Napoleon's tomb, placed his cap over his heart, bowed and gazed at the crypt. Then the master of Europe turned to a favorite aide and said somberly, "You will build my tomb." But construction had already begun on that mausoleum. At its completion in 1945, it would also accommodate some 50 million others. It was called the Third Reich, and its designer was Adolf Hitler. The failed student was destined to be remembered as an architect after all. ■

CHURCHILL

How to stop Hitler? With blood, toil, tears, sweat—and **Winston Churchill**

H E WAS A KINGLY FIGURE, HIS DEEDS FIT FOR A glowing stained-glass window or rousing Shakespearean epic. He was his nation's savior, Britain's greatest statesman, the leader and inspiration of the free world. In war and diplomacy, oratory and literature, above all in his delineation of Western values, his achievements place him in the company of Pericles and Lincoln, of Wellington and Washington.

Yet Winston Churchill was an intensely human hero. He was easily moved to rage or tears; he delighted in mischief and rushed headlong into many an action he was later to regret. If he was an Elizabethan in deed and spirit, he was implacably Victorian in his ideals and dedication to duty. When he became Prime Minister at the nadir of his nation's fortunes in 1940, he had held more Cabinet posts than any other Briton in history and had seen more of war than any of his military advisers. From a lifetime of scholarship, authorship and parliamentary debate, he would soon fashion the soul-stirring prose that was to enshrine immortal deeds in immortal words.

At the end, few who paid him tribute remembered how bitterly he had been reviled in his time. Denounced in turn as charlatan, braggart, turncoat and warmonger, he was many times defeated at the polls, swept from high office, made the scapegoat of others' failures. But if Churchill was sometimes wrong, on the great issues of his times he was most often right. History will forgive his faults; it can never forget the indomitable spirit that swept a people to greatness.

For the Churchills, greatness was a birthright. Winston was born and raised amid the splendors of Blenheim Palace, the 320-room mansion that a grateful nation bestowed on his ancestor, John Churchill, the first Duke of Marlborough, for his victory in 1704 over the French in the Battle of Blenheim. His mother was a beautiful American heiress, Jennie Jerome; his father the brilliant but unsteady Tory politician Lord Randolph Churchill.

School bored young Winston; he was a poor student who most loved playing with his enormous collection of toy soldiers. Fame and glory were always his spur. As a newly commissioned officer in the cavalry, he searched impatiently for battlefields to prove his mettle. But it was a poor time for the molding of heroes; *Pax Britannica* in all its majesty prevailed throughout the civilized world.

Nonetheless, Churchill pushed himself into five wars in as many years. In some of them he managed to double as a war correspondent, thus launching

January 6, 1941

1874 Born in England
1899 Captured in Boer War, he escapes
1914 First Lord of the Admiralty in WWI
1940 As Prime Minister, he rallies England
1945 Hitler is beaten
1965 Dies in London

"Let us therefore brace ourselves to our duties, and so bear ourselves that, if the British Empire and its Commonwealth last for a thousand years, men will still say, 'This was their finest hour.'"

—Speech to the British people, 1940

"We shall not flag or fail. We shall go on to the end. We shall fight in France, we shall fight in the seas and oceans … we shall defend our island, whatever the cost may be. We shall fight on the beaches. We shall fight on the landing grounds, we shall fight in the fields and in the streets, we shall fight in the hills; we shall never surrender, and even if, which I do not for a moment believe, this island or a large part of it were subjugated and starving, then our Empire beyond the seas, armed and guarded by the British Fleet, would carry on the struggle until, in God's good time, the new world, with all its power and might, steps forth to the rescue and the liberation of the old."

—Speech to the House of Commons, 1940

"Never in the field of human conflict has so much been owed by so many to so few."

—On the British airmen in the Battle of Britain, 1940

DECISIVE MOMENTS

JAILBIRD Churchill chased glory throughout the empire, finally finding it in his gutsy escape from a Boer prison camp in 1899. This picture was taken shortly afterward.

INTO BATTLE When Churchill returned from political exile to resume his old post as First Lord of the Admiralty, Hitler's air marshal, Hermann Göring, warned his colleagues, "That means war is really on."

RUINED The Prime Minister surveys the ruins of the House of Commons, destroyed by Göring's bombers in the Battle of Britain, 1940.

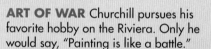

ART OF WAR Churchill pursues his favorite hobby on the Riviera. Only he would say, "Painting is like a battle."

VICTORY! In the nation's darkest hour, Churchill's bulldog bearing and stirring oratory roused Britons to defiance. Said the philosopher Isaiah Berlin: "They conceived a new idea of themselves. They went forward into battle transformed by his words."

LAST HURRAH On his 90th birthday, in 1964, Churchill greets throngs of Londoners who came to cheer him.

the first of his many celebrated careers. After covering British campaigns on India's Northwest Frontier and in the Sudan—where he figured conspicuously in one of history's last great cavalry charges—Churchill also turned out excellent books on the fighting. He had honed his style with extensive reading: Gibbon, Macaulay, Plato, Darwin, Aristotle. By 1899 he had achieved such success as author and correspondent that he resigned his commission and went off to cover Britain's war against the Boer settlers in South Africa.

Ambushed by fame. Churchill first came to public attention as the victim of an ambush, and he never forgot the lesson. Reporting the Boer War, he accepted an invitation to join a rash reconnaissance by armored railway train into enemy territory. The Boers waylaid the train. Churchill was captured, but within five weeks he made a hair-raising escape from the Boer prison at Pretoria, walked unnoticed through the crowded town, stumbled upon the only English settlement in 20 miles and was smuggled under a carload of wool to safety. All Britain acclaimed him a hero.

The hero was soon elected a Tory member of the House of Commons. In February 1901, Winston Churchill rose to make his maiden speech in its chamber, which was to be his stage for more than half a century. At 26, he was a slim, elegant figure, with his family's high forehead and prominent eyes, and his parliamentary style evoked memories of his father. He had the same rolling eloquence, the lightning shafts of wit by which a Churchill could start a storm or turn a tempest back into a teapot. But he had more: in his oratory, the English language and the English spirit came together as fuel and flame.

Churchill's subject: the Boer War. He urged civil rather than military government of conquered areas, to "make it easy and honorable for the Boers to surrender, and painful and perilous for them to continue in the field." These Churchillian themes would recur in succeeding decades: no appeasement of the armed enemy, no revenge on the beaten enemy, look ahead and remember that every action has consequences that affect the goal. He was already a serious politician.

One day in 1904, Churchill entered the House, bowed to the Speaker and, turning his back on the Conservative benches, sat down in the front row of the Liberal opposition, next to David Lloyd George, the fiery, humbly born Welshman who was to influence him profoundly. Churchill was attracted by Liberal positions on trade and social reform: in 1908, as a minister in Herbert Asquith's gifted administration, he worked tirelessly to improve the working-class Briton's harsh existence.

While campaigning in Dundee, Churchill met Clementine Hozier, the granddaughter of a Scottish countess. Sorbonne-educated and a passionate Liberal herself, she was beautiful, intelligent and 10 years younger than Winston. Their wedding in 1908 was a highlight of the social season, and as Winston reported later, they "lived happily ever afterwards."

Ratting and re-ratting. Though immersed in politics, Churchill would continue his career as historian and biographer; his solid biography of his father had appeared in 1906. Winston in those days was probably the most hated man in the House of Commons. The "Blenheim Rat," as his foes called him, was considered a traitor to his class and was ostracized by most of his friends. Then, in the summer of 1911, when imperial Germany gave the first unmistakable signs of belligerency, he turned all his energies to the study of military affairs and foreign policy. From his desk in the Home Office he bombarded the Cabinet with brash, penetrating memos on European strategy. Impressed, Prime Minister Asquith asked him if he would like to take over the admiralty. "Indeed I would," said the 36-year-old minister.

The years that followed tested to the full those Churchillian qualities—daring, prescience, determination—that were to prove his nation's deliverance in two world wars. Churchill built a massive new fleet, converted the navy from coal to oil, pressed development of Britain's first naval aircraft. He also promoted a cumbersome, comic-looking vehicle that was labeled "Winston's Folly"; it later became known as the tank.

Exile. Churchill also pushed a major effort to break the Western Front deadlock, but when it ended in a tragic failure at Gallipoli, he got the blame. He was demoted from the admiralty and resigned from the Cabinet in 1915. Characteristically, he refused to retire and lick his wounds; instead, he volunteered for duty at the front and saw trench warfare firsthand as an infantry officer in France. When the war was over, he was among the first to warn that the Versailles Treaty sowed the seeds of German vengeance; he called it "malignant and silly."

In 1924 Churchill went back to the Tory Party. "Anybody can rat," he explained with a grin, "but it takes a certain amount of ingenuity to re-rat." He was appointed Chancellor of the Exchequer, a post for whose decimal definitives he was not well suited. His first budget was the first link in the deflationary chain that led to a general strike, a nationwide depression and the fall of the second Baldwin government.

Out of the Cabinet, Churchill laid bricks and built dams at his country home, Chartwell. He took up painting, enjoyed the best food and sampled—thoroughly—the best brandy. His joie de vivre was an important element in his political leadership. The forces of dictatorship were pessimistic, hateful, sullen; Churchill loved freedom partly because he knew how to enjoy it. As a British lord once noted, "Mr. Churchill is always prepared to put up with the best of everything."

Later, during the dismal era when Hitler was rising and Britain shuttered its windows to the world, Churchill returned to the House to rumble dire warnings. Thanks to a wide-ranging unofficial network of information gatherers, his knowledge of Hitler's ambitions—and armaments—was extensive. He raged bitterly against Prime Minister Neville Chamberlain's policy of appeasement, arguing that Hitler was essentially a bully who would only respond to force. But in a Britain still shocked by the butchery of the "Great War," he was reviled as a warmonger. Still, in his role as Cassandra, Churchill may have been unheeded, but he was never unheard.

UNCOMMON HOUSE: An aging Churchill at Chartwell, the country home he maintained with the income from his writing

When Britain finally declared war in 1939, the government at last turned to Churchill. He occupied his old desk at the admiralty, and the message flashed to Royal Navy ships around the world: WINSTON IS BACK. In the spring of 1940, as Hitler invaded the Low Countries and the Nazi tide rolled toward Britain, Chamberlain was turned out. With Hitler preparing to pounce, Churchill took the reins with the ringing declaration "I have nothing to offer but blood, toil, tears and sweat."

Defiance. Single-handedly, Churchill rallied his people. No detail was too small to escape his attention. Clad in the siren suit that he invented, a cigar clamped grotesquely in the midst of his cherubic countenance, he never tired of inspecting troops or chatting with victims of the blitz, and often had to be dragged protesting from a rooftop as London shuddered under a Luftwaffe attack. He had frequently damned communism's "foul baboonery," but the Nazi invasion of Russia brought his immediate pledge of unstinting support. "If Hitler invaded Hell," Churchill argued, "I would make at least a favorable reference to the Devil in the House of Commons."

In the hour of victory after World War II, a grateful people was ready to give Churchill any honor he named. He chose instead the one reward the nation was not prepared to give—further service. Above all, war-weary Britons craved a better life. They voted for Labour and the social and economic revolution the party promised. Wounded by defeat, Churchill settled into a new job as leader of His Majesty's Loyal Opposition.

Though out of office, he was seldom out of the limelight. In 1946, speaking as a private citizen at a small college in Missouri, Churchill warned the West that the time had come to close ranks once more against a threat as sinister as any the century had seen: Stalin's Iron Curtain. Summoned by Churchill, Americans acted. In years to come, the U.S. supported NATO, the Marshall Plan and other global burdens that would have been inconceivable a decade earlier. On his return to power in 1951, Churchill saw that his warning had taken effect. When he surrendered office in 1955, the world was as tranquil as it had been at any time in the 40 years since Churchill's Grand Fleet first steamed into action against Germany.

In a lifetime that spanned the Industrial Revolution to the space age, the empire Churchill so valiantly defended had evaporated. *Pax Britannica* had become a *Pax Americana*, sustained by a weight of resolve and physical might that Churchill had fruitlessly implored his own countrymen to accept as the price of peace. Yet his words, his example and his courage were indelibly engraved on the minds of free men and women. With his passing in early 1965, the world was a vastly diminished place, and the world knew it.   ∎

DE GAULLE

Never humble, the Resistance hero earned his claim, "La France, c'est moi"—**Charles de Gaulle**

HIS BANNER, EMBLAZONED WITH THE CROSS OF Lorraine, was drawn from the frescoes of history, and under it Charles de Gaulle waged a lifelong battle for the glory of France. He rescued his nation not once but twice—first from the shame of its capitulation to the Nazis in World War II, second from its own quarreling factions. With the Fifth Republic, he gave France its first strong governmental framework since the days of Louis Napoleon. Even his name, suggestive of both Charlemagne and ancient Gaul, perfectly suited his imperious ways. Winston Churchill once moaned, "Of all the crosses I have had to bear, the heaviest was the Cross of Lorraine."

The son of a philosophy professor who taught in a Jesuit school, Charles chose the army as his profession. At France's military academy, St.-Cyr, his lean 6-ft. 4-in. frame won him the nickname "Asparagus." When World War I broke out several years later, he became a company commander and was wounded three times. Near Verdun, he was struck by shell fire and captured by the Germans. He made three unsuccessful escape attempts before he finally submitted to captivity.

After the war, as France withdrew behind the supposedly impregnable Maginot Line, De Gaulle protested against the purely defensive strategy it epitomized. His theories were vindicated in 1940 when Hitler's fast-rolling panzers outflanked the Maginot Line and knifed into France. As his nation neared surrender, De Gaulle escaped by Royal Air Force plane to London. On June 18, 1940, he spoke to the people of France from London: "Whatever happens," he cried, "the flame of French resistance must not and shall not die!"

De Gaulle had neither following, funds nor authority. The collaborationist Vichy regime condemned him to death as a traitor. No matter: he magisterially insisted that he was the acting chief of a great power and demanded an equal voice with other Allied leaders. When he returned to France in the wake of the Allied invasion in June 1944, he was a national legend. Under his guidance, France began to set up the Fourth Republic, but the hero of the Resistance would not lower himself to join a political party. "De Gaulle is not on the left," he said. "Nor on the right. Nor in the center. He is above."

November 17, 1947

1890 Born in Lille, France
1940 Sets up French Resistance government
1944 Marches into liberated Paris
1958 Takes over French government
1970 Dies in France

By 1958, a tempest born in Algeria threatened to engulf France in civil war. The army, French settlers in Algeria and powerful economic interests in France clamored for De Gaulle to take power. As the condition for his service, he demanded—and received—the right to rule by decree for six months. He had long been convinced that France must free itself of the burden of colonial possessions. He offered France's 12 black African colonies immediate independence and the possibility of a voluntary economic association with France. Then, facing down the military leaders who had helped him to power, he made peace with the Algerian rebels.

In September 1958, De Gaulle submitted a new constitution to the French people that would change the government from a parliamentary system to a presidential one. It was approved, and De Gaulle became the first President of the new Fifth Republic. Under his firm command, France extended recognition to Beijing, built ties with the East bloc, vetoed Britain's entry into the Common Market and generally exasperated friend and foe alike. Though he weathered the strikes that racked France in 1968, he stepped down after losing a vote of confidence in 1969. De Gaulle claimed a synecdoche of self and nation (*"La France, c'est moi"*), which in another man would have seemed absurd. But he earned his boast: Charles de Gaulle *was* France. ∎

ROOSEVELT

Franklin Delano Roosevelt *roused a nation from its creeping paralysis*

THE ENVELOPE BORE A SIMPLE ADDRESS. "TO THE Greatest Man in the World," it said, and the U.S. postal authorities knew just where to deliver it. To the same place where they delivered letters addressed to "God's Gift to the U.S.A." and "My Friend, Washington, D.C."—to the desk of Franklin Delano Roosevelt in the White House. This was not pure sycophancy in the post office. The mailmen also knew where to deliver letters addressed to "Benedict Arnold 2nd" and "Chief Shooter at the Moon, White Father of the Pretty Bubbles."

Roosevelt, the most loved and hated of American Presidents, saved the envelopes. They became part of his famous stamp collection, which eventually numbered more than 1 million different items. With the instinctive frugality of the well-to-do, Roosevelt also collected first editions, ship models, naval prints and campaign buttons. For Franklin Roosevelt was rich. He was born to wealth and ease at an estate above the Hudson River in Hyde Park, New York. Destined for Groton, Harvard, the law and a life of comfortable obscurity, he instead became not only the President and creator of the New Deal but also the architect of a new political coalition that elected him to four terms and remained in control of Washington for more than two decades. As commander of the Grand Alliance that won World War II, he established the U.S. as the unchallenged leader of the free world.

Roosevelt's love for simple joys like stamp collecting was a key element in his strength—a strength that enabled him to overcome a crippling bout with polio that struck him down in the prime of his life, halting his swift ascent to political power and leaving him unable to walk. He had a priceless attribute: a knack for locking up his and the world's worries in some secret mental compartment, and then enjoying himself to the top of his bent. This quality of survival, of physical toughness, of champagne ebullience, was one key to the man. Another was this: no one ever heard him admit that he could not walk.

Roosevelt faced panic with smiling courage, and he fought unprecedented threats to the nation's economy and morale with resourcefulness, energy and a sanguine will to carry on. The intensity of his feeling for what America could be and therefore would be—a feeling that awakened the country to master its own creeping paralysis—prepared the nation for its struggle in the depth of depression. On a far greater scale, for a far greater cause, against a worldwide sense of hopelessness, these same qualities helped Roosevelt guide the Allies to victory in World War II—a victory he died too soon to celebrate.

There were other elements of Roosevelt's success: an immense charm, an instinctive feel for politics, a wide-ranging interest in people and ideas. Not least was the sheer luck so many great leaders appear to be blessed with. "Roosevelt weather" was the envious politician's term for the fact that the sun always seemed to come out when F.D.R. was scheduled to speak.

And then there was his wife, Eleanor Roosevelt Roosevelt. The niece of Theodore Roosevelt, and Franklin's fifth cousin once removed, she was even more extravagantly loved and hated than her husband. In 1933 the *New Yorker* carried a memorable cartoon showing two coal miners looking up goggle-eyed, and one exclaiming, "For gosh sakes, here comes Mrs. Roosevelt." It was hilarious if only because it was so true; soon afterward the First Lady indeed descended into a coal mine. To her critics she was a gadabout and do-gooder, to her admirers she was a dedicated friend of the oppressed, and to everyone she was a marvel of omnipresent vitality. Her discovery in 1918 of her husband's extramarital affair with her social secretary, Lucy Mercer, might have smashed most marriages, but Eleanor and Franklin worked out an arrangement in which she became a kind of mobile ambassador for the wheelchair-bound President.

Squire of the Hudson. Eleanor was a strong woman, but Franklin Roosevelt's life was shaped by an equally powerful figure: that of his mother, the formidable Sara Delano Roosevelt, who had inculcated in the young Franklin her own love of collecting and given him his first stamps. Sara married a widower twice her age, James Roosevelt, 52, a member of the landed gentry of the Hudson Valley and Teddy Roosevelt's distant cousin. Franklin, born in 1882, was her only child, and she kept him in dresses and long curls until he was five. He was 14 before he first went to school, to Groton, and then Harvard. His newly widowed mother moved to Boston to be nearby; she would dote on her son until her death in 1941.

Only an average student at Harvard, Roosevelt did better at Columbia Law School—though he dropped out once he passed the New York State bar exam—then sampled life at the prestigious Wall Street firm of Carter, Ledyard & Milburn. When he married Eleanor in 1905, his mother bought and furnished their house—the first indication that his mother and her daughter-in-law would vie for his attention throughout their lives. The restless young lawyer entered local politics, won a seat in the state senate, made himself a name as a "reformer" by blocking a Tammany Hall candidate for the U.S. Senate. Woodrow Wilson made him Assistant Secretary of the Navy, and Roosevelt went on to win the Democrats' vice-presidential nomination in the doomed 1920 campaign of James M. Cox.

If Roosevelt's ascent had been swift, the tragedy

January 5, 1942

1882 Born in Hyde Park, New York
1921 A polio attack disables his legs
1933 As President, he begins the New Deal
1941 Declares war on the Axis powers
1945 Dies in Georgia

that struck him down in mid-career was even more sudden. In 1921, after two long days of fighting a forest fire and swimming at his summer home on Campobello Island in New Brunswick, he suffered a chill that was misdiagnosed, then the horrifying paralysis of polio. He would never walk unaided again. That a man seemingly so destined for limbo should be wheeled into the White House a decade later was a great triumph of will. A number of his friends came to believe that it was the illness that transformed the amiable aristorat of 1920 into the magnetic leader of 1932. The long struggle endowed him with an extra measure of courage, of resilience, of sympathy for the afflicted.

For years after he was struck down, Roosevelt attempted in vain to restore strength to his lower body. Finally, he aban-

doned the effort and resolved to return to politics. He ran successfully for Governor of New York in 1928 when his mentor, Governor Alfred Smith, ran a failed race for the White House against the Republican Herbert Hoover.

Roosevelt was thus the chief executive of the Empire State when the Roaring Twenties screeched to a halt with the great stock-market crash of 1929. He watched in dismay as Hoover did little to address the Great Depression, which slowly extended throughout the nation. By 1932 national income had plunged by more than half, and unemployment had soared to include one-quarter of the entire work force. FORTUNE magazine estimated that 27.5 million Americans had no regular income at all. More than 1 million of the jobless roamed the country as hobos. Ugly clusters of tin-can shanties known as "Hoovervilles" sprouted, even in the midst of New York City's Central Park. Penniless men tried to sell apples on street corners. Many talked of revolution.

And now there came before the Democratic Convention of 1932 the Governor of New York, a man who was so wasted by polio that he could not stand erect without leg braces, but who promised his stricken nation "a new order of competence and courage" and who declared, "This is more than a political campaign; it is a call to arms."

The call was answered. Roosevelt swept the bewildered Hoover out of the White House by a landslide of 472 electoral votes to 59. In his Inaugural Address he offered not a series of remedies but a new spirit of assurance. It was this spirit that inspired him to seize a phrase from Henry David Thoreau ("Nothing is so much to be feared as fear") for his steadying declaration that "the only thing we have to fear is fear itself."

Spirit of action. The new Congress was ready for bold leadership—ready indeed to give up much of its own authority—and in Roosevelt's legendary first hundred days he won approval of 15 major legislative innovations. The spirit of the hundred days was action, and action now. Many of the New Deal's experiments failed or faltered, but others became part of the steely armature of American life. Social Security, minimum wages, insured bank savings, the right to join labor unions—these are just a few of the lasting results of Roosevelt's first term in office. For better or for worse, Washington took on the basic responsibility for planning and managing society, for maintaining the nation's prosperity and for the equitable sharing of that prosperity.

The new President knew that the actual administration of the New Deal was only part of the answer. No less important was his psychological campaign to cure what had become a national crisis of confidence. Roosevelt instinctively under-stood the immense importance of radio as a means to reach and unite people, and with his sonorous voice he brilliantly exploited the new medium in the periodic "fireside chats" that always began, "My friends …"

Roosevelt crushed Republican Alf Landon in 1936 to win election to a second term. But the innovation and idealism that had marked his first term faded during his second. It became a time of consolidation, of adjustments and repairs; things moved more slowly. Never a modest man, Roosevelt may have been swayed by his landslide victory to believe his power was unlimited. He drew up a plan that would allow him to increase the size of the Supreme Court, a way to circumvent the power of the nine "older men" who had blocked some key programs of his New Deal. The "court-packing scheme" aroused fierce resistance, and not only among Republicans. The ill-advised scheme was defeated in the Senate in 1937.

More ominously, all Roosevelt's programs could not bring the Depression to an end; a recession in 1937-38 set back the recovery. Once again unemployment rose and production sank. As a result, Republicans made a strong comeback in the elections of 1938. Just two years after the landslide of 1936, the New Deal's innovations were drawing to an end, though the nation's new course remained set.

A world at war. The America of the New Deal was still isolationist, justifiably preoccupied with its own enormous problems, but this was a condition that could not last. Like Roosevelt, Adolf Hitler had put Germany's unemployed to work at building autobahns and other showy projects, but now his obsession was to acquire new territory. In 1938 came the Nazis' Anschluss of Austria; that same year Hitler browbeat the British and French into letting him seize the Sudetenland of Czechoslovakia. In 1938 too the Japanese pushed southward across China and captured Canton.

DECISIVE MOMENTS

RISING STAR F.D.R. in 1920 was a comer in the capital. His dreams were crushed by polio in 1921.

STRICKEN Roosevelt on crutches in 1924. Once he became President, he entered into a conspiracy of silence with the U.S. press, and Americans never saw photographs that revealed his disability.

HOME FRONT Roosevelt's mother Sara decorated her son and Eleanor's home and supervised the raising of their children.

The war that ignited Europe in 1939 took two years to reach America. By then, Roosevelt had won an unprecedented third term and become a national leader almost beyond politics. Strongly opposed to Hitler's Germany, but with his hands tied by the country's isolationism, he came up with the innovative Lend-Lease program, which allowed him to ship precious armaments to Britain, and then Russia, without violating the law. Roosevelt realized the war would come to America, and he mobilized the nation, converting entire industries to produce planes, ships and weapons. When the Japanese attacked the U.S. base at Pearl Harbor on Dec. 7, 1941—"a day which will live in infamy," he termed it—the nation was shocked. But thanks to Roosevelt, it was not completely unprepared.

Legacy. The war cost thousands of lives, but it united the nation in a cause that seemed just. And in ways that were only half-understood at the time, the war completed the New Deal. Government spending multiplied more than ninefold and ended unemployment, as the WPA never had. Wartime mobilization rebuilt cities and industries, spurred black migration out of the rural South, beckoned women out of their homes and into factories and created a gargantuan government far beyond the dreams of the New Dealers. The America that emerged from World

COLLEAGUES: Eleanor's earnest idealism sparked the New Deal; she never wrote "I think," it was said, but rather "I feel"

War II was a far different country than the America of the 1920s and '30s. The nation had been transformed, and millions of people—blacks, women, returning veterans—harbored new expectations of what life in America ought to offer them.

But Roosevelt did not live to see that day. The once robust leader was ill when he took the oath of office for his fourth term; he died at 63 in Warm Springs, Georgia—a favorite haunt where he had enjoyed xthe therapeutic waters—on April 12, 1945. The war in Europe ended weeks later.

As historian Doris Kearns Goodwin recounts, it appeared to Eleanor Roosevelt that "a giant transference of energy" had taken place between the President and the people. "In the early days, before Pearl Harbor," Mrs. Roosevelt told her son James, "Franklin was healthy and strong and committed to the Allied cause while the country was sick and weak and isolationist. But gradually, as the President animated his countrymen to the dangers abroad, the country grew stronger and stronger while he grew weaker and weaker, until in the end he was dead and the country had emerged more powerful and more productive than ever before." His wife's view may have been romanticized, but it captures an essential truth about Franklin Roosevelt: with energy, vision and sheer force of will, a crippled man had roused a fallen nation to its feet. ■

THE CHALLENGE The Depression presented Roosevelt with the greatest domestic turmoil a President had faced since Lincoln's Inauguration.

ON COURSE Unlike Churchill and Teddy Roosevelt, F.D.R.—here on the U.S.S. *Houston* in 1938—was no lover of battle, but he proved a steady wartime leader.

STALIN

A communist czar, **Joseph Stalin** *was the ruthless ruler of an empire of fear*

N O TITAN OF HISTORY, NEITHER khan nor caesar nor czar, amassed power so vast or so absolute. A greater empire builder than Peter the Great, he extended Russia's sway over a fourth of the globe and its shadow over the rest. A more terrible tyrant than Ivan the Terrible, he enslaved millions in the name of freedom. His word was gospel, his will law; he repealed truth and denied God. For millions, he was the infallible all. One name wasn't sufficient for the man: born Joseph Vissarionovich Djugashvili, he became the revolutionary known as Koba (Indomitable) and died as the leader known as Stalin (Man of Steel).

Schooled in Siberia. The steeling of Stalin began early and never ceased. He was born in 1879 in a humble cottage (later a shrine) in the tiny town of Gori in Georgia. His father was an alcoholic who beat Joseph mercilessly—until he deserted his family. But his mother worked as a launderer and earned enough money to win him entry to an Orthodox seminary in Tiflis. The priest-to-be was expelled for reading radical literature. He had joined a clandestine socialist group; soon, with czarist police on his tail, Djugashvili went underground and took his first alias: Koba. The young agitator was soon run down, jailed and deported to Siberia. He was 23, and on his

August 16, 1948

1879 Born in Georgia
1917 Bolsheviks take over the government
1929 Begins to collectivize Soviet agriculture
1945 Defeats Hitler, is dominant power in Eastern Europe
1953 Dies in Moscow

way. Siberia was the university of the revolution; there he learned of the struggle between the party's right (Menshevik) and left (Bolshevik) wings. In 1904, Koba escaped from Siberia, traveled hundreds of miles by peasant cart, suffered frostbite and arrived back in Tiflis. While Lenin masterminded the revolution from Geneva and Trotsky formed the first Worker's Soviet in St. Petersburg, Stalin wrote fiery pamphlets in Georgia.

His screeds caught the eye of Lenin, and in 1905 young Koba met the famous revolutionary at a party conference and became a devoted disciple. With the party flat broke, Koba directed "fighting squads" that robbed banks, public treasuries, steamships. His biggest haul: a quarter of a million rubles in a stickup in the main square of Tiflis.

Czarist rule tightened its grip; between 1907 and 1917 Koba spent a total of seven years in prison. During periods of freedom he organized the oil workers in Baku, where he first began using the name Stalin. World War I broke czarist power and brought about the short-lived Kerensky government and the Bolshevik coup d'état in 1917, but Stalin played a modest role in these momentous events. Still, he emerged as one of the members of the party's ruling Politburo. At the end of the civil war, Lenin decided to remove hostile and unreliable elements from the party, and Stalin directed the purges. Soon he was running the party's day-to-day business. Early in 1922 the post of General Secretary of the Central Committee was created for him. The title sounded innocuous, but the job could be made all powerful, and to the rising Stalin, pure power outweighed titular glory.

Power of the purge. When Lenin died, a ruthless struggle for the succession ensued. Flattering a major rival, Trotsky, while scheming against him, Stalin first drove him from power, then from the party, then from Russia. He dealt with opponents on his right just as ruthlessly, and by 1929 he was firmly in control. In that year he began the collectivization of land and the liquidation of the kulaks. The orders were simple, abrupt, brutal: Stalin later told Winston Churchill 10 million had died. His plan never fully succeeded, for the peasants began burning their barns and killing their cattle, threatening the entire economy. It was Stalin's biggest, and perhaps only, political defeat.

In 1934, when the party boss in Leningrad was assassinated, Stalin launched a huge purge. From 1935 through 1938 successive trials were held of Bolsheviks who were not Stalin's sycophants. The purge peaked in 1937, when the top Soviet generals were

MAN OF STEEL: Left, as war leader, Stalin neglected Marxism, stressed patriotism; opposite, Stalin meets with Lenin in 1922. Lenin came to fear his disciple: "Stalin's spite," he said, " ... is a most evil factor in politics." But Lenin died before he could remove Stalin from power

secretly tried and shot. By 1938, when Stalin called a halt and purged the purgers, millions of victims had disappeared.

Stalin learned something from the purges: the power that ideas have over men's minds. Now he burnished his kingdom of fear with the myth of Leninist-Stalinist infallibility. Every Soviet writer, poet, musician and painter was expected to devote his energies to enlarging the myth. Mountains, towns, factories and streets were named for the Man of Steel. Copies of his collected works were printed in the scores of millions.

The Stalin myth was in working order just in time for the Soviet pact with Hitler in 1939, and it survived even that cynical deal. Less than two years later, Hitler double-crossed him and sent the German army sweeping through western Russia. But Stalin's luck held: General Winter stepped in and halted Hitler, just as it had stopped Napoleon 130 years before. Stalin directed the fighting from the Kremlin, drafting every able-bodied man and woman in Russia and holding the nation together until the tide turned.

In 1945 Russian troops swarmed into Berlin, and in the next few years Stalin extended his power over the "liberated" nations of Eastern Europe. When Mao Zedong took control of the Chinese mainland, the addition of China's 400 million to Russia's 200 million was the brightest hour of world communism: Stalin's Marxist-Leninist domain occupied a fourth of the world's land surface, claimed a third of its people. It was the largest empire ever put together by any one man, and at his death in 1953 it was still intact—except that it no longer had Stalin, a man of ceaseless evil and immense success. ∎

DECEMBER 22, 1941 With his devastating surprise attack on Pearl Harbor, Japanese Admiral Isoroku Yamamoto demonstrated the striking power of the naval aircraft carrier.

JULY 13, 1942 As Hitler's tanks rolled across North Africa, cagey panzer commander field marshal Erwin Rommel earned a colorful nom de guerre: the Desert Fox.

MAY 10, 1943 Submarines had fought in World War I, but improved technology—and the strategies of Admiral Karl Doenitz—made Hitler's U-boats a stealthy, potent new weapon.

JANUARY 3, 1944 Visionary leader of U.S. military forces General George C. Marshall would shape the postwar world as Secretary of State; his Marshall Plan resuscitated Europe.

FEBRUARY 1, 1943 Rommel met his match in an equally tenacious foe: British field marshal Bernard Montgomery, who turned back Germany's Afrika Korps at El Alamein.

JULY 26, 1943 Colorful, tough and outspoken, General George S. Patton and his armored divisions slashed through Africa, Italy, France, and held firm at the Battle of the Bulge.

JANUARY 1, 1945 Leadership of history's largest seaborne assault—the Allies' D-day landing in Normandy—made General Dwight D. Eisenhower TIME's Man of the Year 1944.

AUGUST 27,1945 In 1942 General Douglas MacArthur vowed , "I shall return" to the Philippines. He did. After remaking postwar Japan, he tangled with Truman over Korea.

TRUMAN

Fate made him President—and

Harry Truman *took over from there*

WHILE VISITING HARRY TRUMAN in the closing months of his presidency, Winston Churchill spoke bluntly yet generously: "The last time you and I sat across a conference table was at Potsdam [in July 1945]. I must confess, sir, I held you in very low regard. I loathed your taking the place of Franklin Roosevelt. I misjudged you badly. Since that time, you, more than any other man, have saved Western civilization."

If Churchill was deceived at first, so were most of his contemporaries. Sir Winston, in fact, was some years ahead of other historians in his re-evaluation. Truman was one of those public men whose reputations flourish only after years

of retirement. His nondescript appearance, his shoot-from-the-hip partisanship, his taste for mediocre cronies—all the things that in his time led some into considering him too small for the office—have dwindled in importance with the passing decades. What has loomed larger is a sense of the man's courage, a realization that he faced and made more great decisions than most other American Presidents. It was Harry Truman who decided to drop the atom bomb. It was the Truman Doctrine that shattered the long U.S. tradition of peacetime isolation by supporting Greece and Turkey against communist threats. It was Truman's Marshall Plan that committed U.S. resources to the rebuilding of Europe. Later Truman defied the Soviet blockade of Berlin and risked war by authorizing the airlift. Still later he met North Korea's invasion of South Korea by ordering U.S. forces into the field—then fired the legendary general who opposed his Commander in Chief's strategy.

Prarie boy. Harry Truman was the country boy of legend who comes to the big city and outwits all the slickers. Growing up in Independence, Missouri, east of Kansas City, he was innately religious. But like his mother, he was a lightfoot Baptist; he looked on dancing, card playing and bourbon drinking with a tolerant eye. He wore his provincialism as proudly as he would later wear his garish sports shirts. He pos-

sessed some hard inner kernel of conviction—partly moral, partly folk wisdom, partly intellectual—that made him secure.

Though born provincial, he was not born poor; the family farm ran to hundreds of acres. But wheat futures went bad just when young Harry graduated from high school in 1901, and college was out of the question. A congenital eye defect condemned him to thick lenses; reserved, almost withdrawn as a boy, he read every book in the local library. After serving with distinction in France during World War I as a captain in the field artillery, he married his childhood sweetheart, Bess Wallace, and invested his life savings of $15,000 in a haberdashery in Kansas City. He prospered briefly, then went broke during the depression of 1922. Truman proudly paid back all his creditors, although it took years to do so.

His political career began in 1922, when the brother of Kansas City's political boss, Thomas Pendergast, asked Truman to run for county judge in Jackson County, which includes Kansas City. Pendergast's nephew had served in Truman's regiment and admired him. Truman served as an able judge for 10 of the next 12 years; as the highest elected county official, he dealt with roads, hospitals and political patronage. In 1934, at age 50, he was elected to the U.S. Senate. They called him "the Senator from Pendergast."

The snide remark was unfair; Truman was always his own man. Re-elected in 1940, he soon launched a special Senate committee to investigate defense spending, saving the nation billions of dollars during the huge hurry and grab of wartime procurement. By 1944 his stature had grown so impressive that the ailing F.D.R. chose him as his running mate. But his tenure as Vice President was brief: in less than three months, Roosevelt was dead. Truman spoke to reporters the next day, saying, "I don't know whether you fellows ever had a load of hay or a bull fall on you. But last night the moon, the stars and all the planets fell on me. If you fellows ever pray, pray for me."

The buck stops. He was ill-prepared: Roosevelt had not taken him into his inner councils, had not even let him in on the secret of the atom bomb. Truman floundered at first, but he soon took command. On his desk, he placed a sign: THE BUCK STOPS HERE. So did pretensions. When confronted by the great issues, Harry Truman never flinched. The one that brought him the heaviest criticism was the decision to drop the atom bomb. As was his practice, Truman listened to both sides of the argument and then decided. Later he recalled, "We faced half a million casualties trying to take Japan by land. It was either that or the atom bomb, and I didn't hesitate a

April 23, 1945

1884 Born in Missouri
1918 Serves in France during World War I
1934 Elected to Senate from Missouri
1945 Succeeds F.D.R. after three months as Vice President
1972 Dies in Missouri

minute, and I've never lost any sleep over it since."

In the wake of World War II Stalin was pushing hard, backing an armed insurrection in Greece and threatening Turkey. In 1947 the hard-pressed British declared that they could no longer defend freedom in the eastern Mediterranean. Remote as such places then seemed to the U.S., the President proclaimed the Truman Doctrine: the U.S. would aid free countries threatened by communist aggression. Only months later, Truman initiated Secretary of State George Marshall's plan for the economic revival of Europe, which probably staved off imminent revolution in some countries and provided Western Europe with the means to rebuild.

At home, Truman was less successful, facing postwar shortages, inflation, strikes and the hanky-panky of a few subordinates. In early 1948 his popularity was at a low ebb. Panicky party strategists declared that if the Democrats did not appease the South, the party would vanish. Truman responded by proposing an elaborate series of civil rights measures that only further antagonized the South. Then, without major money or support, he set out on a whistle-stop election tour across the country. At each stop he lambasted the "do-nothing" Republican Congress for failing to address the nation's postwar ills. "Give 'em hell, Harry!" the crowds cried. The Democratic left had deserted to third-party candidate Henry Wallace, the South to Strom Thurmond's States' Rights party. The overconfident Republican candidate, Thomas E. Dewey, spent much of his time plotting his future Cabinet. Not until midmorning on the day after the election did an amazed nation learn that Truman had scored the greatest upset in U.S. electoral history.

When South Korea was invaded, Truman reacted with typical dispatch. In a space of 60 hours, he ordered U.S. forces into battle and got U.N. approval. When General Douglas MacArthur tried to bully him from abroad and even challenged U.S. policy, Truman did not hesitate. He recalled the hero of World War II despite a huge uproar. Truman's reaction was characteristic: "General MacArthur was insubordinate, and I fired him. That's all there was to it."

Though eligible, Truman decided not to run for President in 1952; he retired to his home in Independence, wrote his memoirs and built a presidential library. He still ate at lunch counters and took his quick-stepping morning constitutional. Truman was a man of action; deprived of the power to act, he receded from view before his death in 1972. He was, it has been said, perhaps the greatest little man the U.S. has known. In a nation founded on the principle that ultimate wisdom lodges in its citizens, that is no mean accolade. ∎

MAO

A guerrilla who became a god, Mao Zedong *transformed China*

LESS THAN TWO MONTHS BEFORE, MASSIVE EARTH-quakes had devastated three of China's northern cities; more than 250,000 had died in Tangshan, 100 miles east of Beijing. In ancient Chinese folk wisdom, the upheavals would have been read as an augury of other calamitous evils to come, of after-shocks in other spheres. They were. On Thursday, Sept. 9, 1976, loudspeakers throughout China announced that Mao Zedong, Chairman of the Central Committee of the Communist Party, had "passed away" at age 82 "despite all treatment" and "meticulous medical care."

Within minutes of the announcement, all China was in mourning. Mao was the only leader the country had known since his communist armies had swept triumphantly into Beijing to proclaim the People's Republic 27 years before. Mao was not only the architect of China's social revolution but also its guide, prophet and teacher—the man of legend whom millions accepted with blind faith as the font of their country's rebirth to greatness.

Guerrilla fighter and grand strategist, peasant organizer and oracular Marxist philosopher, Mao came to manhood in the 1920s when the once glorious Middle Kingdom was divided, weak, dispirited, a country prey to foreign colonizers and provincial satraps. When he died, China had been unified—admittedly by brutal force and rigid discipline—and was an emergent superpower. The country had regained its once lost pride and was filled with a sense of purpose. It was Mao far more than anyone else who gave it that purpose, and saw that its terrible price was paid. This son of an obscure peasant from the vast hinterland of China was the most influential revolutionary of his generation and, for better or worse, one of the great figures of the 20th century

Mao had a driving energy and a shrewd sense of how to manipulate both friend and foe. After his armies swept victoriously into Beijing in 1949 and inaugurated the communist era, Mao wavered between spasms of intense, hardheaded activism and passive, removed periods of thought and reflection. During the 1960s, at the height of China's "cult of personality," he seemed to have been elevated to the heights of the gods, and when he died he was indeed more a creature of legend than a real person to the 850 million who paid him homage as their leader. Yet he described himself to the American journalist Edgar Snow as "only a lone monk walking the world with a leaky umbrella."

Though Mao subjected himself to such rigors as ice-water

February 7, 1949

1893 Born in Hunan province, China
1934 His guerrillas begin the Long March
1949 Triumphs in civil war and unifies China
1966-69 The Cultural Revolution rages
1976 Dies in Beijing

baths and long hikes, he also had a soft, almost dreamy side; he wrote poems and essays, communicated in allegorical koans. He was hardly immune to the charms of women; in 1994 the memoirs of his longtime personal physician, Dr. Li Zhisui, detailed the harem of adoring concubines with whom the aged leader had dallied. Mao's relations with most people, however, showed a ruthless, selfish quality. Time and again, he coldly thrust aside old comrades-in-arms—including such once trusted deputies as Lin Biao and Deng Xiaoping—because they had either betrayed his ideology or too openly craved a share in his unique power. He was ever wary of the danger that the country's leadership would form a new élite of privilege and power that could destroy his egalitarian vision. His ambition, as radical in its way as that of the Apostle Paul, was to forge "a new man," one free of selfish ideas who would work tirelessly to "serve the people." In pursuit of that goal, he repeatedly plunged China into periods of turmoil, designed to cleanse the ranks of the party and the bureaucracy of élitist ideas and imperious habits.

Yet despite the horrendous human misery he unleashed, in many ways the country's accomplishments under him were staggering. Industrial production increased, and the problem of feeding the country's enormous population was solved. After a relentless process of leveling, China no longer had the egregious gaps between the very rich and the very poor that bedevil much of the Third World. But those gains cost the Chinese dearly. Under Mao, there was no freedom. His persistent demands for ideological purity encouraged the growth of a pervasive apparatus of thought control. Literature and art, dominated by his third wife, the fanatical former actress Jiang Qing, became banal and monothematic—a far cry from the glorious creativity of previous centuries. The party reached into every aspect of personal life, from child rearing to sex habits to clothing styles to marriage, generally by imposing a stern, puritanical morality. Despite Mao's own battle cry, "To rebel is justified," the Chairman—like China's emperors of old—implicitly demanded strict obedience and a kind of filial piety from his people.

The studious guerrilla. Although he carefully nurtured a paternalistic image, the Chairman never got along with his father, a peasant from Hunan province in central China who became a small landlord and grain merchant. The elder Mao felt that five years in primary school was quite enough for his son; young Mao wanted more. Some time after 1906, he ran away from home to resume his schooling in Changsha, Hunan's capital, where his poverty was a stark contrast to his classmates' wealth. There he threw himself into the intellectual and political ferment that followed the collapse of the ruling dynasty in 1911. Earnest, idealistic, energetic and a voluminous reader, the young Mao first entered the wide world outside his native province when, in 1918, he went to Beijing, walking a good part of the way. He had become a communist, and in 1921, when the First Congress of the Chinese Communist Party was convened, he was one of the 12 delegates in attendance.

In 1927 the communist movement underwent a decisive series of reversals. The urban, worker-centered bases of the party were destroyed in an anticommunist coup by a young Nationalist ramrod named Chiang Kai-shek, who was in the midst of a monumental effort to reunite China. Gradually, the center of communist activity shifted to the remote mountainous region of south-central China, where Mao and Marshal Zhu De put together a peasant army and began to build a base. Mao had come to believe the Marxist revolution in China would arise from the rural masses, not urban workers.

These were hard years for Mao and the party; once he had to flee Chiang Kai-shek's troops, leaving his sister and his first wife behind. They were both executed. During this period, Mao developed the formula for guerrilla warfare, which he summed up in one of his most frequently quoted slogans: "The enemy advances, we retreat/ The enemy camps, we harass/ The enemy tires, we attack/ The enemy retreats, we pursue."

The East is red. Those principles soon became articles of survival. In 1934 Mao and Zhu De led the party through the legendary Long March. Pursued by Chiang's Guomindang troops, 100,000 Chinese Red Army soldiers left their base area in south-central China for the rocky hillsides of Yenan, far to the north. Fighting as it marched, the force struggled across 7,000 miles of rugged, largely hostile territory. When Mao reached Yenan in late 1935, only a tenth of his men were left. From these toughened survivors—including Mao's gifted collaborator Zhou Enlai—emerged most of the men who would one day rule the People's Republic of China.

In Yenan, Mao created a new revolutionary base, organizing the peasant masses until he controlled almost 100 million people. From 1937 to 1941, the communists had an uneasy partnership with Chiang's Nationalists in the struggle against Japanese invaders, but cooperation ended after a number of skirmishes between the two armies. A year after the Pacific war ended in 1945, full-scale civil war erupted. For four bloody years, the communists steadily expanded their hold on the countryside until, in the final months of the war, as Mao later put it, "the cities fell like ripe fruit." On Oct. 1, 1949, Mao spoke in communist Beijing. "Our nation will never again be … insulted," he said. "We have stood up." Mao's triumph saw the end of nearly 50 years of chaos and civil warfare in China.

Mao set out to turn China into a socialist state modeled after the Soviet Union. Most Sinologists agree that at least 1 million people were executed over the next six years. Intellectuals, fac-

DECISIVE MOMENTS

PEASANT Mao was born in the hinterland of a China that had changed little over the centuries. He poses on the right with his younger brother, father and uncle at his mother's funeral.

GUERRILLA Mao on horseback in 1947, 13 years after the Long March began and two years before his peasant army would enter Beijing in triumph.

MARXIST Fellow travelers Mao and Stalin were allies, but after Stalin's death a disillusioned Mao reviled the Soviets as "revisionists … renegades … scabs."

tory owners and other "capitalist elements" began the painful process of "thought reform" to purge themselves of "individualist" ideas. Ultimately, countless millions would succumb to the rigors of hard labor in Mao's re-education camps.

Great Slide Backward. In the late 1950s—after a short-lived period of relaxation driven by Mao's call to "Let a hundred flowers bloom"—the Chairman decided to accelerate the pace of social reconstruction by unleashing the Great Leap Forward. It was anything but. Backyard steel furnaces, 18-hour workdays and the herding of half a billion peasants into giant ramshackle communes, combined with three years of bad weather, plunged China into chaos again, and millions starved. The Great Slide Backward also inaugurated serious trouble with Moscow: Mao chafed at the Soviets' ideological bullying, and centuries-old border conflicts were revived.

PERSONALITY CULT: Young Mao had reviled Stalin's deification, but he later embraced idolatry as a political tool

Just as China began to climb back from the Great Leap Forward, Mao unleashed his most traumatic political convulsion, the Great Proletarian Cultural Revolution, an effort to ensure the revival of the nation's revolutionary values. At its height, rampaging hordes of Red Guards crisscrossed the country, obeying Mao's call to "bombard the party headquarters." Every wall in every city was plastered with slogans and posters. Party leaders were humiliated in mass meetings. At this time, Mao's near deification began: his portrait blazed from millions of posters and was worn on badges by virtually all Chinese. His thoughts, excerpted in the Little Red Book, became matter for fervent national veneration.

But the movement swerved into irrationality, and the army had to be called in to quell the Red Guards. In the wake of the upheaval came a seesawing series of purges and counterpurges, including an abortive coup attempt by Mao's designated heir apparent, Defense Minister Lin Biao, who died while fleeing to the Soviet Union.

When order was restored, Mao turned again to thoughts of diplomacy. Realizing he stood alone in his skirmishes with Moscow, he forged a new policy that gradually ended China's isolation from the world and led to Richard Nixon's 1972 trip to Beijing.

Mao's health declined rapidly after that dramatic first visit, and he withdrew behind the walls of his residence in Beijing's Forbidden City. The most successful revolutionary of the century ended his days in the former palaces of the Son of Heaven. From a lean and hungry rebel with a price of 250,000 silver dollars on his head, he had metamorphosed into a red and gold godhead of perfection. Yet even China's man-gods must die someday, their passing foretold by earthquakes. ∎

ANARCHIST A lifelong enemy of bureaucracy in any form, Mao unleashed the Red Guards in 1966 to reform the party. But the radical young leftists' reign of terror sent China into chaos.

ICON Mao led by symbolic gestures. In 1966 he showed his strength at age 73 by swimming in the Yangtze River.

STRATEGIST After breaking with the Soviet Union, Mao turned to the U.S. as a potential ally. Richard Nixon and Henry Kissinger visited Zhou Enlai and Mao in 1972.

KENNEDY

WRITING ON THE CHARACTER OF Napoleon, Ralph Waldo Emerson observed, "He was no saint … and he is no hero, in the high sense." Napoleon had fulfilled an earthly career, at any rate. His life went the full trajectory. One could study the line of it and know, for better and worse, what the man was, and did, and could do. He inhabited his life. He completed it. He passed through it to the end of its possibilities.

John F. Kennedy's bright trajectory ended in midpassage, severed in that glaring Friday-noontime light in Dallas, on Nov. 22, 1963. History abruptly left off, and after the shock had begun to pass, the mythmaking began—the mind haunted by the hypothetical, by what might have been. The myth overwhelmed conventional judgment—and still does, as evidenced by the extraordinary auction of the possessions of Kennedy's late wife, Jacqueline Kennedy Onassis, in New York City in April 1996. In a frenzy of bidding, prices went through the roof: a cigar humidor valued before the sale at $2,500 was sold for $547,500. Buyers insisted they hoped "to buy a piece of his-

tory." But at those prices, they were purchasing mythology. More than three decades after his death, John F. Kennedy's presence in the national memory, in the interior temple, remains powerful, disproportionate to his accomplishments. The truth is, he was not President long enough to be judged by the customary standards.

The mystique. And Kennedy did have his obvious achievements. Merely by arriving as a Roman Catholic at the White House, he destroyed forever one religious issue in American politics. He presided over a change of political generations in America, and did it with brilliant style. He brought youth and idealism and accomplishment and élan—

November 16, 1960

1917 Born in Boston, Massachusetts
1943 Survives crash of PT boat in Pacific
1952 Elected Senator from Massachusetts
1960 Defeats Richard Nixon for presidency
1963 Dies in Dallas

and a sometimes boorish and clannish élitism—to Washington. He refreshed the town and the nation with a conviction that the world could be changed, that the improvisational intelligence could do wonderful things. Yet such almost ruthless optimism had its sinister side, a moral complacency and dismissive arrogance that expressed itself publicly when Kennedy and his élan went venturing into Vietnam, privately when Kennedy went venturing among a series of extramarital sexual partners, including his alleged affair with the girlfriend of a Mafia don.

But after Nov. 22, the record simply went blank. An anguished and fascinating process of canonization ensued. The newly arrived mass medium of television became Kennedy's Parson Weems: the reality of what the nation had lost was preserved with unprecedented, unthinkable vividness on tape. There was the young man born into great wealth; the demanding father and talented family; the bravery of the PT-boat rescue in the Pacific; the picking up of the mantle from his older brother Joseph, fallen in World War II; the American dreamboat campaigning through the primaries among squealing adolescent girls; the wonderfully witty press conferences; the glamorous wife and young children; the one brief shining moment—and then the window in the Texas School Book Depository and the shots, and riderless Black Jack fighting the bridle, and the gallant widow, the little boy saluting. The death of J.F.K. became a participatory American tragedy, a drama both global and intensely intimate. Americans felt Kennedy's death in a deeply personal way: they, and he, were swept into a third dimension, the mythic. Kennedy was turned into a kind of American god.

In a bizarre way, the youngest elected President—who had a problematic tenure that included a mixed bag of one

BEFORE THE FALL: J.F.K. meets the press, above. Below at left, the Kennedys arrive at the Dallas airport on Nov. 22, 1963, on a campaign swing designed to win Southern support

fiasco (the Bay of Pigs) and many missteps and some victories—achieved more in death than in life. In the atmosphere of grief and remorse after the assassination, Lyndon Johnson pushed through Congress much of Kennedy's program, and more: Medicare, civil rights, Head Start and the other programs that came to form Johnson's Great Society.

The record. It is difficult to know whether Kennedy was a visionary or simply a rhetorician. He did have a high sense of adventure and idealism, which he combined with patriotism in the launching of his plan to put a man on the moon and his founding of the Peace Corps and the Alliance for Progress. But his sense of adventure led him into some messy crises: he allowed himself to be talked into the abortive Bay of Pigs invasion of Cuba by military and intelligence experts, and committed American troops to defend South Vietnam without adequately weighing the consequences. Soviet boss Nikita Khrushchev judged him callow and weak after a summit at Vienna, then built the Berlin Wall and installed rockets in Cuba. But Kennedy was a fast learner: he belatedly rose to the challenge, and made Khrushchev back down in Cuba.

At home as abroad, Kennedy's performance was mixed. Faced with growing confrontations between blacks and whites

as Martin Luther King Jr. and others fought for equal rights, Kennedy's response was deflected, inconsistent. While pronouncing civil rights to be a moral issue, he acquiesced to an FBI investigation of King. He pushed for a civil rights bill but died before it could become law.

A judgment on Kennedy's presidential performance inevitably ends in a perplexity of conditional clauses: if he had lived … if he had won a second term. It is possible that the abrupt end of his term in office, his assassination, much more profoundly affected the course of America than anything he did while he was in the White House. There was a kind of dual effect: his death enacted his legislative program and at the same time seemed to let loose monsters, to unhinge the nation in some deep way that sent it reeling down a road toward riots and war and assassinations and Watergate.

The couple. Kennedy did imagine a better America, a fairer place, a more excellent place. He even believed—undoubtedly with a strong assist from his wife—that it was part of his task as President to lift American culture, so the Kennedys brought Pablo Casals and Igor Stravinsky and Bach and Mozart to the White House. That was a novel notion in American politics, novel at least since the days of Thomas Jefferson.

Jacqueline Bouvier Kennedy was her husband's equal—and often his superior—in her polish and presence. When the Kennedys visited France and dazzled Paris with their youthful grace, Jack introduced himself by saying, "I am the man who accompanied Jacqueline Kennedy to Paris." She managed to radiate glamour and a conspicuous shyness at the same time. Her interests were always arty; during her senior year in college her essay on the great Russian ballet impresario Serge Diaghilev earned her *Vogue* magazine's Prix de Paris, a contest that awarded the winner a year in Paris and an internship with the magazine.

During the 1,000 days of Kennedy's presidency, the First Lady's greatest impact was on style. She redid the White House, replacing routine reproductions with authentic period pieces and fabrics. The redecoration was a triumph celebrated on TV when the First Lady led a correspondent through the rooms, explaining her inspirations; 80 million people tuned in. Jackie also revolutionized dress for a female public figure. She loved slacks and shorts and riding habits, and for formal wear favored top couturiers like Halston, Givenchy, Balenciaga. Prefiguring her later involvement in landmark preservation, she managed to save historic 19th century town houses around Washington's Lafayette Square that were slated to be destroyed to make way for an office building. Beneath her elegant veneer there was steel. In the wake of the assassination, she refused to take tranquilizers, fearing they would blunt her reactions and interfere with her planning—because plan the funeral she did. The riderless horse, the eternal flame, the wailing Irish bagpipe—all were her idea.

With her gallantry in the days following her husband's murder, Jacqueline helped create the myth of John F. Kennedy, and that myth will undoubtedly outlive the substance of what he achieved. History remembers not so much what he did as what he was: he has become an endless flame, kept alive in a special vault of the national imagination. ∎

JOHNSON

*The one thing **Lyndon Johnson** couldn't legislate was victory in Vietnam*

H E WAS PERHAPS THE MOST EFFECTIVE FLOOR leader the U.S. Senate has ever had, an all-time master at getting what he wanted. Lyndon Baines Johnson was often described as being an arm twister, but he wasn't. Instead, with his long, strong fingers, he would take firm grasp just above an elbow and then squeeze—hard. Johnson had other techniques for making men feel at a disadvantage: he might peer closely at someone's face and say, "My ole daddy always told me never to trust a man who can't look you straight in the eyes." But his favorite approach was pure persuasion. "Come now, and let us reason together," he was fond of saying, after *Isaiah*, and he could reason on behalf of the national interest with rare intensity and eloquence. For Lyndon Johnson had a dream for America—for a bountiful America that bestowed its blessings on all citizens, old and young, black and white, those born to wealth and those arisen from poverty.

In his presidency, L.B.J. moved America a long way toward realizing his dream. Yet Americans never came to love him as much as he loved the country, and for all his achievements, he was finally driven from office. All Presidents learn to live with vilification, but Johnson got more than his measure. He was denounced as vain, tyrannical, vindictive, sly and crude. The attacks were so harsh and sweeping because Johnson resembled a cast of characters more than a single person.

There was folksy Lyndon, winding up a whistle-stop address with "Ah wish Ah could stay and do a little sippin' and whittlin' with you …" There was Lyndon the manipulator of men, devising plots so byzantine that not even his aides knew what he had in mind. Most of all there was Lyndon the patriot, who could say—because he wanted to believe it, in defiance of the facts—that his great-grandfather had died at the Alamo with Jim Bowie and Davy Crockett. His patriotism made him implacable on Vietnam, the tragedy that pulled him from office. He was determined that "I'm not going down in history as the first American President to lose a war." He related Vietnam to Texas: "Just like the Alamo, somebody damn well needed to go to their aid. Well, by God, I'm going to Vietnam's aid!"

From the hills to the Hill. Johnson was shaped and shadowed for life by the hill country of Texas. To him the world was just Johnson City grown big. He loved to relate lugubrious tales of family poverty, even though the Johnsons were actually quite well off by the standards of the Texas of his time. Lyndon's father had earned a teacher's certificate and was active in state politics as well as farming. Lyndon married Claudia ("Lady Bird") Taylor, the daughter of a wealthy rancher. Once out of col-

lege Johnson taught briefly, then landed a job as secretary to Representative Richard M. Kleberg, son of the owner of the gigantic King Ranch.

After that, except for a brief time out to serve in the Navy during World War II, it was politics all the way for L.B.J. One of his earliest sponsors in Washington was Representative Sam Rayburn of Texas, who was later to become one of the most powerful Speakers in the history of the House. An ardent New Dealer, Johnson was named Texas director of Franklin Roosevelt's National Youth Administration.

In 1937, in a special election to fill a vacancy caused by death, Johnson ran for Congress as an all-out F.D.R. man against a field of five anti–New Deal candidates. He won, and was re-elected five times. Then in 1948, in a tight, vicious contest in which each side accused the other of vote stealing, L.B.J. was elected to the U.S. Senate. Thereafter the Senate became his true home, a place where his personal flaws became formidable weapons, making him a force to be reckoned with, a man to be feared, a leader to be respected for his superb political instincts. As Senate majority leader for six years, Johnson was the architect and deliverer of such Dwight Eisenhower legislation as the Civil Rights Act of 1957 and the National Aeronautics and Space Act of 1958.

The Great Society. The 1,000 days of the Kennedy Administration were days of frustration for Vice President Johnson, who had been nominated primarily to balance the ticket and win Southern votes, and from that penumbra he emerged, President by accident, as a whirlwind of creative energy unleashed. As his memorial to the slain Kennedy,

January 1, 1965

1908 Born near Johnson City, Texas
1937 Elected to House of Representatives
1953 Elected leader of Senate Democrats
1963 Becomes President after J.F.K.'s death
1973 Dies in Texas

a cornucopia of liberal legislation poured fourth in housing, antipoverty programs, education, conservation, Medicare—particularly after L.B.J.'s crushing defeat of Senator Barry Goldwater in 1964. With the historic Civil Rights Act of 1964 and Voting Rights Act of 1965, Johnson brought blacks fully into the nation's electoral process and helped them obtain equality in housing and employment. To the end, his stand on America's most complex social problem was unwavering.

In the exuberance of the moment, much of the Great Society legislation passed under Johnson's leadership was too hastily conceived—the product of goodwill more than of good planning. A New Dealer to the end, Johnson operated on Depression-forged beliefs in government spending as a cure-all, and his emphasis on federally funded programs to attack the nation's social ills would later become the target of Republican conservatives like Ronald Reagan and Newt Gingrich.

In the quagmire. Johnson's personal pronouncements were sometimes eccentric ("Never trust a man whose eyes are too close to his nose") and sometime pungent (he would keep J. Edgar Hoover as head of the FBI, he said, because "I'd rather have him inside the tent pissing out than outside pissing in"). He was consumed by strange, dogged passions: he once flew to Vietnam and told U.S. troops to "come home with that coonskin on the wall." Relaxation on his L.B.J. Ranch back home in Texas meant roaring around the dirt roads at high speed in his Lincoln Continental, while regaling guests with stories of Texas life. He jetted around the world in less than

five days in 1967 and wound up dropping in on the Pope to see if His Holiness could help free U.S. war prisoners.

Overshadowing Johnson's character and achievements, however, was the "brushfire" war he inherited in Vietnam, which soon began to breed campus revolt and riots that would scar America's cities. Month after month, optimistic war bulletins from the White House were followed by news of slaughter in the field, giving birth to the "credibility gap." Deeper and deeper Johnson plunged the nation into the morass, bringing the total U.S. troops in Vietnam close to a staggering half-million by the time he left office in 1969—with no end in sight. Angry war protesters chanted, "Hey, hey, L.B.J.—how many kids have you killed today?" Johnson agonized but would not budge. He became a virtual prisoner in the White House. A poetaster-politician, Senator Eugene McCarthy, made Vietnam an issue and won 20 of the 24 delegates at stake in New Hampshire's Democratic primary in 1968. Less than two months later, a distraught Lyndon Johnson gave up, announcing that he would not run for re-election.

He returned to his beloved Texas hills, supervised the building of the massive L.B.J. Library in Austin and devoted himself to his 300-acre ranch, gradually increasing his cattle herds through shrewd trading at local livestock auctions. Following his death from a coronary occlusion in 1973, he was laid to rest under the giant live oak trees in the family cemetery near the Pedernales. Beyond a nearby stone wall, the howitzers of the Texas National Guard fired a 21-gun salute—in a cow pasture. Lyndon Johnson would have liked that. ■

SORROWS:
Johnson's tenure as President began and ended in sadness. Above left, he takes the oath of office aboard Air Force One after J.F.K.'s assassination; at right, he works on his 1968 statement that he will not run for another term

NIXON

To his long list of "enemies," add

a name at the top: Richard Nixon

RICHARD NIXON'S FIRST CONSCIOUS MEMORY WAS of falling—falling and then running. He was three years old, and his mother had taken him and his brother out riding in a horse-drawn buggy, and the horse turned a corner too fast going home. The boy fell out. A buggy wheel ran over his head and inflicted a deep cut. "I must have been in shock," Nixon recalled later, "but I managed to get up and run after the buggy while my mother tried to make the horse stop." The only aftereffect, Nixon said, was a scar, and that was why he combed his hair straight back instead of parting it on the side.

In a sense, Nixon spent his whole life falling and running and falling again. A symbol of the politics of anger, he was also the only man in U.S. history ever to be elected twice as Vice President and twice as President. As President he achieved much: the U.S. withdrawal from Vietnam, the resumption of relations with China, the first major arms agreement with the Soviet Union. Yet he will always be remembered as the chief perpetrator—and chief victim—of the Watergate scandal, as the only President ever to resign in disgrace.

Learning to bluff. The hallmark of Nixon's youth had been poverty—poverty and family illness and endless work. His father Frank was a combative and quarrelsome Ohioan who moved to Yorba Linda, California, in 1907. There in 1913 his pious Quaker wife Hannah gave birth to Richard, their second son. When Dick Nixon was 12, his younger brother Arthur

died of meningitis; later Harold, the eldest son, was stricken with tuberculosis, draining the family finances and sending Nixon into the work force at an early age. Upon graduating from high school, Nixon had to turn down a scholarship from Harvard (Yale was also interested) and attend a tiny local school, Whittier College. Duke University Law School was just starting when it offered the young college graduate one of 25 scholarships available to a class of 44. There he lived in a $5-a-month room; later he shared a one-room shack that had no plumbing or electricity.

Returning to Whittier in California, Nixon was taken into the law firm of a family friend., began joining clubs and making speeches. He even signed up for the local theater group, where he met a schoolteacher named Thelma ("Pat") Ryan. It took two years of courtship before she agreed to marry him in 1940; she used her own savings to buy the wedding ring.

After Pearl Harbor, Nixon joined the Navy—despite his Quaker upbringing—and served creditably as a supply officer in the South Pacific. He became a master of bluffing in stud poker and saved a stake estimated at as much as $10,000 by war's end. He invested half of it the following year to launch his political career. Pitted against Jerry Voorhis, a popular liberal Democrat, Nixon implied—falsely—that Voorhis was a communist. This kind of smear was to become a Nixon trademark. To one of Voorhis' supporters, Nixon later offered a rationale: "Of course I knew Jerry Voorhis wasn't a communist, but I had to win. The important thing is to win."

Win he did. His climb to national office was spectacularly fast, spurred on by the exposure he gained as a member of the House Committee on Un-American Activities as it investigated Alger Hiss as a communist informant. He ran for the Senate in 1950 against Helen Gahagan Douglas, a former actress and ardent New Dealer. Again smear tactics helped Nixon win: she was "pink right down to her underwear," he proclaimed. He had hardly begun serving in the Senate before G.O.P. leaders turned to him as a running mate for the immensely popular General Dwight Eisenhower. But during the campaign the press discovered that Nixon had a secret slush fund of $18,000 provided by California businessmen. At Eisenhower's urging, Nixon went before a national TV audience with an impassioned defense of his honesty, claiming the only personal present he had received was a "little cocker spaniel dog in a crate ... our little girl ... named it Checkers." Hundreds of thousands of listeners wrote in support of Nixon, and Ike settled his future by saying publicly, "You're my boy!"

The Veep. Eisenhower won 55% of the vote, and the freshman Senator from California, only 39 years old, found himself Vice President. He traveled the world conferring, orating, debating. In Moscow to open a U.S. trade exhibit in 1959, Nixon got into a finger-pointing argument with Soviet leader Nikita Khrushchev in the kitchen of an American model home.

As Eisenhower's inevitable successor, Nixon was nominated to run against the Democrats'

August 25, 1952

1913 Born in Yorba Linda, California
1952 Vice President
1968 Elected President over Humphrey
1971 Trip to China
1974 Resigns presidency in disgrace
1994 Dies at 81

COMRADE! Sharing a 1971 toast with Zhou Enlai

"I HAVE NEVER BEEN A QUITTER": Defiant on his darkest day, Nixon flashes a victory sign on departing the White House

telegenic John F. Kennedy. The vote was incredibly close, with Kennedy winning 50.4% of the popular vote and Nixon 49.6%. He accepted the bitter defeat and returned to California. Then his legendary political shrewdness abandoned him. He let himself be talked into running for Governor against the popular Edmund G. ("Pat") Brown and tried to imply that Brown was a dangerous leftist. Nixon lost, and it was after this crushing defeat that he blew up at reporters and announced, "You won't have Nixon to kick around anymore."

Only 49 by then, he decided to move to New York City and make some money. He joined a prosperous Wall Street firm but never really retired from politics. He stumped for Barry Goldwater in 1964, and when that campaign ended in disaster, he became the logical man to reunite the splintered party in 1968. In a year of ghetto riots and political assassinations, Nixon promised "peace with honor" in Vietnam and "law and order" at home. He was reassuring enough to beat Hubert Humphrey and the Vietnam-burdened Democrats.

Nixon's first term included some surprisingly liberal innovations: he cut military spending, tied Social Security increases to the cost of living, instituted "revenue sharing" to funnel federal tax money back to states and cities. And he startled the world by journeying to Beijing to open U.S. relations with the aging Mao Zedong. But his achievements were overshadowed by Vietnam. Nixon had campaigned on a promise to end the war "with honor," meaning no surrender and no defeat, but the communists had shown no interest in negotiation. Antiwar protests grew in size and violence, particularly after he ordered

bombing raids and made a temporary "incursion" into Cambodia. When the peace treaty was finally signed, it was too late to salvage America's interests in Vietnam.

Nightmare. Nixon brought to the White House an extraordinary permanent anger and resentment. His fears led to the drawing up of an official "enemies list," the use of "dirty tricks" in his successful 1972 re-election campaign against George McGovern and the creation of a group of "plumbers" to stop press leaks from the White House. It was this group that bungled the break-in at Democratic National Headquarters at the Watergate apartment complex. But it was Nixon and his aides who bungled the handling of the affair, engaging in the elaborate cover-ups and deceit of the "long national nightmare" of Watergate. When public opinion, the Supreme Court and senior members of his own party finally abandoned him, Nixon resigned from the presidency on Aug. 9, 1974. For anyone else, departure in disgrace from the highest office in the land would have served as a public farewell. But Nixon, who proudly stated, "I have never been a quitter," climbed once more out of the abyss, re-creating himself as an elder statesman before his death at 81 in 1994.

In his last meeting with his staff before his resignation as President, Richard Nixon burst into tears. "Always remember," he said, "others may hate you, but those who hate you don't win unless you hate them—and then you destroy yourself." Gifted in many ways but always nursing an inner kernel of hatred, Richard Nixon had destroyed himself. ∎

GORBACHEV

*First **Mikhail Gorbachev** made the U.S.S.R. disappear—then he followed*

THE 1980S CAME TO AN END IN WHAT SEEMED like a magic act, performed on a world-historical stage. Trapdoors flew open, and whole regimes vanished. The shell of an old world cracked, its black iron fragments dropping away, and something new, alive, exploded into the air in a flurry of white wings. The wall that divided Berlin and sealed an international order crumbled into souvenirs. The cold war, which seemed for so long part of the permanent order of things, peacefully deconstructed before the world's eyes. After years of numb changelessness, the communist world came alive with an energy and turmoil that took on a bracing dynamic of its own.

The magician who set loose those forces was a career party functionary, faithful communist, charismatic politician, international celebrity and impresario of calculated disorder named Mikhail Sergeyevich Gorbachev. In a novel alliance with the free forces of world communication, Gorbachev became the patron of change: Big Brother's better twin. In Warsaw his portraits, like icons at a holy festival, waved amid a swarm of

Czechs. In East Germany the young chanted, "Gorby! Gorby!" to taunt the police. In breaking the chains of Soviet repression, Gorbachev knew he was releasing forces that might escape his control. And sure enough, his ride on the tiger of reform ended when he was devoured by the energies he set loose.

Child of struggle. The man who would overturn the legacy of Stalin and Lenin was born in the small farming village of Privolnoye in the south of the Russian republic in 1931—the height of Stalin's brutal drive to force Soviet peasants into collective labor farms. The Gorbachevs survived the worst of the upheaval by being on the winning side: Mikhail's grandfather helped organize a collective farm. Not long after the turmoil of collectivization died down, the Soviet Union was hit by the second trauma of Gorbachev's boyhood: the Nazi invasion. Mikhail was 11 years old when German tanks rumbled into nearby Stavropol; his father fought at the front for four years. When Gorbachev traveled to school in Moscow in 1950—five years after the war's end—he saw that "everything lay in ruins."

At Moscow State University, Gorbachev studied law, succumbed to the Stalin cult and fell in love with fellow student Raisa Maximovna Titorenko. They married early in 1954. Though he trained as a lawyer, Gorbachev was more interested in politics. A true believer among cynical careerists, he rose fast in the party when he returned to Stavropol, becoming first secretary of the Stavropol territory in 1970, at age 39. He was an incorruptible bureaucrat, open and accessible with the local farmers, even popular with journalists.

Gorbachev attracted important party patrons, and by 1977 he was featured in a front-page interview in *Pravda*. In 1978 he met party boss Leonid Brezhnev, and less than a month later he was plucked out of Stavropol to become, at 47, a member of the national hierarchy, ranking 20th among all Soviet leaders. The aging Kremlin leadership was looking for new blood.

When Brezhnev died in 1982 and Yuri Andropov came into office with plans for reform, he began grooming Gorbachev as a key lieutenant in his clean-up campaign. But Andropov's tenure was brief, and after his death in 1984 the party's Old Guard made a final stand, choosing the ailing Konstantin Chernenko, 72, as General Secretary. Through much of that brief year in power Chernenko was so sickly that

Gorbachev, his deputy, ran the country.

In March 1985, Gorbachev officially became General Secretary of the party. Soon Russia was learning the two tenets of Gorbachev's new line: *glasnost* and *perestroika*. *Glasnost*—openness—freed the press and the people to discuss Soviet social problems honestly for the first time. *Perestroika*—restructuring—was more difficult to achieve. Initially Gorbachev believed he could restructure the country by replacing hacks with doers, offering real rewards for hard work and cutting back on the consumption of vodka. It took two years for him to discover that the problems were much deeper and that the solutions would have to be far-reaching and disruptive.

Gorbachev was more successful in his initiatives with the nations of Eastern Europe. Those regimes had long taken it for granted that their Big Brothers in Moscow would provide the brute force that was the substitute for political legitimacy in the Marxist-Leninist system. Now all of a sudden, the No. 1 man in the Kremlin was saying he would not back them and they had to find a way of making a genuine social compact with their own people or fall. Hence the amazing events of 1989, when one after another the communist dictatorships of Eastern Europe came tumbling down: in Hungary, in East Germany, in Czechoslovakia, even in hard-line Bulgaria.

Dustheap of history. At home, Gorbachev now faced the paradox of *perestroika*: freedom, so crucial to his principles and strategy, emboldened his critics and opponents. The Soviet Union hovered at the edge of definitive change, and the push that sent it over the brink came in August 1991. While Gorbachev was at his vacation retreat in the Crimea, a group of hard-line communists took him into custody, sent tanks into the streets of Moscow and banned demonstrations. But the coup was curiously halfhearted. Its leaders even failed to take the populist President of the Russian republic, Boris Yeltsin, into custody. When Yeltsin climbed onto a tank in front of the Russian Parliament Building to denounce the coup, and Soviet troops refused to fire on him, the plotters fled. A haggard-looking Gorbachev returned to Moscow to find that Yeltsin had become the effective leader of the forces of reform.

In the wake of the coup attempt, the Communist Party temporarily went underground, its leadership disbanded, its offices padlocked. Gorbachev resigned in late December, and atop the Kremlin the flag of the Soviet Union was hauled down on the last day of 1991 and replaced by the Russian flag. Gorbachev turned to a life of speechmaking, globe trotting and attempts to regain the spotlight. Like Theodore Roosevelt, he seemed doomed to spend his later years in fruitless attempts to regain control of the levers of power. His belated entry into Russia's presidential race in 1996 met with little enthusiasm: as one newspaper reported, he was "tanned, fit and disregarded." History's regard would be higher. ∎

January 1, 1990

1931 Born in Privolnoye, Russia, U.S.S.R.
1985 Becomes General Secretary of Party
1991 Hard-line coup fails; U.S.S.R. breaks up, and he resigns
1996 Fails in run for presidency of Russia

YEARNING TO BREATH FREE: President Ronald Reagan called the U.S.S.R. an "evil empire" but came to support Gorbachev. Reagan's successor, George Bush, continued that policy

JANUARY 3, 1938 In a long career, China's Chiang Kai-shek opposed the Manchu dynasty and Japanese invaders but lost his most important battle—against Communist Mao Zedong.

JUNE 21, 1943 Founding his fascist party in 1921, Italy's Benito Mussolini dreamed of creating a new Roman Empire, but his alliance with Hitler led to Italy's defeat—and his death.

NOVEMBER 22, 1954 For five decades Ho Chi Minh fought for a free, unified Vietnam, first against the French, then the U.S., but he did not live to see North Vietnam's victory in 1975.

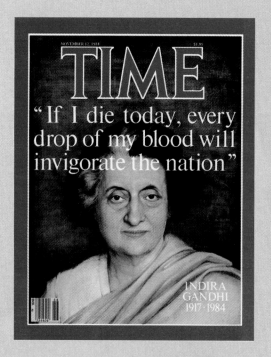

NOVEMBER 12, 1984 Daughter of Indian leader J.P. Nehru, Indira Gandhi became a powerful Prime Minister who helped give birth to Bangladesh. She was assassinated in 1984.

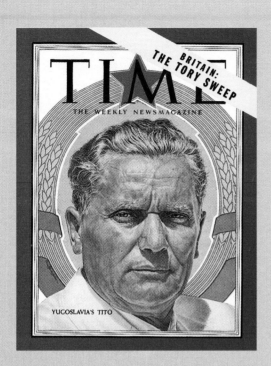

JUNE 6, 1955 Partisan leader against Nazi invaders in WW II, Josip Broz Tito held the Yugoslav federation together after the war and successfully charted independence from Stalin.

JANUARY 26, 1959 After Fidel Castro led a tiny band of rebels to victory over dictator Fulgencio Batista, he turned Cuba into an outpost of communism 90 miles from the U.S.

MAY 14, 1979 Iron-willed Prime Minister Margaret Thatcher led a conservative revolution in Great Britain and faced down Argentina over the Falkland Islands in 1982.

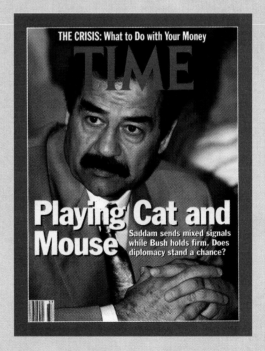

AUGUST 13, 1990 An old-style dictator who ruled through fear, Iraq's Saddam Hussein fought Iran in the 1980s, then was smashed by U.S.-led allies after he invaded Kuwait in 1990.

THE AC

Nelson Mandela, 1994

TIVISTS

If politics is the art of the possible, activism is the pursuit of the ideal. Activists wear the harness of dreams; they are men and women so bound to an abstract vision that they will pay any price to achieve it. For Nelson Mandela, the price was 27 years in prison; for Mohandas Gandhi, the price was life. Some activists share a secret, silent conversation that unites them in common cause: Gandhi learned from Thoreau and Tolstoy; Mandela and King and Walesa learned from Gandhi. But there are other activists and other ideals: Maria Montessori fought to free minds; Billy Graham battled to save souls. And there is a dark activism too, an activism that insists its vision must be achieved no matter the cost, an activism that embraces expedience—and becomes terrorism. ■

GANDHI

A warrior who needed no weapons, **Mohandas Gandhi** *drove the British from India with "soul force"*

WHEN MOHANDAS GANDHI WAS in London in 1931 pleading for Indian independence, a small British girl started to ask for his autograph. Then she drew back shyly before the strange little dhoti-clad man with the cavernous mouth, jutting ears and scrawny neck. With a child's candor, she looked up at her mother and asked, "Mummy, is he really great?"

Mohandas Gandhi *was* great, but he was a human being perhaps more scarce than great men: he was a good man. He disturbed people by his goodness. He called himself "a Hindu of Hindus," and yet he put many a professing Christian to shame. "The spirit of the Sermon on the Mount," wrote the man who fitted the rubrics of the Beatitudes more comfortably than most Christians, "competes almost on equal terms with the *Bhagavad-Gita* for the domination of my heart."

June 30, 1947

1869 Born in Porbandar, India
1893 Goes to South Africa to practice law
1915 Returns to India to fight for civil rights
1947 England grants India independence
1948 Assassinated

From the Russian novelist and pacifist Count Leo Tolstoy and the American hermit-naturalist Henry David Thoreau, Gandhi learned the doctrines of non-violence and organized disobedience to unjust power. He combined the elements into a belief of Christlike simplicity: oppose hate with love, greed with openhandedness, lust with self-control; harm no feeling creature. Fragile tools, but Gandhi used them to wrest from the British Empire its greatest diadem, the Indian subcontinent, and to become the father of modern India.

"A half-naked fakir." Mohandas Karamchand Gandhi was eight years old—a skinny, timid schoolboy in the northwest India town of Porbandar on the Arabian Sea—when Queen Victoria was proclaimed Empress of India at the Great Durbar in Delhi in 1877. His frail body never grew beyond 110 lbs., but his youthful conscience matured into a towering spirit that laid the mighty British low. Winston Churchill, the last lion of Victoria's empire, once called Gandhi "a half-naked, seditious fakir ... These Indian politicians," he said in 1930, "will never get dominion status in their lifetimes." Seventeen years later,

LAWYER In 1900 the 23-year-old Gandhi, with a new law degree from London, went to South Africa to begin his legal career. There he first felt the full weight of the British Empire's rigid racial code.

ADVOCATE Appalled by the plight of South Africa's large Indian minority, Gandhi ignored his lucrative law practice to lead successful non-violent protests that dismantled anti-Indian laws.

HUSBAND In an arranged marriage—a practice he later crusaded against—Gandhi and his wife were wed when both were 13. After the birth of a fourth son, they ceased sexual relations at Gandhi's suggestion.

ASCETIC In 1931 Gandhi calls on Prime Minister Ramsay MacDonald at 10 Downing Street. Though his love of simplicity was genuine, Gandhi carefully deployed the power of his humble clothes and frail bearing as a weapon in his war with the mighty British Raj.

DIPLOMAT In 1947 Gandhi meets with Viscount Mountbatten, Britain's chief representative in India, to discuss details of the British withdrawal. "Imperialism is the Great Satan of our day," he argued.

POLITICIAN Gandhi talks policy with his long-time associate Jawaharlal Nehru in 1946. As independence neared, Gandhi found he had lost control of the process he created; free India was baptized at birth in the blood of religious war.

Gandhi had achieved not merely dominion status for India, but complete independence from the hated British rule.

Gandhi first felt the full weight of the white man's color bar when he went to South Africa as a London-educated vakeel (barrister) at age 23. More and more he neglected a lucrative law practice to lead his fellow Indians in a fight against local anti-Indian laws. Deciding that manual labor was essential to the good life, he came to believe Indians would find peace only through making their own clothes on the charka (spinning wheel). He moved to a farm settlement to work the ground and began to publish a newspaper, *Indian Opinion.* Mobilizing local Indians for his first civil disobedience campaign, he won repeal of some anti-Indian laws from an obstinate South African government. In 1915, at age 45, he returned to Bombay, the hero of India.

Leader in a loincloth. The first year after his return, Gandhi toured much of India. Walking among the people, the gentle ascetic in loincloth won the hearts of millions of Indians. "Gandhi says" became synonymous with "the truth is" for many a villager. The peasants began calling him Mahatma (Great Soul); he claimed he hated the honorific. Gandhi found that India's "struggle" for independence rested in the hands of a few well-educated Indians. Their Indian National Congress was then a polite debating society; Gandhi converted it into a mass movement. Indian peasants did not worry about independence until Gandhi told them to. He began to preach and practice the two beliefs that would become the revolutionary tools of his movement: ahimsa (nonviolence), which he claimed was the first principle of life, and satyagraha—"soul force," or conquering through love, the only proper way of life.

Those Gandhi called "the dumb, toiling, semi-starving millions" could understand him when he cried for their freedom; they could not always understand him when he told them they must not use violence to win that freedom. When he saw the bloodshed that followed an early call for resistance in 1922, Gandhi was overwhelmed with remorse. He called off his campaign and imposed on himself a five-day fast.

The pattern repeated itself in later years. The ways of passive action—the sari-clad women lying on railway tracks, the strikes, the banner-waving processions—would lead to shots in the streets, to burning and looting. Gandhi always punished himself for his followers' transgressions by imposing a fast on himself. And with each fast, each boycott, each imprisonment, Gandhi came closer to his goal of a free India. He spent a total of 12 years in jails of the British Raj, which feared to leave him free, feared even more that he would die in British hands and enrage all India. With the same weapons he got in some blows at his favorite social evils—the treatment of the untouchables under the Hindu caste system, child marriages, the use of alcohol and the inferior status of women in Indian society.

In 1930 Gandhi and 70 volunteers marched from Ahmadabad by a circuitous route to Dandi on the gulf of Cambay to protest a British tax on salt that affected every household in India. There, at 6 a.m. on April 6, he waded into the sea, dipped up water in an earthen jar and evaporated it over a small fire, leaving crude but illegal salt. Several of Gandhi's lieutenants were arrested early in the campaign, but he was not taken into custody until the first week of May. By that time the crusade had spread widely, amid much rioting. The salt march brought Gandhi and his cause to the attention of the world; TIME named him Man of the Year for 1930. The next year Gandhi was released from jail. The British still ruled India, but the independence movement had grown enormously.

In 1942, at the height of World War II, Gandhi called once more for Britain's total withdrawal from India and threatened a mass campaign of civil disobedience to achieve it. Again the British arrested him; again Indians rioted; again his power over the Indian people only grew during his 21 months in jail.

By the end of the war, the British Empire was exhausted; the time for India's freedom had come at last. Yet with Gandhi's greatest victory—the arrival of independence on Aug. 15, 1947—came his greatest defeat. The subcontinent was partitioned into two nations, Hindu-majority India and Muslim-majority Pakistan. Seething with fear and religious fanaticism, India spurted blood: in all, some one million died in the months following the British withdrawal.

Independence without unity between religions was as ashes in Gandhi's mouth. He continued to work to reunite Pakistan and India. But in the last half-year of his life he found not only Muslims but also many of his own Hindus opposed attempts at reconciliation. On his 78th birthday, Gandhi spoke sadly, "The time was when whatever I said, the masses followed. But today I am a lone voice in India."

TWILIGHT: Gandhi went to his death believing he had failed

Target of hatred. Four months later, on Jan. 30, 1948, in New Delhi, Nathu Ram Vinayak Godse, editor of the extremist newspaper *Hindu Rashtra,* approached Gandhi as his grandnieces helped him to his outdoor prayer pavilion. After a brief exchange of words, Godse shot Gandhi three times at close range; he died 28 minutes later. With supreme irony, violence broke out again in India after Gandhi's death, as his admirers exacted a blood price from the Hindu extremists.

The world that revered few men had revered Gandhi—but, he feared, not enough to follow where he pointed. He died believing his "lone voice" was unheard. He was mistaken, for the power of his message would endure to move men and nations decades after his death. Adapting Gandhi's beliefs and tactics, activists like Nelson Mandela and Martin Luther King demonstrated that his soul force would long resound. ∎

MANDELA

Captivity ennobled **Nelson Mandela**—*and once free, he freed his people*

JUST A SHORT STROLL FROM NELSON MANDELA'S modest country house in South Africa's Transkei region is the even more humble village where he was born. The round thatched huts of Qunu have no running water or electricity, and shy herd boys wielding sticks tend the skinny cattle the same way young Rolihlahla Nelson Mandela did some 70 years ago. Walking across the green hills above the village one morning in 1994, Mandela recalled a lesson he learned as a boy. "When you want to get a herd to move in a certain direction," he said, "you stand at the back with a stick. Then a few of the more energetic cattle move to the front, and the rest of the cattle follow. You are really guiding them from behind." He paused before saying with a smile, "That is how a leader should do his work."

No one would suggest that so charismatic a figure as Nelson Mandela, a doughty and energetic 77 in 1996, leads from behind. Yet for close to three decades he led the struggle to topple South Africa's apartheid regime from a series of prison cells, gradually accumulating in isolation the moral authority, world recognition and—in Gandhi's term—"soul force" that would ultimately lead to his personal liberation as well as the freeing of his people from white rule.

On one level Mandela is merely a man of extraordinary courage whose commitment to racial justice never flagged during those long years of imprisonment. On another level he is an astute politician—a word he proudly uses to describe himself—who skillfully negotiated with President F. W. de Klerk to arrange the transition to a fully democratic South Africa, then won election to its presidency by an overwhelming margin. But on a more transcendent plane, where history is made and myths are forged, Mandela is a hero, a man who, like those described by author Joseph Campbell, has emerged from a symbolic grave "reborn, made great and filled with creative power."

Mandela witnessed the dynamic of leadership early on, for he was born to a royal family of the Thembu tribe of the Xhosa people. Several times a year, his guardian, Chief Jongintaba, the regent of the Thembu, presided over what were essentially tribal town meetings. People came from far and wide to Chief Jongintaba's royal seat, the Great Place at Mqekezweni. These meetings lasted days, and did not end until everyone had had a chance to speak his mind. Rolihlahla sat on the fringes and watched as his guardian listened in thoughtful silence. Only at the end would Chief Jongintaba speak, and then it was to nurture a consensus. A leader, Mandela learned, does not impose a decision. He molds one.

Mandela matured into a combination of African nobility and British aristocracy. He has the punctilious manners of a

February 5, 1990

1918 Born in Transkei, South Africa
1961 Founds militant wing of A.N.C.
1962 Jailed for subversive activities
1990 Freed from jail
1994 Elected President of new nation

Victorian gentleman. (His aides sometimes chastise him for rising from his chair to greet everyone who approaches him.) His patrician nature was prominently on display during his negotiations with De Klerk for a new constitution in 1991. At the end of the first day of meetings, Mandela—then only a year out of prison—gave De Klerk a withering dressing down: "Even the head of an illegitimate, discredited minority regime, as his is, has certain moral standards to uphold." His wrath is cold, not hot; he does not explode at his foes, he freezes them out.

At the same time, Mandela possesses a common touch that no amount of political coaching can inculcate. When he speaks at banquets, he makes a point of going into the kitchen and shaking hands with every busboy. When he lived underground as an outlaw in the early 1960s and wanted to elude the police, his colleagues marveled at how he blended in with the people. He usually disguised himself as a chauffeur; he would don a long dustcoat, hunch his shoulders, and suddenly this tall, singularly regal figure was transformed into one of the huddled masses moving along the streets of Johannesburg. Even today, at rallies or meetings, the poorest South African feels he has the right to greet and address his leader.

Though he may be a natural mass leader, Mandela does not exhibit all the attributes associated with such charismatic figures. Yes, he may plunge into ecstatic crowds at rallies, pump hands, toss off a few steps of the *toyi-toyi*, the stomping dance of the South Africans. But when he begins to speak, the cheers usually turn to good-natured but puzzled silence. Not for Mandela the soaring metaphors of Martin Luther King; he addresses his audiences in the sober, didactic style of an organic-chemistry professor. He refuses to tell his listeners what he thinks they want to hear. To black audiences, he declares that democracy and majority rule will not change the material circumstances of their lives overnight. At the same time, he informs white audiences that they must take responsibility for South Africa's troubled past, and will have to reconcile themselves to its uncertain future.

Spear of the nation. As a boy, Mandela was taught to rule; it was anticipated he would someday head the Thembu tribe. Instead he became a lawyer, graduating from the University of the Witwatersrand, then joining the anti-apartheid African National Congress party. With classmate Oliver Tambo, he set up the first black law practice in South Africa in 1952. Defiantly working from a whites-only downtown neighborhood, the two young lawyer-activists specialized in representing blacks who failed to carry the passes that were required of nonwhites in white neighborhoods.

Mandela and Tambo helped form the Youth League of the

A.N.C. in 1944, and three years later they drew up a program of action calling for strikes, boycotts and acts of civil disobedience. In 1955 they supported the Freedom Charter, an economic credo many thought socialist. Mandela abandoned the peaceful methods espoused by then A.N.C. leader Chief Albert Luthuli after the Sharpeville Massacre in 1960, in which police killed 69 black protesters. Oliver Tambo left to establish a headquarters in exile, and Mandela stayed behind to set up the A.N.C.'s underground military wing, Umkhonto we Sizwe (Spear of the Nation), and launch a sabotage campaign. After 17 months on the run, he was nabbed in 1962. In 1964 he and seven others were convicted of sedition. His sentence: life in prison.

Mandela was sent to Robben Island, a penal colony across from Cape Town Harbor, where he would be held for more than two decades before being moved to a less harsh prison, Victor Verster, outside Cape Town. During the first 10 years he spent in jail, Mandela swung a pickax in a limestone quarry, breaking boulders into gravel. But the severe conditions only strengthened his resolve; typically, he directed his anger to a crusade for better prison conditions.

Several interesting changes occurred during Mandela's long, long, incarceration. For one thing, his enforced isolation slowly transformed him into a mythic figure. Incommunicado, without the opportunity to speak out on specific issues, Man-

ROOM WITH A VIEW: Revisiting his cell on Robben Island

dela in his silence became South Africa's most persuasive presence: an inspiration to blacks, a recrimination to whites. What is more, he sensed the moral power his confinement had conferred. Mandela had always been willing to talk; violence was his recourse when the other side would not listen. One day in 1986 he sat down and wrote a letter to the government proposing a dialogue on the nation's future. This gesture received a secret, surprisingly willing response from President P.W. Botha, a hard-liner on apartheid who nonetheless had begun to sense his country's escalating dilemma.

Pariah state. Apartheid was collapsing of its own inherent absurdity. Moreover, the outlawed A.N.C.'s 1984 call to make South Africa "ungovernable" had been answered by a surge of black demonstrations and acts of civil disobedience. To put down such unrest, the government had to use increasingly brutal police and military actions, many of them filmed by news cameras and televised to appalled viewers around the globe. These ugly spectacles increased international pressure for economic sanctions against South Africa. Whites saw their nation becoming an international pariah.

Botha realized he needed Mandela and arranged a meeting with him in July 1989, slipping him out of prison for the purpose. The two issued a joint communiqué committing

FIREBRAND Rejecting nonviolence after the Sharpeville Massacre of 69 blacks in 1960, Mandela founded the guerrilla wing of the African National Congress. Living underground and committing acts of violence, he was dubbed "the Black Pimpernel" by the white press.

PRISONER During his incarceration, Mandela organized protests against conditions in prison. Offered his freedom by the Botha regime in 1985 if he would renounce the A.N.C.'s struggle, Mandela defiantly replied, "I cannot give any undertaking. Only free men can negotiate."

muniqué committing themselves to peace. A month later, Botha was nudged out of office; De Klerk succeeded him and announced, "Our goal is a totally changed South Africa." He delivered on his promise in memorable fashion: on Feb. 11, 1990, before the eyes of a wondering world, the now legendary Nelson Mandela walked out of Victor Verster prison—free at last.

Rainbow nation. Four years later, on April 27, 1994, Mandela triumphed in his long quest to end apartheid. At 12:01 a.m., white rule in South Africa came to an end, as cheering crowds in the nine new provincial capitals hailed the raising of a new flag with six colors symbolizing the people, their blood, their land, the gold under the ground, the sky—and peace.

A few days later, in a remarkably peaceful election, lines of determined blacks stretched a mile or more at polling places to cast their first votes. Nelson Mandela was overwhelmingly elected President of the new nation. Yet he was magnanimous in victory, including in his coalition Cabinet not only his longtime A.N.C. colleagues but also F. W. de Klerk and tribal leader Mangosuthu Buthelezi, whose Zulus would be a key constituency of the new South Africa.

Mandela's inauguration on May 10 transformed Pretoria

FIRST PERSON

"We stand here today as nothing more than a representative of the millions of our people who dared to rise up against a social system whose very essence is war, violence, racism, oppression, repression and the impoverishment of an entire people ... Because of their courage and persistence for many years ... all humanity will join together to celebrate one of the outstanding human victories of our century That triumph will finally bring to a close a history of five hundred years of African colonisation ... Thus it will mark a great step forward in history and also serve as a common pledge of the peoples of the world to fight racism wherever it occurs and whatever guise it assumes."

—*Nobel Peace Prize speech, 1993*

from a dour police state to a city of brotherly love. Blacks and whites embraced, old political adversaries shook hands, and the crowds at a mixed-race concert swayed in unison to Zulu drummers, Afrikaner fiddlers and English-singing rock bands. A flight of South African air force jets streaked by overhead, streaming smoke trails of the six colors of the new "rainbow nation."

Yet there was one cloud in Mandela's sky: his marriage to his wife Winnie did not survive his years in prison. Increasingly prominent and radical, she became embroiled in a series of scandals. She was charged with engaging in corruption and ultimately convicted of kidnapping, but to Mandela—who had generally supported her actions—only her sexual infidelity mattered. He was granted a formal divorce early in 1996.

If there has been a consistent criticism of Nelson Mandela over the years, it is that he is too willing to see the good in people. Yet this flaw grows out of his great strength, his generosity of heart toward his enemies. He defends himself by noting that thinking too well of people can make them behave better than they otherwise would. Astonishingly, the man who spent 27 years in prison at the hands of a heartless regime still believes in the goodness of the human heart. ∎

FREE MAN In February 1990 Mandela walks to freedom with his controversial wife Winnie. They were divorced in 1996.

NEGOTIATOR After months of arduous talks, Mandela and F.W. de Klerk agreed to a new constitution. They shared the Nobel Prize for Peace in 1993.

CANDIDATE Citizen Mandela takes to the hustings on the way to a sweeping election victory in May 1994. Once President, he named De Klerk and Zulu leader Buthelezi to his coalition Cabinet.

BEN-GURION

*How **David Ben-Gurion** turned the Promised Land into the state of Israel*

THE LUSTIEST CHEERS AT THE VAST MIL-
itary parade in Jerusalem in May 1973
marking Israel's 25th anniversary
were neither for the tanks passing the
reviewing stand nor for the Phantom
jets whooshing overhead. Instead, the
crowds cheered loudest for a slight,
aging, white-thatched man being
helped to a seat of honor among the dignitaries. He
was David Ben-Gurion, Israel's longtime leader,
first Prime Minister and, in a sense, its George
Washington. Out of the Prime Minister's office for
10 years and in complete retirement for three,
Ben-Gurion, in that appearance, gave Israelis a
chance to acclaim his role in the birth, growth and
maturity of their country. As it turned out, the
independence-day parade was his last hurrah: the
87-year-old leader died seven months later.

With his white hair foaming up from each side
of his thrusting head, Ben-Gurion looked like an
Old Testament patriarch. A Zionist and Socialist, a
prophet with a pistol, he was both realist and visionary.
Through half a century of Turkish, British and international
rule in Palestine, he dreamed of and worked for a Jewish
state. It was Ben-Gurion who suggested the name of the
country and proclaimed its birth in 1948, who carried out
unpopular decisions in the state's early days and who imprint-
ed on Israel the strength of his own personality.

It was quite a personality. Ben-Gurion's moods covered the

August 16, 1948

1886 Born David
Gryn in Russia

1906 Arrives in Pales-
tine, changes name

1935 Becomes leader
of Zionist movement

1948 Proclaims new
state of Israel

1973 Dies in Israel

full range from stormy to stoical. He was at times
arbitrary, vindictive and magnanimous. He had a
disarming smile, but the deep-set brown eyes
under the delta-like shock of white hair always
burned. Innocent of humor, he had no small talk
and no interest in anybody else's. He did not drink
or smoke, rarely went to concerts, disliked movies.
He was adored by Israelis in general, but loved by
only a few who knew him intimately—most notably
his wife Paula—and he was disliked by some political adversaries (Golda Meir would refer to him
only as "that man"). Aloof even from old colleagues,
his private passion was reading philosophy—Spin-
oza, the Greeks, the ancient Buddhist texts.

Lion cub. He was born David Gryn, and he
set out from Russia in 1906 and landed illegally at
Jaffa to begin a new life as a Zionist pioneer. Once
in Palestine, Gryn followed a practice of the early
settlers and changed his name to Ben-Gurion,
Hebrew for "Son of a Lion Cub." Eager to work the
land, he settled in the Galilean village of Sejera and insisted
in later years that farming there had been his greatest joy.
Friends, however, described a less than expert plowman who
spent most of his time reading and studying.

Ben-Gurion soon left the land for the labor movement,
organizing Jewish workers and writing for a small labor
weekly. Eventually his political activities on behalf of Zionism
so angered Turkish authorities that they exiled him and for-
bade his return. He went to the U.S., met and married a Pol-
ish-born Brooklyn nurse named Paula Munweiss. After he
became famous, she liked to tease him by saying he had
spent part of their wedding night at a Zionist meeting.

When the British replaced the Turks in Palestine under a
League of Nations mandate, Ben-Gurion returned. Moving
from labor activities to Zionist planning, he was elected chairman of the political arm of the World Zionist Organization.
Early on he had been hopeful that Palestine's Jews and Arabs
could live together in peace, but by the mid-1930s he had
come to think of Palestine as a strictly Jewish state, and he
devoted himself to planning the immigration and armed
strength necessary to accomplish it.

Birth of a nation. It was Ben-Gurion who created the
Haganah, the underground Jewish army. After World War II
he developed a strategy to end the British mandate, stepping
up the illegal immigration of Jews from Europe in the face of
stern British opposition, while Jewish terrorists carried out a
continuous assault on British personnel and bases. This desperate plan succeeded, and the birth of the new nation of
Israel was proclaimed by Ben-Gurion in Tel Aviv the very day
the last British soldier left the territory.

FATHER OF HIS COUNTRY: Ben-Gurion's twin shocks of white hair gave him the look of an Old Testament patriarch; opposite, on May 14, 1948, under a photograph of Zionist prophet Theodor Herzl, he proclaims "the establishment of a Jewish state in Palestine to be called Israel"

The Jews of this new nation of Israel danced for joy, yet Ben-Gurion knew that five Arab armies were massed against his people, and that the proclamation he had read was their call to war. He acted as Defense Minister as well as Prime Minister, and his ill-armed, illegally trained forces smashed the Arab invaders with stunning success. At the same time, he prevented civil war by ordering Israeli solders to fire if the Jewish terrorist group Irgun Zvai Leumi (National Military Organization) attempted to land weapons for itself from the freighter *Altalena* in defiance of his decree that "there shall be one army, one nation, one people." The Irgun, headed by Menachem Begin, backed down and obeyed.

Ben-Gurion stamped his own indelible style on the new state. It was egalitarian, as he was, and an open-necked sports shirt became a kind of national costume still favored by Israel's leaders. The army had a special place in his heart, and it was Ben-Gurion who developed the Israeli warfare strategy based on pre-emptive strikes. He also approved the capture and public trial of Nazi war criminal Adolf Eichmann, so that young Sabras (native-born Israelis) would have a better understanding of what the Holocaust had meant.

At his home in the pioneer Negev kibbutz of Sde Boker, after his retirement, Ben-Gurion spent his time writing his memoirs, reading philosophy and watching trees that he had planted swaying in the desert wind. His final wish, granted by a grateful nation after the unavoidable panoply of a state funeral—which the old lion would have scorned—was to be buried by his wife's side in the soil of Sde Boker. ∎

KHOMEINI

Iron-fisted mystic **Ayatullah Khomeini** *heralded a newly militant Islam*

THE DOUR OLD MAN SHUFFLED TO THE ROOFTOP and waved apathetically to crowds that surrounded his modest home in the holy city of Qum. The hooded eyes that glared balefully from beneath his black turban often turned upward, as if seeking inspiration from on high—which, as a religious mystic, he indeed was. To Iran's Shi'ite Muslims, Ayatullah Ruhollah Khomeini was an ascetic spiritual leader whose teachings were law. To the West he was a fanatical foe whose judgments were harsh and whose reasoning was surreal. Yet to millions of all faiths around the world, the Ayatullah was most significant as the prophet of a rejuvenated Islamic fundamentalism. Just as Mao Zedong had proclaimed to the world on gaining power that China had "stood up," so too the Ayatullah was the herald of a new breed of extremist Muslims, militant in their determination to shape their own destiny.

Khomeini was learned in the ways of Islamic law and Platonic philosophy, yet he would remain astonishingly ignorant of cultures other than his own. Rarely had so improbable a leader shaken the world. Only a few years before the Iranian revolution, Khomeini was an austere theologian almost totally unknown in the West. For decades he had nursed an inflexible devotion to a few simple ideas and developed a finely tuned instinct for articulating the passions and rages of his people. Khomeini was no politician in the Western sense, yet he possessed the most potent of political gifts: the ability to rouse millions to both blind adulation and blind fury.

Sign of God. Khomeini's career traced the classic trajectory of 20th century rebels: from agitation to arrest, from arrest to exile, from exile to triumphant return. His nemesis was the ruling family of Iran, personified in the figure of Shah Mohammed Reza Pahlavi, who ruled through the strong support of the U.S. In 1963 Iran was swept by riots stirred up by its powerful Islamic clergy. The Shah suppressed the disturbances, in part by jailing one of the instigators, an ascetic theologian named Ruhollah Khomeini, who had recently attained the title of Ayatullah —"sign of God," a popularly bestowed honorific. Khomeini had drawn crowds to fiery sermons in which he denounced the Shah as a traitor to Islam. In 1964 he was arrested and exiled, first to Turkey, then to Iraq, where he continued to preach against the idolatrous Shah and to promulgate his vision of Iran as an "Islamic republic."

By 1978 the Shah had alienated almost all elements of Iranian society. Westernized intellectuals were infuriated by rampant corruption, workers by the selective prosperity that raised glittering apartments for the rich while the poor remained in mud hovels, the clergy by Westernized gambling casinos and bars. Everyone hated the secret police, the SAVAK. But the U.S. regarded the Shah as a valuable ally and funneled to him money and weapons.

Late in 1978, small anti-Shah demonstrations swelled into protest marches of hundreds of thousands in Tehran. At the outset the revolt had no visible leaders. But even in exile Khomeini was well known inside Iran for his unyielding insistence that the Shah must go. When demonstrators began waving the Ayatullah's picture, the frightened Shah pressured Iraq to boot Khomeini out. It was a fatal blunder; in October 1978 the Ayatullah settled outside Paris, where he gathered a circle of exiles and for the first time publicized his views through the Western press.

Return of the prophet. Khomeini now became the active head of the revolution. Cassettes of his anti-Shah sermons sold like pop records in bazaars. When he called for strikes, his followers shut down the banks, the postal service, the factories, the food stores and, most important, the oil wells, bringing the country close to paralysis. The Shah imposed martial law, but to no avail. In January 1979 the Shah and his Empress went off into exile, leaving behind a "regency council." But Khomeini announced that no one ruling in the Shah's name would be acceptable, and Iran was torn by the largest riots of the entire revolution. Now his time was at hand, and the Ayatullah returned to Tehran to a tumultuous welcome: "The holy one has come!" The vast, adoring throng stalled Khomeini's motorcade so that he had to be lifted over the heads of his adulators by helicopter. He withdrew to the holy city of Qum and

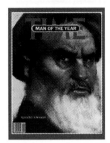

January 7, 1980

1900 Born in Khomein, Iran
1963 Exiled for leading anti-Shah protests
1978 Moves to France
1979 Returns to lead Iran; approves taking of U.S. hostages
1989 Dies in Qum

appointed a government. But it quickly became apparent that real power resided in the revolutionary *komitehs* that had sprung up all over the country and took orders only from the 15-man Revolutionary Council headed by Khomeini.

In power, Khomeini and his followers displayed a retaliatory streak, and revolutionary courts condemned enemies to death or life imprisonment. Troubled by ethnic minorities, Khomeini seized upon a successful student attack on the U.S. embassy in November 1979 as a way of directing popular attention away from the country's increasing internal problems. When the U.N. and the world court condemned the seizure of the embassy, it was Iran against the world—indeed, all Islam against the "infidels." Glorying in his power over the West, a defiant Khomeini successfully held his 50 American hostages for 544 days, watching in delight as President Jimmy Carter's helicopter-rescue attempt fizzled in the desert. When the hostages had finally lost their purpose, he released them—but not until the very day Carter yielded the presidency to Ronald Reagan.

Khomeini soon found new enemies, this time within the Islamic world; he became embroiled in a lengthy war with Iraq that was not settled until 1988. Early in 1989, the Ayatullah again surfaced to surprise the West, denouncing Salman Rushdie's novel *The Satanic Verses* as blasphemous, and issuing a *fatwah* (death sentence) that drove Rushdie into an underground exile that continues in 1996, seven years after Khomeini's death in June 1989.

The Ayatullah's funeral was a bizarre spectacle. As a frantic crowd of nearly 1 million mourners gathered around the open wooden coffin containing his remains, the corpse spilled to the ground, bare feet protruding from beneath a white shroud. Revolutionary Guards had to beat back the adoring crowds to bury the body. Yet even in death Khomeini managed to excoriate his enemies, raging in his will against "the atheist East" and "the infidel West." Like the Ayatullah himself, the intense passions he ignited could not easily be put to rest. ■

REVOLT IN THE DESERT: Born the son of an Ayatullah, Khomeini, at left in 1952, became one of six grand Ayatullahs of Iran's Shi'ite Muslims. After his return from exile in Paris, center, he approved the seizure and mistreatment of U.S. hostages by students

KING

Born to the nightmare of racism, Martin Luther King *dared to dream*

F
OR THE REV. MARTIN LUTHER KING JR., DEATH AT the hands of a white bigot came as a tragic finale to an American drama fraught with classic hints of inevitability. Propelled to fame in the throes of the U.S. blacks' mid-century revolution, he gave it momentum, steered it toward nonviolence and served as its eloquent voice. Yet the movement he served with such power and zeal was beginning to pass him by even before his death. Nonviolence was beginning to seem outmoded to the increasingly militant black community. Behind his back, King's black denigrators called him "de Lawd"; in public they called him an Uncle Tom. And in the years since he was gunned down on the balcony of a Memphis motel in March 1968, both his achievements and his personal character have been assailed.

Yet if ever there were a transcendent symbol of the dreams, hopes and achievements of African Americans, it was Martin Luther King. Bridging the void between black despair and white unconcern, he spoke so powerfully of, and from, the wretchedness of his people's condition that he became the moral guidon of civil rights, not only to Americans but also to the world beyond. The courage and eloquence that brought him TIME's designation as its Man of the Year for 1963 and the Nobel Prize for Peace in 1964 have endured. His legacy as America's foremost spokesman for civil rights in this century is secure.

January 3, 1964

1929 Born in Georgia
1957 Rides victory in Montgomery bus boycott to national fame
1963 Triumphant Birmingham protests and March on Washington
1968 Killed by white racist in Memphis

Born in 1929 to a middle-class Georgia family active for two generations in the civil rights cause, he was the second child and first-born son, named after his father, Michael Luther King. The elder King, pastor of Atlanta's Ebenezer Baptist Church, changed both their names when Martin was five to honor the Reformation rebel who nailed his independent declaration to the Castle Church. The small cruelties of bigotry left their scars despite King's warm, protective family life. As an adult, he still recalled the curtains that were used on the dining cars of trains to separate white from black. "I was very young when I had my first experience in sitting behind the curtain," he says. "I felt just as if a curtain had come down across my whole life. The insult of it I will never forget." A bright student, he zipped through high school, entered Atlanta's black Morehouse College at 15 and searched for "some intellectual basis for social philosophy." Thoreau's essay "Civil Disobedience"

"Right temporarily defeated is stronger than evil triumphant."

—Nobel Peace Prize speech, 1964

"Before the Pilgrims landed at Plymouth, we were here. Before the pen of Jefferson etched across the pages of history the majestic words of the Declaration of Independence ... we were here. If the inexpressible cruelties of slavery could not stop us, the opposition we now face will surely fail. We will win our freedom because the sacred heritage of our nation and the eternal will of God are embodied in our echoing demands."

—"Letter from a Birmingham Jail," 1963

"I've looked over, and I've seen the Promised Land. I may not get there with you, but I want you to know tonight that we as a people will get there."

—At a Memphis rally the night before his death, 1968

"So even though we face the difficulties of today and tomorrow, I still have a dream. I have a dream that one day this nation will rise up and live out the true meaning of its creed ... that all men are created equal. I have a dream that one day even the state of Mississippi, a state sweltering with the heat of oppression, will be transformed into an oasis of freedom and justice. I have a dream that my four little children will one day live in a nation where they will not be judged by the color of their skin but by the content of their character. I have a dream today. And if America is to be a great nation, this must become true. So let freedom ring."

—March on Washington, 1963

showed him the goal, and King picked the ministry as a proper means to achieve it. At Crozer Theological Seminary in Chester, Pennsylvania, he discovered the writings of Mohandas Gandhi, whose faith in nonviolent protest and doctrine of satyagraha—"soul force"—became King's lodestar.

Moving on to Boston University, King gained a doctorate and a bride, Antioch College graduate Coretta Scott, and in 1954 he took his first pastorate in Montgomery, Alabama. There, late in 1955, a seamstress's tired feet precipitated the first great civil rights test of the South's white power structure and launched King's galvanic career. Mrs. Rosa Parks' arrest for refusing to give her seat on a town bus to a white man ended 382 days later with the capitulation of the Montgomery bus line to a comprehensive Negro consortium and the U.S. Supreme Court. King, too new to Montgomery to have enemies in the usually fragmented Negro community, became its chief. His leadership was more inspirational than administrative, but it was marked by profound courage. One night a dynamite bomb was tossed onto his front porch while he spoke at a rally; he returned home and faced down a mob of enraged blacks, eager for revenge: "We believe in law and order. We are not advocating violence. We want to love our enemies." The crowd dispersed, and a white policeman who was present later said, "I owe my life to that nigger preacher."

The initial triumph in Montgomery annealed King's philosophy. When the following years brought sit-ins and freedom rides, King was there with organizational support. He formed the Southern Christian Leadership Conference and midwifed the Student Nonviolent Coordinating Committee, two of the most effective agents of civil rights change in the 1960s.

Battle in Birmingham. King's horizon grew, and with it his clout. In 1963 he marched into Birmingham, tactically prepared, and flayed that citadel of Dixie bigotry on national television. Public Safety Commissioner Theophilus ("Bull")

Connor became the white villain for King's black heroes. Day after day, men, women and children in their Sunday best paraded cheerfully downtown to be hauled off to jail for demonstrating. Connor arrested them at lunch counters and in the streets, wherever they gathered. Still they came, rank on rank. At length, on Tuesday, May 7, 2,500 blacks poured out of church, surged through the police lines and swarmed downtown. Armed with clubs, cops beat their way into the crowds. An armored car bulldozed the milling throngs, while fire hoses swept them down the streets. King had created a crisis, and Connor had made it a success. The whole world was watching—and the spectacle brought aroused whites flocking to the civil rights movement in a stream that continued to grow until black victories began to dam its flow. "The civil rights movement," said President Kennedy in a later meeting with King, "owes Bull Connor as much as it owes Abraham Lincoln."

By now, King was swamped with speaking engagements. One of the century's great orators, he married the cadences of classic Southern Baptist preaching with the democratic idealism of Jefferson and Lincoln and marshaled his memorable phrases as his most powerful weapons in his war against prejudice. He reached his peak as a public speaker with his unforgettable peroration at the Lincoln Memorial at the March on Washington in August 1963: "I have a dream!" he cried, and it seemed the dream was becoming a reality, so powerfully did he evoke its contours.

Although 1965 marked the enactment of voting rights by the U.S. Congress and another successful civil rights campaign—this time in Selma, Alabama—it also brought the deadly rioting in Watts, the black ghetto in Los Angeles. To many blacks, the pace of gain was too slow and too meager: like Gandhi before him, King was outpaced by the expectations he had helped unleash. He went north, turning his battle toward economic issues in New York City, Cleveland and Chicago.

More and more, King diffused his aims. He inveighed

LEADER King was a 28-year-old minister in 1957 when he made national headlines by leading the successful boycott of the Montgomery bus system.

PRISONER Dressed for arrest, King is picked up for "loitering" at a protest during the 1957 bus boycott. In 1963 he would write one of his most famous statements on civil rights—the "Letter from a Birmingham Jail"—on scraps of paper smuggled out of a prison cell.

against the Vietnam War, saying it hamstrung the civil rights drive and President Lyndon Johnson's war on poverty. Calling at one point for a $4,000-a-year guaranteed family income in the U.S., he threatened national boycotts and spoke of disrupting entire cities by nonviolent camp-ins. His newly emphasizd goals: "Economic security; decent, sanitary housing; a quality education."

In his lifetime King was deified by his admirers, demonized by his enemies. If something of a saint, he was also a sinner: FBI Director J. Edgar Hoover actually taped episodes of his marital infidelities to blackmail him, and in 1990 scholars charged he had plagiarized sections of his doctoral thesis.

Death in Memphis. In the spring of 1968, King threw himself into a minor labor dispute in Memphis, where 1,300 predominantly black garbage collectors were striking for higher pay. Ironically, when blacks rioted during his first march, King felt that his nonviolent philosophy had been besmirched, and he wanted to withdraw. Only at the urging of his aides did he consent to return.

When he came back to Memphis, he found a different sort of challenge. Some newspapers had emphasized during his absence that the prophet of the poor had been staying at the luxurious Rivermont, a Holiday Inn that charged the then grand sum of $29 a night for a suite. To repair his image, King checked into the black-owned Lorraine, a nondescript, two-story cinderblock structure near Memphis' renowned Beale Street, where he and his entourage paid

GOOD SHEPHERD: Walking with children to integrate a Mississippi school

$13 a night for their green-walled, rust-spotted rooms. On April 4, when King walked out of Room 306 onto the second-floor balcony of the Lorraine to take the evening air, he was shot through the neck by a heavy-caliber bullet fired from the rooming house across the street. He was pronounced dead within an hour—at age 39. His assassin, James Earl Ray, a white supremacist, was apprehended and sentenced to 99 years in prison.

Throughout King's oratory ran a dark premonition that he would be slain. And with reason. By 1964 his home had been bombed three times and he had been jailed 14 times. In Harlem in 1958, a deranged black woman stabbed him dangerously near the heart. He had been pummeled and punished by white bullies in many parts of the South. In simmering Philadelphia, Mississippi, he had declared, "Before I will be a slave, I will be dead in my grave." That epitaph hardly symbolizes what King stood for: life and love—not death and despair.

King flung luminous words into the face of white America: "We will match your capacity to inflict suffering with our capacity to endure suffering. We will meet your physical force with soul force. We will not hate you, but we cannot in all good conscience obey your unjust laws. We will soon wear you down by our capacity to suffer. And in winning our freedom, we will so appeal to your heart and conscience that we will win you in the process." In his death, as in his life, Martin Luther King—eyes on the prize—moved all Americans a long way toward that goal. ∎

MARCHER
King leads the 1965 march for voting rights in Selma. By 1968 his nonviolent tactics seemed dated and ineffective to more militant blacks.

TARGET King stands with colleagues Jesse Jackson and Ralph Abernathy on a motel balcony in Memphis; minutes later he was shot.

ORATOR
King's "I Have a Dream" speech at the 1963 civil rights March on Washington electrified the crowd and moved the conscience of the nation.

SCHWEITZER

Renouncing his glittering gifts, **Albert Schweitzer** devoted his life to giving

ALBERT SCHWEITZER WAS NINE DECADES old when he died in 1965, a fitting age for a life so worthy and a span sufficiently protracted beyond his main achievements that he himself had heard all the possible praise and criticism that could be said of him. His apostles painted him as a saint; they turned his ethic of reverence for life into reverence for Schweitzer. His detractors found his philosophy uselessly pretentious, his medical practice frightfully outdated, his racial attitudes outmoded. The world weighed these extremes, consulted its feelings and struck a balance on his humanity: he died admired by mankind, and his legacy of dedication to others endures.

Like Winston Churchill, Schweitzer was a true polymath. He was a virtuoso organist who once played before jammed churches and concert halls in Europe. He was a musicologist whose biography of Bach and edition of his organ works became standard texts. He was a philosopher who thought deeply about the crisis of Western culture. He was a Protestant minister and biblical scholar whose historical criticism of the New Testament early in the century turned out to be a theological blockbuster. Above all, he was a man who decided to turn his back on the world's glittering prizes and become a doctor of medicine in order to serve his fellow man.

Growing up the son of an evangelical pastor in the little Alsatian village of Günsbach, young Albert was punished repeatedly because he refused to accept such advantages as an everyday overcoat, new gloves, or leather shoes, which poorer boys did not have. An indifferent student, he flourished when he entered the University of Strasbourg, and one morning when he was 21, he made a momentous decision: "I would consider myself justified in living until I was 30 for science and art, in order to devote myself from that time forward to the direct service of humanity." For a youthful idealist, there was nothing particularly unusual about this decision—except that he acted upon it. Without telling anyone of his plan, he set out upon such a decade of activity as would have done credit to an ordinary man's lifetime. Three years later, his first philosophical book, *The Religious Philosophy of Kant*, was published. The same year he became a preacher. In 1903 he began the work that was to make his reputation international—*The Quest of the Historical Jesus*. The book was a milestone in modern theology that searingly exposed the futility of 19th century attempts to extricate the "real Jesus" from the Gospel Christ. And even as he preached and wrote, his career as a concert organist and Bach scholar was flourishing.

On Oct. 13, 1905, Schweitzer posted letters to his parents

July 11, 1949

1875 Born in Alsace, Germany
1896 Vows to devote his life to others
1899 Begins preaching in Strasbourg
1913 Begins his medical missionary work
1965 Dies in Africa

and a few intimates breaking the news that at the beginning of the winter term he would take up the study of medicine, and would spend the rest of his life as a doctor in equatorial Africa. The hubbub that resulted astonished him; he was burying talents that had been entrusted to him, his friends and family cried. Unconvinced, for the next seven years Schweitzer studied for his M.D. while continuing to preach and to play the organ concerts of the Bach Society in Paris each winter. In June 1912, he married Helene Bresslau, the daughter of a Strasbourg historian who had equipped herself for their life together by becoming a trained nurse. On Good Friday of 1913 they set out for Africa—where, said Schweitzer, the need was greatest and the hands stretched out to help were the fewest. In Africa he saw the greatest unpaid debt of Western civilization, to the black man the white man had wronged.

Lambaréné is a tiny French Protestant missionary settlement in the midst of a lake and river system 1½ days by boat from Africa's west coast. When the Schweitzers reached it they found the need for a doctor even greater than they had anticipated. Before their instruments could be unpacked, they were besieged by the sick. As news of the white doctor and nurse spread, patients came from as far as 200 miles to see them. None of the buildings Schweitzer had expected to be ready had been put up; his first surgery was a windowless chicken house with a leaky roof. But in spite of the heavy labor of constructing new buildings—in which he served as wood cutter, foreman, carpenter and architect—Schweitzer treated some 2,000 cases during the first nine months after he arrived in Africa.

For 52 years Schweitzer would toil at Lambaréné. During the evenings, he sometimes practiced on the ant-proofed piano given him by the Bach Society when he left Europe. His jungle hospital began as one man's noble effort to follow the example of Jesus; it became a bizarre institution tailored to the idiosyncrasies of a spiritual dictator. Because Schweitzer revered all life, not a fly was swatted at Lambaréné; goats, pigs and traveler ants shared the squalid huts of the patients. Only with reluctance did he admit electricity to the operating room; sanitation consisted of open sewers flushed by the tropical rain. To the end, Schweitzer wore a pith helmet, spoke French and German, but did not bother to learn the local dialects. A racial paternalist, he believed the African to be a "child of nature" who could not be trusted and wanted only to be left in the primitive security of tribal life. Feet of clay? Yes. But the world will always have the memory of a giant who tried in his singular way to love as Jesus loved, who oddly but honestly lived his beloved Goethe's song:

The deed is everything
The glory naught.

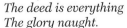

DALAI LAMA

*The Chinese drove **the Dalai Lama** into exile,*

but his serene spirit is not so easily moved

NIGHT HAD SETTLED UPON THE ROOF OF THE world. With a jingling of harnesses and the clip-clop of hooves, a small caravan wound slowly up the 17,000-ft. pass. Ahead lay the snowy summits of the Himalayas, an ocean of wind-whipped peaks and ranges that have served Tibet as a rampart since time began. Cavalrymen with slung rifles spurred forward; state officials in furs, wearing the dangling turquoise earrings of their rank, sat tiredly in the saddle; rangy muleteers in peaked caps with big earflaps goaded the baggage train up the steep path. They listened for the sound of gunfire behind them, a sign that the pursuing Chinese had clashed with their rear guard. Passing a cairn of rocks topped by brightly colored prayer flags, each pious Tibetan added a stone to the mound. The little group was charged with a divine responsibility: to ensure the escape from Tibet of the "God-King" in their midst.

He was born Tenzin Gyatso. To his people he is the Yeshi Norbu, the precious Wish-Fulfilling Gem. Elsewhere in the world he is known by his Mongol title, Dalai Lama (Ocean of Wisdom). As the incarnation of Avalokitesvara, the Bodhisattva of mercy, he is, in Tibetan eyes, a living god. Yet in the more than 30 years since that April night in 1959 when the 23-year-old Dalai Lama fled from Tibet, he has remained a transient on a refugee's passport. Dependent on the kindness of foreigners, he decorates certain of their gatherings but—because

of fear of China—is generally kept out of politics. His visits with top U.S. officials are unofficial; Beijing roars at the merest mention of a challenge to its rule over Tibet, which dates from its invasion and takeover of the country in 1950. The Dalai Lama's humble sermons often fall on unheeding ears.

Two years old when he was deemed by spiritual elders to be the 14th earthly incarnation of Avalokitesvara, the Dalai Lama spent most of his youth enclosed within the cavernous Potala Palace in Lhasa, Tibet's capital. But following his flight to India in the wake of a failed Tibetan revolt against China, the monk has showed himself to be a shrewd and vigorous negotiator, confronting Chinese leaders with a pragmatic pacifism they cannot budge. At the same time, he embodies humility and compassion, proudly describing himself as "Just a Buddhist monk, no more, no less."

Only the Dalai Lama can give Beijing the legitimacy it needs to rule Tibet—and he will do so purely on his terms. Alarmed that resentment of the Chinese has destroyed "the basic good quality of Tibetans," he cautions them against vengeance. When rebellion flared in Lhasa in 1989 and China imposed a brutal crackdown, he reacted from his headquarters in Dharmsala in northern India more in sorrow than in anger. "We honor more than 1 million Tibetans who have died as the result of four decades of Chinese occupation," he declared. "No amount of repression, however brutal and violent, can silence the voice of freedom and peace." At the same time, he cautioned his countrymen that "there's no use to feel hatred. Hatred destroys our own happiness." Later that year, the Dalai Lama's advocacy of nonviolence was recognized with the Nobel Peace Prize. The happiness of the Ocean of Wisdom, it appears, is indestructible. ∎

SUMMITEER:
The 14th Dalai Lama is framed by the Himalayas; beyond the peaks lies occupied Tibet

April 20, 1959

1935 Born in Tibet
1940 He is enthroned while a regent rules
1950 China invades and takes over Tibet
1959 Flees to India after failed uprising
1989 Awarded the Nobel Peace Prize

MOTHER TERESA

Embracing Calcutta's sickness and squalor, **Mother Teresa** *found a hope that inspired the world*

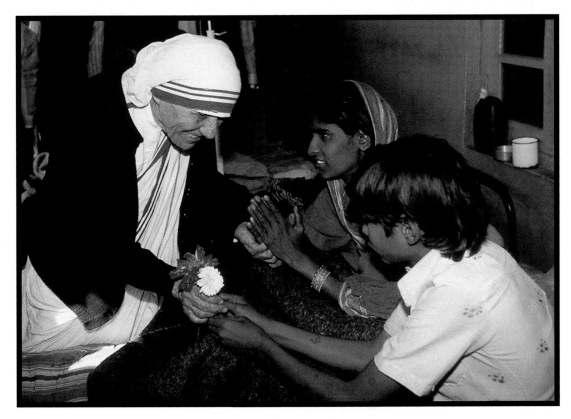

December 29, 1975

1910 Born in Skopje, Yugoslavia
1928 Arrives in India as a young nun
1950 Founds the Missionaries of Charity order in Calcutta
1979 Awarded the Nobel Peace Prize

RICH IN SPIRIT:
Nuns in Mother Teresa's order live in strict poverty, in sympathy with the plight of the poor

H ER RADIANT FACE, CREASED WITH THE CARES OF human devastation, is a common sight at places of suffering: Bhopal, Beirut, Chernobyl, Armenia's earthquake zone, famine-racked Ethiopia, the black townships of South Africa, her AIDS hospice in New York City. Back home, passing through Calcutta's mean streets, she is a fierce and indefatigable ministering angel in a white-and-blue sari, striving against unspeakable human squalor. Few 20th century individuals have done more to rouse compassion for the wretched of the earth than the "ordinary" nun Mother Teresa, who has been proclaimed a saint by admirers from every faith.

From the Roman Catholic sisters who follow her, Mother Teresa requires not only poverty, chastity and obedience but also a fourth vow, service to "the poorest of the poor." More than 3,000 sisters of the Missionaries of Charity have joined her to pursue that rigorous path, aided by brothers in a separate men's order and a host of lay "co-workers." Together, Mother Teresa and her followers operate a network of some 350 missions, spread across scores of nations, that administer hospices, food centers, clinics, orphanages, leprosariums and refuges for the insane, retarded and aged.

Born Agnes Gonxha Bojaxhiu, the daughter of an Albanian grocer, Teresa joined the Sisters of Loreto and was sent to India at 18. After 19 years as a teacher and then principal of a high school for privileged girls, in 1946 she received a "call within a call"—that is, a special vocation within her nun's

vocation—during a train ride, in which she felt God directing her to the slums. "It was an order," she told colleagues.

The year after India, her adopted homeland, won independence, Teresa also struck out on her own. Attracting a dozen disciples, she founded the Missionaries of Charity in 1950. The order's first project, still in operation, was the Nirmal Hriday (Pure Heart) center. Located next to a temple to Kali, the Hindu goddess of destruction, it is a shelter where the sisters bring aged street dwellers so that they can either recover their health or die with dignity. Mother Teresa's work spread across India, then overseas and eventually even to Albania and other postcommunist lands. Long revered within her church, she became a universal symbol of humanitarianism in the 1970s, and honors have flowed to her endlessly. Awarded the 1979 Nobel Peace Prize, she said, "I accept in the name of the poor," then requested that the traditional banquet be canceled so that its cost could go to the needy.

Stooped and a mere 5 ft. tall, Mother Teresa has a peasant's simplicity and tenacity. To those who favor political reforms over charity or dismiss her efforts as futile, she merely replies, "God has not called me to be successful. He has called me to be faithful." Despite her celebrity, she is neither an orator nor an intellectual. But her joy and faith touch almost everyone who meets her. Said a fellow nun: "Mother is very ordinary. When people meet her, they are so surprised by her ordinariness. But she allows God to work through her, and he has done extraordinary things." ∎

DEWEY

Rejecting hand-me-down verities, **John Dewey** *sought new truths*

R IGHT FROM THE START, THE RUMPLED-LOOKING GRADuate student from Vermont made a deep impression on President Daniel Coit Gilman of Johns Hopkins University. But President Gilman did think that the young man was off on a wrong track. "Don't be so bookish," Gilman thundered. "Get out and see more people." Student John Dewey listened politely to his president, then ignored the advice. He had long since made up his mind that he would keep right on studying; his ambition was to become a philosopher.

In time, the young scholar more than realized his ambition. A shy, shuffling figure, Dewey in his long life managed to exert as much influence on education and thinking in the U.S. and around the world as any man of his time. Teachers and judges became Deweyites, and so did millions of ordinary men and women who did not even know who he was or what his theories were.

Born in 1859, the year in which Darwin's *Origin of Species* appeared, Dewey marked the crest of a tide that had begun to swell with the French Revolution. No man so completely summed up the raw, rationalistic credo of his century—belief in the here and now, in the necessity for perpetual adjustment to change, in the idea that man has no provable end, only "ends that are literally endless." For 65 years after his Johns Hopkins days, Dewey preached his doctrine. Tugging at his mus-

June 4, 1926

1859 Born in Burlington, Vermont
1899 Publishes *The School and Society*
1904 Begins teaching at Columbia University
1916 Publishes *Democracy and Education*
1952 Dies at 92

tache and rumpling his hair, he lectured in a gentle voice, pausing now and then in his classroom at Columbia University in New York City to glance at his fistful of notes or to gaze distractedly out the window. But however labored his delivery, his message took hold. Philosophy, he declared, could not lean on eternal verities, or summon up answers, for there are no ultimate answers to be summoned. "The moment philosophy supposes it can find a final ... solution," said he, "it ceases to be inquiry and becomes either apologetics or propaganda."

In such a world, said Dewey, the philosopher (and, for that matter, the educator) should not concern himself with God or the existence of absolutes. His target is man and society, where nothing is either good or bad, but only better or worse. Values are not eternal, they are perpetually born, and to Dewey the philosopher can only assist at their birth, shaping values as they arise to meet the needs of the present. He may take hints from the past, but the only real test of an ideal is how it can be expected to work out in the future. Thus, for experimentalist Dewey and his followers, action became a sort of giant laboratory, where values could be run through a series of streamlined tests. "The method we term 'scientific,'" said he, "forms for the modern man ... the sole dependable means for disclosing the realities of existence."

That being the case, education also had to change. For just as the world learns by experience, so do children. Mere memory is not enough: children have to act as well as read, to solve everyday problems, as if school were society in miniature. The aim of education is not knowledge alone, but growth—and growth was the important thing in Dewey's world. As writer and teacher, he drummed his philosophy of growth into two generations of Americans, and for millions the popular version of his doctrine became the one true gospel. But for many others, his sole achievement was that in trying to light the way he merely succeeded in putting out the stars.

In his own life, however, he at least practiced what he preached: he worked tirelessly in behalf of the poor, thrust himself to the forefront of the fray wherever he spotted a Cause. "As the philosopher has received his problem from the world of action," he once wrote, "so he must return his account there for auditing and liquidation." In 1952 Dewey finally settled his account. At 92, he left this world still growing—and other philosophers still wrestling with the question, Growing for what? ∎

MONTESSORI

Finding young minds in chains and shackles, **Maria Montessori** *found new ways to free them*

THE YOUNG WOMAN WHO SHOWED UP at the new housing project in the slums of Rome one day in the early 1900s was supposed to be no more than a medical adviser for the children of the tenants. But as soon as she saw her little charges, she knew that she would have to be a good deal more than that. The 50 children were a bedraggled and obstreperous lot, "naughty because of mental starvation." There and then, physician Maria Montessori decided to give them a whole new type of school.

In time, the Casa dei Bambini, founded in 1907, became one of the sights of Rome, for the young *dottoressa* in the floppy hat seemed to perform miracles with children. The Argentine ambassador paid a call, as did the Queen Mother of Italy and a whole procession of Italian professors. Within a few short years, the Montessori Method became the talk of educators all over the world.

The daughter of a civil servant, Montessori was long used to causing talk. She had started out as a mathematical prodigy; later she shocked her friends—and the chauvinistic male students who taunted her—by becoming the first woman ever to receive an M.D. from the University of Rome. At the psychiatric clinic of the university, she threw herself into the study of children with learning problems and started experimenting with new ways of educating them. From such beginnings, she developed a theory to apply to all children, and put it into effect for the first time at her little slum school in Rome.

To Montessori, the ordinary schoolroom, with its pupils "nailed to their seats," was the very opposite of what it should be. Her own theory had one "fundamental base—the liberty of the pupils in their spontaneous manifestations." The teacher's primary task, she believed, was to release the children's natural individuality, to arouse their interest with special games and devices and then to let them teach themselves. The classroom had to be specially furnished for the purpose, "with little low windows, little tables, little armchairs, and low cupboards, within reach ..."

In such an atmosphere, Montessori argued, children would want to learn, and gradually train their own senses by building blocks, by buttoning buttons and finally by tracing letters from a cardboard alphabet. Once they got to that point, they could begin to grasp abstractions—reading by the time they were four, algebra at five, cube roots at six.

Over the years, Montessori carried her children's crusade far beyond her native land. In the long black dresses she often wore, she stumped the nations of Europe, working and lecturing from 8 in the morning until 8 at night. Then, in the 1930s, her

February 3, 1930

1870 Born in Rome
1894 First woman M.D. from U. of Rome
1907 Opens first Casa dei Bambini
1934 Flees Italy's Fascist government
1952 Dies in the Netherlands

crusade began to slow. In Italy, Benito Mussolini closed her schools because of her anti-Fascist leanings. In the U.S., educators became more and more absorbed with the equally radical ideas of Columbia's John Dewey. Even some of her own followers betrayed her; they transformed her doctrine of guided freedom into a doctrine of unguided anarchy, and many educators turned away in disgust.

Though old and exiled, Montessori continued to preach. She wandered to Barcelona, where she had to be rescued during the civil war, then to India, where she was interned as an enemy alien. Settling in the Netherlands, she set up a new training center. Wherever she went, her message was always the same: "You must fight for the rights of the child," she would exclaim, and hundreds of educators were still inspired to take up the cry.

Her fight came to an end in the Netherlands, where she died in 1952. Maria Montessori had helped revolutionize the concept of primary education, but at 81, she had no intention of stopping there. Her last words were directed to her adopted son Mario, who had gradually taken over her work: "What are *you* planning for the reform of the world?" ∎

SANGER

Unbearable! Defying society's conventions,
Margaret Sanger *crusaded for birth control*

Sanger in 1936

1883 Born in
Corning, New York
1912 Works as nurse
in New York City slums
1916 Opens first birth
control clinic
1937 Mailing of birth
control matter allowed
1966 Dies at 82

FAMILY PLANNING BY CONTRACEPTION WAS THE CAUSE. Margaret Sanger was its champion. Early in the century, when she raised the banners of her lonely crusade, she was lacerated from the pulpits as a "lascivious monster" bent on murdering unborn children. Birth control, a phrase she invented, was unmentionable, immoral, illegal. It was a federal crime merely to send information about it through the mails. She was arrested eight times. Her zeal led to the breakup of her first marriage. Yet when she died in 1966 at age 82, her vision had been realized beyond her dreams. Birth control, which to her meant the right of every woman to control the size of her own family, had become accepted in the U.S. and—despite the formidable opposition of the Vatican—was spreading rapidly throughout the world.

Margaret Sanger grew up in Corning, New York, the sixth of 11 children. Her mother died of tuberculosis at 48. Margaret came to New York at 17, married architect William Sanger, joined the Socialist Party and toiled as a nurse in the teeming tenements of New York City's Lower East Side. On a swel-

tering day in July 1912, Nurse Sanger made her way through pushcarts to a cramped flat in a Grand Street building. Sadie Sachs, 28, a mother of three, was near death as a result of a self-induced abortion. She pleaded with Nurse Sanger and the doctor: "Another baby will finish me. What can I do to prevent it?" The doctor's gruff reply: "Tell Jake to sleep on the roof." Three months later, Sadie Sachs was dead—of another self-induced abortion. Margaret Sanger had a cause.

In 1913, in birth control clinics in France and Scotland, she listened and learned, then returned to publish a magazine called *Woman Rebel*. Its motto: "No Gods. No Masters." Her first editorial promised future stories on birth control; postal inspectors grabbed up copies, and she was indicted for sending birth control information through the mails. Deciding she needed time to prepare her defense, she left her three children with a nurse and fled to Europe. By the time she returned to stand trial a year later, she had begun to attract public support. Besides, the first issue of *Woman Rebel* had only promised illegal stories; it had not delivered them. The government withdrew its indictment.

In 1916 Sanger opened the nation's first birth control clinic in Brooklyn. On the first day, 150 pram-pushing women from the neighborhood lined up to pay the 10¢ registration fee. Nine days later, the clinic was raided by policemen and—to her disgust—a policewoman. Sanger was convicted of disseminating birth control information and imprisoned for 30 days.

A radiant, vivacious redhead scarcely 5 ft. tall, Sanger left scores of suitors in her wake. Divorced from her first husband in 1922, she married machine-oil magnate J. Noah H. Slee—but only after planking down a premarital platform to ensure her independence: she would continue to call herself Margaret Sanger, and she and Slee would occupy separate apartments in the same house. The agreement shocked conventional minds, but the marriage held firm.

Throughout the 1920s and 1930s, the use of contraceptives spread, although they remained illegal, and it was considered boldly wicked to admit using them. All the while, Sanger fought futilely for a federal "Doctors Bill" that would open the mails to birth control information and devices. Finally, in 1937, after a new Japanese birth control device Sanger had ordered sent to an associate was seized by U.S. Customs, the government decided it would not carry the case to the Supreme Court. The mails were opened for good, although it was not until 1965 that Connecticut became the last state to lift its ban against birth control clinics.

Margaret Sanger started on a personal crusade to secure the freedom of the individual woman, whom she termed a "brood animal for the masculine civilizations of the world." Along the way she became a role model for thousands of women who fought to control their own destinies—and achieve Sanger's goal of making every child a wanted child. ∎

MAN'S WORLD: Sanger, left, and her sister in court in 1916, after police arrested her and closed her first birth control clinic

APRIL 7, 1952 Seven years after F.D.R.'s death, Eleanor Roosevelt continued fighting for a host of social causes. She both advocated and personified women's struggle for equality.

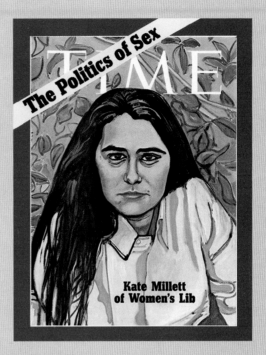

AUGUST 31, 1970 The radical activism of the 1960s transformed "feminism" into "Women's Lib." Writer and theorist Kate Millett was a strong voice in the new movement.

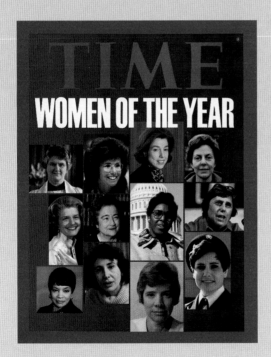

JANUARY 5, 1976 As more women advanced in a host of professions, TIME named 12 prominent U.S. figures, from legislator to athlete to judge, as Women of the Year 1975.

MARCH 9, 1992 The cycle comes full circle: by the 1990s, feminist leaders Gloria Steinem and Susan Faludi were battling the resistance provoked by the success of their revolution.

GRAHAM

With his resounding call to believe,

Billy Graham *has moved multitudes*

SOMETHING IN THIS MAN, SOMETHING IN HIS urgent voice and eager eyes, in the message and the messenger, overwhelms even those who are predisposed to distrust him. Long ago, Billy Graham gave up the shiny suits and Technicolor ties of the brash young evangelist; the silver mane is thinner now, the step may falter a bit, he no longer prowls the stage like a lynx. In his preaching as well, the temperatures of hellfire have been reduced, the volume turned down. Graham, 78 in 1996, is saving his strength: he is fighting Parkinson's disease, a progressive nervous disorder that has already made it impossible for him to drive or write by hand. But while he has learned to number his days, Graham intends to make the most of them: "The New Testament," he notes, "says nothing of Apostles who retired and took it easy."

Numbers, poets complain, are soulless things, the anonymous rungs of infinity. But it is hard to talk about Billy Graham, the great reaper of souls, without talking about numbers. This is the man who has preached in person to more people than any human being who has ever lived. His mission began in country churches, trailer parks and circus tents in the 1950s, then moved through cathedrals and stadiums and the world's vast public squares, where he has called upon more than 100 million people to "accept Jesus Christ as your personal Saviour."

There may have been more clever preachers and wiser ones, those whose messages seemed safer, their logic more sound. But never in history has a preacher moved so many people to act on the "invitation," that mysterious spiritual transaction that concludes every revival meeting. Over the years, nearly three million individuals have stepped forward, according to his staff's careful count.

Graham's first blitz of Australia in 1959 is perhaps the best example of his power. Over a period of five months, he preached to one-fourth of the current population; respondents to his "altar call" numbered more than 1% of the Australian citizenry. Sydney's crime rate dropped by nearly half just after the crusade and remained low for years; alcohol consumption dipped 10%, and a previous rapid increase in out-of-wedlock births halted. In the two decades following the crusade, one-fourth of the Australians training for the clergy were people who had come forward at his meetings. "I don't know why God has allowed me to have this [power]," Graham says. "I'll have to ask him when I get to heaven."

From the start, Graham presented to skeptics and believers alike a raucous, muscular Christianity, full of fire and

October 25, 1954

1918 Born in North Carolina
1934 He "makes his decision for Christ"
1949 Earns national fame for his preaching
1996 He and his wife receive a Congressional Medal

free of doubt. Born on a North Carolina dairy farm to pious parents who believed in spanking, Bible readings and persistent instruction in clean living, Graham has always emphasized that each person is sinful before God, a predicament that can turn to redemption through faith in Jesus Christ and his death on the cross.

The young Billy dreamed of being a baseball player, but after a conversion experience as a teenager, he dedicated his life to preaching the Gospel. Early on, friends sensed in him an ability to move people that owed less to intellect than to the tug of sincerity. His call to faith was vibrant and virile; so loud and fast was his delivery that journalists called him "God's Machine Gun." Skeptics sniffed at his "Christian vaudeville"; Harry Truman called him a "counterfeit" and publicity seeker.

Graham learned to weather the adverse effects of both derision and applause; through the years he became America's perennial deus ex machina, perpetually in motion, sweeping in to lift up spirits befuddled by modernity. When Presidents needed to pray, it was Graham they called; he ministered to Dwight Eisenhower in the White House, spent the night with the Bushes on the eve of the Gulf War. Since Graham's rise to national fame in the late 1940s, other high-wattage preachers have come and gone—some falling into moral and financial disaster—but Graham's simplicity, probity and refreshing lack of pomposity have earned him admirers of all faiths. In 1996 his status as America's prime minister was certified again when he was awarded a Congressional medal and addressed a rapt audience of admiring legislators in the Capitol. Further proof of a tenet Graham has long preached: his God offers hope even to those who may appear beyond salvation. ∎

JOHN XXIII

Thanks to **Pope John XXIII,** *his church is less Roman—and more Catholic*

CT. 28, 1958. *"TU ES PETRUS"* (Thou art Peter), sang the choir, and the ancient hymn set off a roar that swept across St. Peter's Square down to the Tiber's banks: *"Viva il Papa!"* Angelo Giuseppe Cardinal Roncalli—until today, the Patriarch of Venice—was now His Holiness John XXIII, the 262nd Supreme Pontiff of the Roman Catholic Church. Beneath his jeweled miter and glistening white robes, Roncalli was a square, strong rock of a man. But he was nearly 77, and he had been chosen for the papacy in part because a College of Cardinals deeply divided between conservative and liberal wings expected the elderly prelate hadn't long to live.

Pope John would indeed have a short reign of less than five years. But far from being the caretaker the church expected, during his brief time in office John created an atmosphere of ferment, unleashing forces that would reshape his ancient church and touch the spiritual lives of countless people around the globe—not only Roman Catholics but people of all other faiths.

Pope John was an intuitive being who revered people, not ideas. For 500 years, the Roncallis had worked the vineyards and wheat fields around the village of Sotto il Monte (Beneath the Mountain), eight miles from the Lombardy town of Bergamo. The natural rhythmic influence of his first years on the farm formed him for all time. Sober and responsible as a youth, he was only 11 when he decided to be a priest. He won a scholarship to the Pontifical Seminary in Rome, was ordained at 25 and said his first Mass in St. Peter's Basilica.

The young Father Roncalli toiled in minor church positions in Rome and Bulgaria. From 1934 to 1944 Archbishop Roncalli was Rome's man in 98%-Muslim Turkey, where he became adept at diplomacy. In 1945 he was transferred to war-ravaged France, only because the Holy See did not want to spare a top man for that messy post. But the French were charmed by Roncalli's humility and his sparkle as a raconteur—as well as by his reputation as "a heavy fork." In 1953 Pius XII gave him a red hat and the see of Venice. Roncalli loved the ancient city of canals—and the worldly Venetians loved him—but he would serve there only five years before becoming Pope.

All his life John made a point of meeting and fraternizing with non-Catholics and "anyone who does not call himself a Christian but who really is so because he does good." While in Turkey, John helped rescue Jews escaping from Nazi Germany. When a group of Jews visited him after he became Pope, he simply repeated the biblical greeting "I am Joseph, your brother." He welcomed historic guests to the Vatican: the first Greek Orthodox sovereign since the days of the last

January 4, 1963

1881 Born in Sotto il Monte, Italy
1904 Ordained a priest in Rome
1958 Named Pope
1962 Convenes Second Vatican Council to renew the church
1963 Dies in Rome

Byzantine emperor, the first Archbishop of Canterbury since the 14th century, the first chief prelate of the U.S. Episcopal Church, the first Moderator of the Scottish Kirk, the first Shinto high priest, a black Baptist minister from America.

In a position that had previously seemed remote and unworldly, John demonstrated such warmth, simplicity and charm that he won the hearts of Catholics, Protestants and non-Christians alike. His frequent sallies out of the Vatican earned him a nickname from admiring Romans: "Johnnie Walker." He pronounced himself embarrassed at being addressed as "Holy Father," and admitted that he could not get used to thinking of himself in the plural. "Don't interrupt me—I mean us!" he once joked. When Jacqueline Kennedy came to visit the Vatican, John asked his secretary how to address her. The reply: "'Mrs. Kennedy' or just 'Madame,' since she is of French origin and has lived in France." Waiting in his private library, the Pope mumbled, "Mrs. Kennedy ... Madame; Madame ... Mrs. Kennedy." But when the doors opened on the U.S. First Lady, he stood up, extended his arms and cried, "Jacqueline!"

In his greatest achievement, the convening of the council called Vatican II in 1962, John left his personal stamp upon a church that had seemed unchanged for centuries. His revolutionary goal: to bring the mother church of Christendom into closer touch with the modern world, and to end the division that had dissipated the Christian message for four centuries. John set out to adapt his church's whole life and stance to the shattering changes in science, economics, morals and politics that were sweeping the modern world; to make it, in short,

WALKABOUT: John loved to escape the stuffy confines of the Vatican and mingle with every-day people. Here he visits prisoners in a Rome jail; opposite, he prays at the opening of the Second Vatican Council.

more Catholic and less Roman. By revealing in Catholicism the deep-seated presence of a new spirit crying out for rejuvenation, the council shattered the Protestant view of the Roman Catholic Church as a monolithic and absolutist system.

As 2,500 bishops from all over the world came to Rome to deliberate, Pope John encouraged "holy liberty" in the expression of their views. Their voice, heard in the great debate of St. Peter's nave, spoke for John's instincts and not for the conservative Italians of the Roman Curia who govern the church in the name of the Pope. The Curia did not want the council to take place. One Curia man, according to a Vatican story, told the Pope, "We can't possibly get a council ready by 1963." "All right," said John, "we'll have it in 1962."

John died two years before the council ended, but the forces he set in motion left his church vastly changed. The council fathers approved liturgical reforms that, among other things, enabled the world's bishops to decide for themselves whether they wished the Mass to be said in the language of their own countries. The council also opened the way for more tolerant Catholic positions on church-state relations and religious freedom, while it tempered hierarchical authority by giving the laity a bigger role in the church.

John gave the world what neither science nor diplomacy can provide: a sense of its unity as the human family. By bringing Christianity to a new confrontation with the world, by salving the wounds of centuries and by renewing the sense of the optimism at the heart of the Christian message, the "heavy fork" altered the Christian family forever. ∎

JOHN PAUL II

*When **Pope John Paul II** talks, the whole world listens—like it or not*

THE ROMAN CATHOLIC CHURCH WAS IN A STATE of shock. On Aug. 26, 1978, it had crowned Albino Cardinal Luciani as Pope John Paul I, succeeding Pope Paul VI. Then, only 33 days later, the frail, 65-year-old new Pope had died—and from around the world, the Cardinals who had come together two months before to vote for a Pope hastily reassembled to conduct another election. This time, with the shock of John Paul I's death firmly in mind, the College of Cardinals elected the youngest man to become Pope since 1846. But their choice startled the world for more profound reasons: for the first time in 456 years, the heavily Italian College of Cardinals had not elected one of their countrymen to the papacy. The new Pope was a Pole—Karol Cardinal Wojtyla of Cracow—the first non-Italian to head the church since the botched term of Holland's Adrian VI had put a "Dutch Curse" on the papacy.

A newspaper in Lima, Peru, greeted Wojtyla's election with the headline LABORER POET ACTOR PRIEST POPE. That and more: quarryman and factory worker in his youth, member of Poland's anti-Nazi underground, professor of philosophy and ethics, pastor with an unaffectedly common touch. On top of that, he was more of an athlete than any Pope in memory, a man who loved to ski, kayak and canoe, to climb mountains and hike, to play guitar and sing around a campfire.

The news from Rome electrified Poland, a nation whose fervor for Roman Catholicism had been unsurpassed for a millennium, and which in 1978 was impoverished and chafing under the grip of the atheistic U.S.S.R. In the Pope's home see of Cracow, historic political and cultural center of the nation, people of all ages flocked into the streets, singing and shouting and hugging one another. At Wawel Castle, where Polish kings once lived, the Zygmund Bell, rung only on historic occasions, pealed joyously, as did the bells in all of Warsaw's churches.

No one was more surprised by his election than the robust Wojtyla. Only days before, as the conclave was convening, he had carried his scarred satchel into his less-than-choice assigned lodgings in the Vatican's Apostolic Palace and had waved off a request from TIME to sit for a photographic portrait, laughingly advising the journalists, "Don't worry, I'm not going to become Pope." No infallibility here: a few days later, the Pole was elected on the eighth ballot of the College of Cardinals, which had first turned to Holland's Johannes Willebrands and then to Wojtyla as it sought to break a deadlock between factions favoring liberal and conservative Italian candidates.

In the years since 1978, John Paul II has more than lived up to the great expectations that greeted his election. His impact on the world has been enormous, ranging from the global to the personal. Taking the papacy to the people, he has covered more than half a million miles in his travels. Many believe his support for Lech Walesa's trade union Solidarity in his native Poland was a precipitating event in the collapse of the entire Soviet bloc. In 1994 *Crossing the Threshold of Hope*, his meditations on topics ranging from the existence of God to the mistreatment of women, became an immediate best seller in 12 countries—while a recording of the Pope saying the rosary in Latin against a background of Bach and Handel ascended the pop charts in Europe.

When John Paul talks, it is not only to his flock of nearly 1 billion; he expects the world to listen. And the flock and the world listen, not always liking what they hear. For though the Pope is widely loved and admired, he is also scorned. However much John Paul's energy and personal charisma have refreshed the Pope's relationship with his followers, his has been a conservative papacy. Declaring "the Pope must be a moral force," he has preached a strict line against church liberals, against Liberation Theology, against the ordination of women, against homosexuality and especially against abortion and birth control.

This Pope can impose his will, and there was no more formidable and controversial example of this than the Vatican's intervention at the United Nations International Conference on Population and Development in Cairo in September 1994. There the Pope's emissaries defeated a U.S.-backed proposition John Paul feared would encourage abortions worldwide. The consequences, his critics predicted, could be global and catastrophic; still he could not be swayed. Yet even those who contest the teachings of John Paul—and there are many—do not argue with his personal integrity and his power to move and inspire people of all faiths.

The road to Rome. Wojtyla's early years in Poland were hard. His mother died when he was nine, and he was brought up by his father, who subsisted for the most part on an army sergeant's pension. Though many Cardinals and Popes have been trained from early youth in the hothouse atmosphere of minor seminaries, Wojtyla went to an ordinary high school. He attended Mass each morning and headed a religious society, but equally strong adolescent passions were literature and the theater. He was the producer and lead actor in a school troupe that toured southeastern Poland doing Shakespeare and modern Polish plays.

The Pope-to-be entered the Jagiellonian, the historic university of Cracow, where he majored in philology, but after the Nazi occupation shut down the school he spent World War II working in a stone quarry and a chemical factory. He had an

June 18, 1979

1920 Born in Wadowice, Poland

1946 Becomes priest; Soviets control Poland

1978 Named first non-Italian Pope in 456 years

1981 Assassination attempt in Rome

PRIEST Coming of age during the Nazi Occupation of Poland, Wojtyla first studied for the priesthood at an illegal underground seminary, and risked his life to shelter Jews from the Germans.

ATHLETE An enthusiastic and dedicated outdoorsman, Bishop Wojtyla loved hiking, canoeing, kayaking—and especially skiing. Here, a few months before becoming Pope, he sports ski goggles on the slopes of Poland's Tatras mountain range.

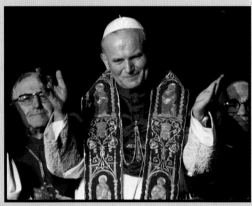

POPE In his first appearance in 1978, the new Pope blesses a startled crowd of Italians. *"Un Papa straniero!"*—a foreign Pope—they shouted.

VICTIM John Paul's peripatetic version of the papacy left him exposed to crowds in his open "Popemobile." In 1981 he was severely wounded by gunman Mehmet Ali Agca in St. Peter's Square.

PILGRIM Since his election in 1978, John Paul has traveled more than half a million miles to visit his flock. Here, on his first visit to the U.S., in 1979, he welcomes a young hitchhiker to his "Popemobile."

CONFESSOR Two years after the assassination attempt, John Paul met with his assailant, whom he blessed and forgave.

active social life, and at least one steady girfriend. A devout tailor interested him in the writings of St. John of the Cross, Spain's 16th century Carmelite mystic, and in 1942, the year after his father died, Wojtyla decided to begin studies for the priesthood at an illegal underground seminary.

That was risky enough, but he was also active in the anti-Nazi resistance. Says a high school classmate: "He lived in danger daily of losing his life. He would move about the occupied cities taking Jewish families out of the ghettos, finding them new identities and hiding places. He saved the lives of many families threatened with execution." Meanwhile he took a major role in an underground theater company whose anti-Nazi and patriotic dramas boosted Polish morale.

Ordained a priest in 1946, just as the Soviet-backed Communist Party was beginning to smother all opposition, Wojtyla did two years of doctoral work in philosophy in Rome. During this period he spent considerable time ministering to Polish refugees in Belgium, Holland and France. Returning to Poland as a parish priest, he studied ethics and then taught moral theology at Cracow's Jagiellonian. In 1954 he began teaching at the Catholic University of Lublin, where he soon became head of the ethics department; in 1962 he was named Archbishop of Cracow. Bishop Wojtyla first established the international contacts that were to make him Pope during John XXIII's Second Vatican Council, where he made eight speeches, the most memorable in favor of religious liberty. Church honors followed: a Cardinal's red hat in 1967, election as one of three Europeans on the council of the world bishops' synod in 1974, an invitation to conduct the Lenten retreat for Pope Paul VI's household in 1976.

Wojtyla was an avid outdoorsman who loved canoeing and kayaking. But his great passion was skiing: before becoming Pope he used to take a week off yearly to schuss in the Tatra mountain range. An American woman who once broke her leg while skiing there remembers being serenaded in the nearby hospital by a group of fellow skiers; only later did she learn that the guitarist was Bishop Wojtyla. As Pope, John Paul continued skiing and hiking until 1994, but he will never ski again. After he took a fall, he was given an artificial femur; he now walks with a cane, and his left hand shakes. Advancing age has finally slowed him down.

John Paul, superstar. Pope John XXIII had amazed Romans by his frequent journeys out of the Vatican into the streets of Rome; John Paul II took the papacy to the world, and his frequent travels redefined the relationship between the Pope and his flock. Within months of becoming Pope he had emerged as an incandescent figure, a superstar whose very appearance made people feel that they had been lifted above the drabness of their own lives into a realm where they felt capable of better deeds, better lives. The Vatican had once seemed distant, remote, walled-off; now here was the Roman Pontiff plunging into crowds, raising children high in the air, hugging the pilgrims who came to see him. Babies were blessed; grandmothers wept and swooned. Teenagers flocked

to cheer his approach like rock fans afflicted with Beatlemania.

Always in his travels, John Paul conveyed a tangible sense of strength and an extraordinary, low-burning joy—joy in the signs of national pride and faith he saw before him, joy in being a Christian, joy in being human. During his first visit to America, in October 1979, he celebrated an outdoor Mass in Iowa before a huge crowd of 350,000 worshippers. An envious Protestant minister in the crowd turned to his Catholic neighbor and said, "You got a Pope who knows how to pope."

To forgive, divine. Two years later, in May 1981, the world recoiled in horror when John Paul was shot in the chest as his open "Popemobile" drove through a crowd of pilgrims in St. Peter's Square at the Vatican. The hardy Pontiff survived and managed to turn even that savage act into a moment of grace.

Thirty-one months later, in a bare, white-walled cell in Rome's Rebibbias prison, John Paul tenderly held the hand that had held the gun that was meant to kill him. For 21 minutes, he sat and talked with his attacker, Mehmet Ali Agca, a Muslim extremist. Then John Paul blessed the young man and forgave him for his action. Asked the awed prisoner: "Tell me why it is that I could not kill you?" The act was a perfect economy of drama. The Pope's deed, not his words, spoke, and it spoke with the full authority of his moral life and the danger to which Agca had subjected it. The message: "Forgive us our trespasses, as we forgive those who trespass against us."

It was Joseph Stalin who facetiously asked Winston Churchill at the Yalta Conference: "The Pope? How many divisions does he have?" As John Paul has demonstrated throughout his papacy, he needs no divisions. His power rests in the word, not the sword. He is an army of one, and his empire is both as ethereal and as ubiquitous as the soul. ∎

GRIEF: The Pope prays at Auschwitz, "The Golgotha of the modern world"

WALESA

Uniting Poles to strike in solidarity,

Lech Walesa *made tyranny tremble*

LIKE POLAND, THE COUNTRY HE CAME TO PERSONIFY, Lech Walesa bears the scars of two of the century's most oppressive regimes. The Nazis killed his father, and then the Soviet "liberators" strangled his freedom. But the courageous young electrician from the windswept shipyards of Gdansk on the Baltic Sea refused to play the victim. Leading a revolt against communist rule, he became an international symbol of the individual's struggle for freedom and dignity, and the triumphs of his Solidarity labor movement lit fires of hope throughout Eastern Europe that culminated in the collapse of the Soviet Empire in the early 1990s.

Again and again, Walesa's roller-coaster career has plunged him from the heights to the depths. In 1981 Solidarity won a smashing victory over Poland's repressive communist regime, and he was designated TIME's Man of the Year. Yet December of that year found him a captive of the government, his rev-

olution seemingly extinguished. In 1990 he was elected President of a Poland free at last of Soviet sway, but in 1995 he was ousted by voters who had tired of his high-handed ways—in favor of a former minister from the last communist regime.

Walesa was born in a clay hut during the Nazi occupation in the village of Popow, between Warsaw and Gdansk. His carpenter father Boleslaw was conscripted by the Nazis to dig ditches during the war and died in 1946 from the exposure and beatings he suffered. His mother Feliksa seemed to have had the most effect on him. As the parish priest remembered her: "She always had to be the most important person around and was a fantastic organizer." Her headstrong son also liked being in charge. "I had something in me that made me the leader of the gang," he says. "I was always on top."

Spark of revolt. His nation seemed always to be on the bottom. Emerging from German occupation in World War II only to find itself annexed by Stalin, Poland chafed and rebelled. In 1956 workers rioted to protest food shortages; in 1968 intellectuals protested censorship. Neither movement changed things. In 1970 an even bloodier uprising flared in the port cities along the Baltic coast. The movement was centered on Gdansk's Lenin shipyard, where Walesa had begun to work as an electrician in 1967. He became a leader of the protest, but when fellow workers occupied the police headquarters, he persuaded a crowd of 20,000 not to attack the

STRIKE! Deeply religious, Walesa was guided by faith in himself and his destiny; he had no qualms about speaking for all Poles: "We eat the same bread," he would tell the crowds

nearby prison. Later, police and army units opened fire. Scores of workers died, and Walesa still claims he did not lead his fellow workers with enough vigor or wisdom then.

Eight years later, the surprise election of Karol Cardinal Wojtyla as the first Polish Pope caused an explosion of national pride in heavily Roman Catholic Poland that created the psychological climate from which the Solidarity movement would emerge. The spark that ignited the revolution was a government decree raising meat prices in July 1980. Once again, the workers reacted with angry protests, but the movement still had no focus. In the Lenin shipyard, the anger was just about to die out when a stocky man with a shock of reddish-brown hair and a handlebar mustache clambered over the iron fence to join the strikers. They all knew Lech Walesa. He was an unemployed electrician, fired eight months earlier for trying to organize an independent trade union.

Gates of hope. Walesa took charge and became the head of an interfactory strike committee that eventually became the bargaining voice for most of the 500,000 strikers across the nation who had joined the revolt. The Lenin shipyard and Walesa's new Solidarity labor union became the emotional center of an extraordinary national movement. Festooned with flowers, white-and-red Polish flags and portraits of Pope John Paul II, the plant's iron gates came to symbolize the heady mixture of faith, hope and patriotism that sustained the workers through their vigil. As the world wondered if Soviet tanks would crush them, Walesa and his fellow strikers stood their ground; like soldiers before battle, they received Communion from priests. Through it all, Walesa's plucky courage and infectious good humor helped keep spirits high. But he was also a strict leader: alcohol was forbidden, property respected, discipline maintained.

January 4, 1982

1943 Born in Popow in occupied Poland
1970 Plays major role in failed labor uprising
1980 Emerges as leader of Solidarity
1990 Voted President in free elections
1995 Rebuked at polls

Walesa's firmness paid off: the government team finally gave in to almost all the worker's demands. In addition to the right to strike and form unions, the Warsaw regime granted extraordinary concessions: the press was unfettered, freedom of movement was unchained, and thousands of schoolbooks that falsified Polish history were thrown out.

But Moscow was appalled at the virus of liberty it saw in Poland. The clampdown came in December of 1981 in classic communist fashion: Walesa was hustled out his apartment in Gdansk at 3 a.m. to seclusion, while olive-drab tanks and armored personnel carriers moved through the snow-filled streets. Thousands of Solidarity members, dissidents, intellectuals, artists and some 30 former government officials were rounded up.

Walesa was released the following November, after the government outlawed Solidarity. But the union and its leader were not so easily extinguished. In 1988 widespread strikes and other economic problems forced the government to enter into negotiations. Early in April 1989, Walesa won approval for still more reforms. In relatively free elections two months later, Solidarity candidates won overwhelming victories; in December 1990 Walesa was elected President of Poland.

But once in office, the man who had led the fight against the tyranny of the Kremlin seemed to be studying one of their old playbooks. Walesa had always been stubborn and proud, and his rule amounted to a one-man obstinarchy; he presided over six different governments and repeatedly sought to bypass democracy and rule by decree. Ironically, he was beaten in the presidential election in 1995 by Aleksander Kwasniewski, a minister in Poland's last communist government. Walesa's roller-coaster career was enduring another jolting passage. But he could afford to enjoy the ride: his place in history was secure. ■

OCTOBER 1, 1923 A Briton who came to the U.S. in 1863, labor leader Samuel Gompers headed the American Federation of Labor and won breakthrough victories for the union cause.

MARCH 15, 1926 Supreme Court Justice Oliver Wendell Holmes Jr. served for 30 years on the highest U.S. bench; for his incisive arguments he was known as "the great dissenter."

DECEMBER 13, 1968 As leader of the Palestine Liberation Organization, Yasir Arafat fought for a Palestinian homeland—first with terrorism, then by making peace with Israel.

SEPTEMBER 19, 1969 Russian-born, U.S.-educated Golda Meir moved to Palestine in 1921 and fought for a Jewish state. She served as Israel's Prime Minister from 1969 to 1974.

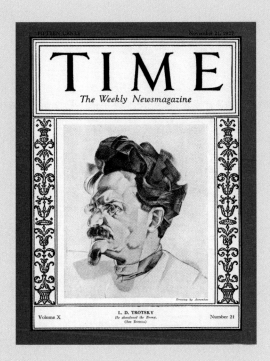

NOVEMBER 21, 1927 Firebrand Marxist Leon Trotsky helped Lenin bring the Bolsheviks to power in Russia and led the Red Army in the war that followed, but was purged by Stalin.

AUGUST 8, 1960 Heir to Trotsky as a prophet of revolution, physician Che Guevara helped Fidel Castro win the Cuban revolution; he died leading guerrillas in Bolivia in 1967.

NOVEMBER 28, 1983 Colonialist in Burma, chronicler of urban poverty, Loyalist fighter in Spain, Cassandra of totalitarianism: writer George Orwell took the century's pulse.

JANUARY 5, 1987 Taking up the mantle from her martyred husband, Corazon Aquino led a popular revolution that ousted corrupt Filipino leader Ferdinand Marcos in 1986.

THE PIO

The century's sound track was the breaking of barriers. The pioneering spirit found new frontiers in unexpected places: not only in the air but also under the sea and deep within the human consciousness. The spirit that urged Edmund Hillary to climb Mount Everest and drove Jacques Cousteau to explore the seas also animated Freud and Jung, the great spelunkers of the mind. And it touched ballplayer Jackie Robinson and environmentalist Rachel Carson, who fought to overcome a different kind of barrier: outworn habits of thought. Pioneers are connoisseurs of risk, yet their code calls for silence about their motives. When mountaineer George Mallory was asked why he tried to conquer Everest, he offered the answer that defines the breed: "Because it's there." ∎

NEERS

Hillary & Tenzing, 1953

LINDBERGH

A daring solo flight by **Charles Lindbergh** *put wings on the frontier spirit*

SOME STILL SAY IT WAS NO MORE THAN A STUNT, a daredevil adventure that no man who was concerned about his safety and his future should have attempted. But if so, Charles Lindbergh's 1927 pioneering solo flight across the Atlantic in a single-engine plane that cruised at less than 100 m.p.h. was surely the most glorious stunt of the century—one of those magnificently eloquent gestures that awaken people everywhere to life's boundless potential. After his flight the young pilot was romanticized as an argonaut of the air age, a Ulysses from Minnesota. But Lindbergh was a much more complex person than the one-dimensional hero created by the press. He had an authentic explorer's spirit, and in later years he contributed to the development of aeronautics, worked on the frontiers of medical research and became an early and ardent supporter of the conservation movement. Though his life was shadowed by tragedy and controversy, he is remembered as a trailblazer of the machine age and an authentic hero.

Wine of the gods. Lindbergh's father, a populist Republican Congressman from Minnesota, taught him to be totally self-reliant, and the son always had a vigorous contempt for the herd mentality. Itching to fly since he first saw an airplane as a child, Lindbergh spent 1½ years at the University of Wisconsin. Then, unable to sit any longer in a classroom, he enrolled in a flying school. "In flying, I tasted a wine of the gods," he later wrote. The young pilot was soon barnstorming the country, offering plane rides at $5 a head. Later he flew an airmail route between St. Louis and Chicago, a hazardous adventure in the primitive flying machines of the 1920s. A natural flyer, he was ineluctably drawn to aviation's biggest prize: $25,000, offered by a New York hotel owner for the first successful solo completion of the 3,600-mile flight between New York and Paris. With the backing of some young St. Louis businessmen and $2,000 from his own savings, Lindbergh ordered a plane built to his peculiar specifications; it was in effect one giant gasoline tank with wings, a propeller and a bucket seat. He named it *The Spirit of St. Louis,* and in May 1927 flew it to New York.

Other flyers were waiting for good weather to try the distance. Learning that Atlantic squalls would soon lift, Lindbergh decided to be first and lifted off from Long Island's Roosevelt Field even before the weather turned. The *Spirit* was so weighted with fuel that it cleared the telephone lines at the end of the runway by only 20 feet. He flew over Nova Scotia and Newfoundland, past the southern tips of Ireland and England, then—fighting sleep—over the Channel to France.

Even before he landed, some mysterious chemistry, an interaction between his own personality and public need and desire, had caught the imagination of millions. For the 33⅓ hours of the flight, many people on both sides of the Atlantic talked of little else but the chances of the man who had already been dubbed "the Lone Eagle." Shortly after 10 p.m. on May 21, he circled Le Bourget Airport, but was puzzled by what looked like enormous traffic jams on the nearby roads. He quickly found out the cause; even before the *Spirit's* propeller stilled, both Lindbergh and his plane were engulfed by joyfully hysterical Parisians.

The hysteria did not stop for years thereafter, but Lindbergh managed to retain his simple dignity. He was the kind of man whom Americans instinctively appreciated and liked: practical and resourceful, with a mechanical turn of mind, full of animal spirits, empty of all pretension, built around a steel-tough core of reserve and self-respect. The Lindbergh name was magic all over the world; the extent of his fame at the time is impossible to understand at century's end, when the culture of celebrity has permeated daily life.

A hero in exile. Two years after his flight, Lindbergh, now an aviation consultant, married Anne Morrow, the pretty, bright daughter of Dwight Morrow, a New York City banker then serving as U.S. ambassador to Mexico. Earnest, poetic, adventurous Anne Morrow had much in common with earnest, adventurous (but not poetic) Charles Lindbergh. She was a writer, destined for fame on her own, and they settled down to a quiet life in New Jersey. Peace was short-lived, however. In 1932 the Lindberghs' first and then only child, 20-month-old Charles Jr., was kidnapped from a second-floor nursery. Ten weeks later, the body was found in a shallow grave in some woods near the Lindbergh home. After one of the most celebrated trials of the century, Bruno Richard Hauptmann, a Bronx carpenter, was convicted and electrocuted for the murder.

Throughout their ordeal, the Lindberghs were hounded by the press, which treated their tragedy with savage sensationalism. Lindbergh already disliked the intrusive media, and the coverage of the kidnapping story left him completely embittered. Finally, he packed up his family (there were eventually five other children) and moved to Britain and then France, where he stayed until the eve of World War II. At this time he came to work closely with Dr. Alexis Carrel, a Nobel laureate in medicine. The two developed a perfusion pump for keeping the heart and other organs alive.

Lindbergh went to Germany in 1938 and was decorated by Field Marshal Hermann Göring with the Order of the German Eagle. Impressed by the progress of Nazi Germany's air

January 2, 1928

1902 Born in Detroit, Michigan
1927 Is first to fly solo across the Atlantic
1932 His son is killed
1941 Joins isolationist group America First
1974 Dies at 72, is buried in Hawaii

machine, and equally appalled by the lack of preparedness in Britain and France, Lindbergh returned to the U.S. and fought to convince the nation that it must vastly upgrade its air power. In 1941 he joined America First, an isolationist group that urged the U.S. to stay out of the war. Britain and France were doomed, he said, and Germany and the Soviet Union would eventually destroy each other. Though Lindbergh immediately volunteered for service after Pearl Harbor, President Franklin Roosevelt would not forgive his isolationist stand and refused him a uniform. As a civilian consultant to the War Department, however, Lindbergh was able to perform valuable service in improving planes and fighting techniques, both at home and on the battlefields of the South Pacific. But Lindbergh never recanted his isolationist stance, and though he was not an anti-Semite or a fascist, as some charged, he remained appallingly insensitive to the true evils of the Hitler regime.

After the war Lindbergh continued his career as a high-level consultant in the airline industry and took great interest in the U.S. space program. After a trip to Africa in 1964 he became a passionate conservationist and traveled the world in the cause of the environment. In his last years his favorite spot was a simple five-acre retreat on the Hawaiian island of Maui. It was there, on a cliff overlooking the Pacific, that the Lone Eagle was buried following his death in 1974. ■

DECISIVE MOMENTS

FRENZY Alerted by ground spotters who had seen his plane pass over Ireland and England, a crowd of 100,000 met Lindbergh in Paris.

CO-PILOT Two years after his solo crossing, Lindbergh married Anne Morrow, a gifted writer who chronicled their travels in best sellers and later traced their lives in her autobiography.

THE BURDEN On his return to the U.S., some 4 million New Yorkers showered the "Lone Eagle" with ticker tape. A private person, Lindbergh came to hate the intrusiveness of both the public and the press.

THE TRAGEDY In a trial sensationalized by the press, Bronx carpenter Bruno Hauptmann was found guilty of kidnapping and murdering Lindbergh's son.

ISOLATED Lindbergh visited Nazi Germany in 1938 and was given a medal by Luftwaffe boss Göring. Lindbergh returned to America in 1939 as an ardent, outspoken isolationist. When war came, F.D.R. refused his request to serve in the military.

EARHART

Soaring through life, **Amelia Earhart**
slipped the bonds of gravity and gender

MANY MYSTERIES SURROUND THE death of pioneering aviator Amelia Earhart, who disappeared with navigator Fred Noonan in 1937 somewhere in the South Pacific. But there is no question as to why Earhart courted danger throughout her life and set out on her fatal round-the-world flight; she identified her motivation in the title of her book *The Fun of It.* And she had fun. She was the second person after Lindbergh to fly the Atlantic solo, first to fly from Hawaii to the U.S. mainland. She set altitude and speed records, co-founded an airline, wrote books and—tellingly—designed practical fashions for women. For beneath the fun, Earhart knew she was not simply a pioneer flyer, but was also opening doors for women to succeed in professions long reserved for men.

Born in Kansas in 1898, Earhart went east to study at Columbia University, then west to be with her parents, who had moved to Los Angeles. In California she took her first airplane flight and set off, with characteristic exuberance and pluck, to become an aviator. Flying machines were still a novelty—indeed, the air age was only 15 years old—when she took her first solo flight in 1918. Two years later, she set a woman's altitude record of 14,000 ft. and then returned to the East to begin a career in social work, but when she was offered a chance to go along as a passenger on a transatlantic flight—primarily for publicity value—she immediately signed on.

Amelia Earhart thus made national headlines as the first woman to cross the Atlantic, with Wilmer Stultz and Louis Gordon in the *Friendship.* After that she settled down to learn flying as well as she could. She flew for fun, flew for publicity. She learned to fly so well that she became the world's foremost female aviator. And she became a good friend of Eleanor Roosevelt, who shared her belief that women should not stand in the shadow of men. In 1931 she married publisher George Palmer Putnam, who encouraged her career, which evolved from publicity-oriented stunts to an interest in the scientific aspect of flying. She became a consulting member of Purdue University's faculty, specializing in aeronautics and careers for women, and in 1936 she acquired a Lockheed Electra that was described as a "flying laboratory" equipped with up-to-the-minute flying and navigating devices.

Earhart still yearned to achieve one goal: the circumnavigation of the globe by air. She set off from Miami on June 1, 1937, with colleague Fred Noonan, a onetime airline navigator. Their "flying laboratory" was far less advanced than advertised: with Noonan sitting behind Earhart, they exchanged messages back and forth with a long bamboo pole.

The two flew leisurely to South America, Africa, India, Australia. On July 1 they left Lae, New Guinea, for the "worst section"—the 2,550 miles of open ocean to tiny Howland Island, where no plane had ever been. Strangely, Earhart did not reveal her position along the way, though the Coast Guard cutter *Itasca* at Howland heard from her about once an hour. Her final message said she had only half-an-hour's gas left and could not see land. But she still gave no position. When the plane failed to arrive at Howland, and it became clear it was down, the *Itasca* steamed hopelessly in search with no idea of where to look. It turned up no trace of Earhart, Noonan or the plane. An extensive search over the next few weeks also found no trace of the aviators.

The disappearance of Amelia Earhart remains one of the century's unsolved enigmas. Over the years it has generated expeditions, scholarly research—and some overly imaginative TV shows. It has been argued that the Earhart trip had a hidden agenda: to spy on Japanese installations in the Pacific. Many believe she was captured and executed by the Japanese. Serious scholars claim to have found evidence of plane crashes on various Pacific islands. The mystery endures. And though her death was a tragedy, one suspects that the high-spirited Earhart would have enjoyed the endless conjecture, and even the more absurd hypotheses that surround her disappearance, if only for the fun of it. ■

Earhart in 1937

1898 Born in Kansas
1920 Sets woman's altitude record
1932 First woman to fly the Atlantic solo
1931 Marries publisher George Putnam
1937 Disappears over the South Pacific

WRIGHT

How to make machines fly? With the right stuff—and **the Wright brothers**

O N THAT COLD DECEMBER DAY IN 1903, a gusty north wind was blowing across the dunes of North Carolina's coast. The wind blew sand into the eyes of Wilbur and Orville Wright as they moved their awkward flying machine out of its shed at Kitty Hawk. A dismal-looking horse and wagon waited nearby. A man sat on the wagon seat, leaning patiently forward, his hands hanging loosely between his knees, the reins looped over a crooked finger. He was a local undertaker.

The flying machine was called *Flyer 1.* It resembled a great, wide box kite, with struts supporting vertical and horizontal rudders far out in the rear. The engine was at one side of the flyer's seat, so that if the plane tumbled it would not fall on him. Two skids projected in front to prevent the plane from

somersaulting on landing. Orville, a short, neat man with a heavy mustache, stretched himself flat on his stomach on the lower wing, between the two chain-driven propellers. The 12-h.p. engine coughed, spat and began to clatter. With Wilbur running alongside holding one wing, the plane teetered down its wooden launching rail and rose unsteadily into the air. For 12 seconds it lurched slowly forward like an uncertain kite, dipping and bobbing a few feet above the ground, then settled back on to the cold sand.

Three more flights were made that day, the brothers taking turns at the controls. The longest sustained flight was 59 seconds, for a distance of 852 feet. Then the wind picked up the plane, rolled it over and wrecked it. But the Wright brothers, bicycle mechanics from Middle America, had proved that man could conquer the air. In classic American fashion—in a pattern that would give birth to such age-defining products as the Model T and the Apple personal computer—a breakthrough that would fundamentally alter society was the product of inspired tinkering by dedicated shade-tree mechanics.

Though Orville was four years younger, he and Wilbur had worked as a team since they were both boys. Sons of a United Brethren bishop (there were two other brothers and a sister), they liked to make things for themselves. Frustrated with formal learning, they quit high school and opened a bicycle shop in their hometown of Dayton, Ohio, in 1892. In 1896 they read about the fatal crash of Otto Lilienthal, a German scientist who had been experimenting with gliders. They became interested in the notion of powered flight and sent to the Smithsonian Institution for all the information there was on flying. There wasn't much. They asked the Weather Bureau to recommend a place where the wind blew steady and strong over the unobstructed ground. The bureau suggested Kitty Hawk.

For three years, they battled Kitty Hawk's mosquitoes and sandflies and flew their gliders off a high dune called Kill Devil Hill. They sewed the sateen for the wings on a neighbor's sewing machine. For power, they crafted a 12-h.p. water-cooled engine. They built the first wind tunnel out of an old starch box, tried hundreds of different wing shapes and found that practically all published data on flying were useless. Two things, they learned, happened to a moving plane—wind pushed it up from below and a vacuum sucked it up from above. If the plane was slightly curved and tapered from front to back, the suction force was about three times the pushing force. They figured out a way to warp the wings to keep the plane on an even keel (the principle of later ailerons).

But even after their historic flight on that December day, recognition was slow. By 1905 the brothers were sustaining flights of almost an hour in their latest machine, *Flyer 3*. Yet not until 1909 did the U.S. Army buy a plane for the Signal

December 3, 1928

1867 Wilbur is born near Millville, Indiana
1871 Orville is born
1903 First successful flight at Kitty Hawk
1912 Wilbur dies
1915 Orville sells the company and retires
1948 Orville dies

Corps. The general public was also slow to realize that the flying machine was a practical fact. Then the medals and kudos poured in. The Wrights set up a factory and began to make money. They hauled a plane to Europe, where kings and queens attended their demonstrations. President William Howard Taft received them with fanfare in the White House. Shy, low-spoken, Midwestern-bred men, the Wrights were embarrassed by the fuss. Once, after enduring the ramblings of several long-winded speakers at a dinner in France, Wilbur rose and remarked, "The most talkative bird in the world is the parrot. But he is a poor flyer."

In 1912 Wilbur was stricken with typhoid fever and died. A saddened Orville sold the company and his patents to Eastern capitalists in 1915. Orville had conceived the plane as a convenience for private citizens. Thanks to his pioneering, every nation would be made a neighbor—or so he had thought. He watched with pride and considerable dismay as planes became bigger and faster. The use of airplanes in World War I made it clear that he and his brother had unwittingly created an instrument of destruction that would loose unimagined violence upon the world.

The rush of aerial development passed Orville by. He built himself a laboratory in Dayton and spent his time puttering in it. After 1918 he rarely flew. He had fractured a hip in an early crash, and any vibration caused him excruciating pain. Occasionally an aircraft company asked his advice. He still loved to build gadgets—a rolling roof and self-opening doors for his summer lodge in Canada, an automatic record changer, a line of mechanical toys that his brother Lorin manufactured. He lived alone—neither he nor Wilbur ever married. Said the old-fashioned Orville: "You can't support a wife and a flying machine too." In 1948, three years after the *Enola Gay* dropped an atom bomb on Hiroshima, Orville Wright—begetter of an age—suffered a heart attack and died. ∎

MAGNIFICENT MEN: Above left, the brothers, 6 years after the first flight at Kitty Hawk, right; opposite, Wilbur at the controls

APRIL 18, 1949 Flying an experimental X-1 craft, Chuck Yeager—who was later celebrated in Tom Wolfe's *The Right Stuff*—was the first human to fly faster than the speed of sound.

FEBRUARY 17, 1958 After World War II, rocket scientist Werner von Braun, designer of Germany's V-2 missiles, came to America and jump-started the fledgling U.S. space program.

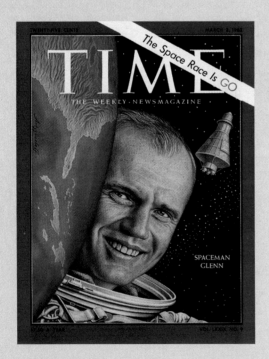

MARCH 2, 1962 John Glenn became the first U.S. astronaut to orbit the earth, though his triumphant flight almost ended in tragedy when his heat shield was dislocated before re-entry.

JULY 25, 1969 When the *Eagle* landed in the Sea of Tranquillity on July 20, 1969, American Neil Armstrong left his footprints on history as the first human being to walk on the moon.

APRIL 21, 1961 After its surprise launch of the Sputnik satellite in 1957, the U.S.S.R. sped far ahead in space when cosmonaut Yuri Gagarin became the first to orbit the earth.

MAY 12, 1961 Racing to catch the Soviets, the U.S. responded with the Mercury program. With a brief suborbital flight, Alan Shepard became the first American in outer space.

APRIL 27, 1970 With ingenuity and rare courage, U.S. astronauts James Lovell, Fred Haise and John Swigert patched up their crippled *Apollo 13* craft and flew it back to earth.

FEBRUARY 12, 1986 The U.S. suffered the worst disaster in the history of space exploration when a shuttle craft exploded after lift-off. All seven *Challenger* astronauts died.

COUSTEAU

Jacques Cousteau *is the Columbus and the conscience of the oceans*

THE WATER MAY BE THE TRANSLUCENT SURF OFF Bermuda, an ice-skimmed quarry in Vermont, the Pacific rolling in majestic rhythm toward the shores of San Diego. Around the world, swimmers sink beneath the waves to fly like spirits through an alien realm. That humans are here at all, exploring a world forbidden to man for millenniums, is largely because of the work of a visionary Frenchman named Jacques-Yves Cousteau. He is the Columbus of the submarine world, at once the pioneer, prophet, poet—and foremost promoter—of the deep. As the developer of the Aqua-lung, he set divers free to roam in the kingdom of the fish. As captain of the *Calypso*, he became an internationally recognized exponent of marine conservation. As an author and expert in underwater photography, he became the avatar of ocean exploration.

Cousteau has said, in his best Barnum-of-the-barnacles mode, "From birth, man carries the weight of gravity on his shoulders. He is bolted to earth. But man has only to sink beneath the surface and he is free. Buoyed by water, he can fly in any direction—up, down, sideways—by merely flipping his hand. Under water, man becomes an archangel." Such raptures of the deep could only come from the mouth of an aesthete or an ascetic—and Cousteau is somewhere in between. His 6-ft. body has always been lean. His face, hollow-cheeked, cleft by the lean curve of an aristocratic nose and scoured by furrows, might have been carved by the sea itself.

Young Cousteau graduated second in his class from France's naval academy, and after a car crash left his arms badly injured, he spent hours working their strength back by swimming in the Mediterranean. There in 1936 a fellow naval officer gave him a pair of goggles used by pearl fishermen. Cousteau put his head beneath the surface, and as he tells it, his life instantly changed: "There was wildlife, untouched, a jungle at the border of the sea, never seen by those who floated on the opaque roof." Cousteau explored the jungle, learning to spear fish with curtain rods and knitting needles. But he was still tethered to the surface by the need for air. Looking for a better way to supply it, he tried an oxygen lung based on a design developed by the British as early as 1878. He almost killed himself. He did not know the fatal flaw of oxygen; it becomes toxic at depths below 30 ft. Twice he had convulsive spasms, and was barely able to drop his weights and make the return to the surface.

Cousteau allowed World War II to distract him only briefly and at intervals from his search. After

March 28, 1960

1910 Born near Bordeaux, France
1943 First successful test of his Aqua-lung
1951 First voyage of the *Calypso*
1979 His son Philippe dies in a plane crash
1996 *Calypso* sinks

France's surrender, he stayed in the navy in Occupied France, but worked for the Resistance. Under the eyes of the indifferent Germans, he worked with a brilliant engineer named Emile Gagnon to develop a lung that would automatically feed him safe, compressed air at the same pressure as the surrounding water so that he could swim with both arms. One day in 1943 Cousteau waddled out into the Mediterranean under the 50-lb. Aqua-lung, and realized his dream. He was free: "I experimented with all possible maneuvers—loops, somersaults and barrel rolls. I stood upside down on one finger and burst out laughing, a shrill, distorted laugh. Nothing I did altered the automatic rhythm of the air. Delivered from gravity and buoyancy, I flew around in space."

Cousteau could scarcely wait for the war to end to develop his new discovery. He sold the French navy on the virtues of the Aqua-lung and got leave for government-backed oceanographic work on

SEA CHANGE: Jacques Cousteau, captured in his native habitat. "When a person takes his first dive," says the veteran explorer, "he is born to another world"

the 360-ton *Calypso*, a converted minesweeper from the British Royal Navy. Aboard the *Calypso*, he gathered the material for the books and films that brought sudden fame to diving and himself. *The Silent World*, published in the U.S. in 1953, sold more than 5 million copies around the world.

Cousteau turned to prowling about the skeletons of ships on the ocean floor, thus bringing potent new tools to the science of marine archaeology. One of his first finds was a 1,000-ton Roman freighter that sank 10 miles off Marseilles around 205 B.C. Increasingly his work turned to science. But he was always more interested in being an explorer than a research scientist, in getting information from the deep, not interpreting it. As an admiring oceanographer once put it, "Cousteau's patron saint should be Ulysses, not Aristotle."

Over the years, the rewards have been many: expeditions to explore waterways around the globe, more than 100 documentary films of ocean life, more than two dozen books, three Oscar awards, 10 Emmys, induction into the Académie Française. But Cousteau has known tragedy as well. His son and heir apparent Philippe was killed in a plane crash in 1979; later he parted ways with Jean Michel, his eldest son and close collaborator, and the two went to court over the commercial use of the family name. In January 1996 the *Calypso* sank in shallow waters off the port of Singapore after being hit by a barge in the shipyard where it was berthed.

As his knowledge of the oceans grew, Cousteau underwent a final transformation. He became an outspoken opponent of uncontrolled exploitation of marine resources, the conscience of the sea. Turning 86 years old in 1996, he is spending less time under the waves and more time at international conferences, where he argues for population control and reduced consumption of natural resources. After years of being the spokesman for underwater life, he insists, "I'm now fighting for my own species. I finally understand that we ourselves are in danger. The notion of sustainable economic development … is impossible; it's an illusion. Our Western model is not valid for a world of limited resources." The man who has been compared to Columbus and Ulysses is spending his final years in a different role: as an aging King Canute, defiant against the rising tide of human exploitation. ∎

HILLARY & TENZING

In the century's peak experience, **Edmund Hillary and Tenzing Norkey** *conquered Mount Everest*

AN EXPECTANT BRITAIN WAS HOLDING ITS BREATH in early June 1953 for a great moment: the coronation of Princess Elizabeth as its new Queen. But half a world away, another crowning moment was about to occur. On coronation eve, a heartbroken message flashed from the foot of Mount Everest in the Himalayas: "BAD SNOW CONDITIONS ... EXPEDITION ABANDONED BASE CAMP TWENTY-NINTH." But the cable was a ruse, coded to prevent a leakage of the great news that the British ambassador to Nepal was relaying to London. Decoded, the message ran, "HILLARY & TENZING CLIMBED MAY 29TH."

Thus, with laconic drama, the ninth British Everest expedition told of the conquest of earth's highest spire—all 29,028 ft. of it. Everest had been tamed by Edmund Hillary, a beekeeper who had begun climbing in his native New Zealand, and the Sherpa mountaineer Tenzing Norkey, who had herded yaks above 20,000 ft. from the age of 10. In reaching the roof of the world, they had done what Columbus and Lindbergh had gloriously done before them: asserted that puny man can measure all things earthly.

The expedition assembled in March, aided by 350 porters; by late May only the seven men of the core team remained, sleeping with oxygen tanks in Camp VIII, at 25,850 ft. The last climb was 3,000 ft. In the final exhausting stages, two assault teams (each with two men) had been "babied" for the final attack. Team No. 1 got the order to go and vanished upward, into the clouds. No human had been higher and lived, but the pair lacked the strength to go on. Back they came.

Team No. 2 was Hillary and Tenzing. They dragged themselves up to 27,900 ft. and there, on a rocky ledge, they spent a gale-swept night in a ragged tent. At 6:30 they thawed out their boots and buckled on all that remained of the precious oxygen. The summit was hidden in clouds, but they knew it lay ahead and above. On and up they stumbled, like flies on a whitewashed wall. As fast as one hump was cleared, the next blocked the view. Both men were slowing down when suddenly it loomed into view—one last narrow snow ridge running up to a peak beyond which nothing was higher.

They made it, roped together, and stood on top of the world. Gravely they shook hands, and Tenzing hugged Hillary like a bear. What did it feel like to be there? Said Hillary (soon to be Sir Edmund) in his stiff-upper-lip mode: "Damn good." Said Tenzing: "I thought of God and the greatness of his work."

They returned to camp, too exhausted to speak, but their comrades forgave them. On both bearded, icicle-festooned faces, a broad grin told the story that Everest at last had yielded. The king of mountains had been conquered, and the next day a Queen was crowned. ∎

BECAUSE IT'S THERE: Above—and above it all—Tenzing stands at Everest's crest; below, the mountain beaters celebrate

Hillary in 1955

1919 Hillary is born in New Zealand
1953 Climbs Everest
1958 Journeys by land to South Pole
1985 Becomes ambassador to India
1995 Meets his namesake, Hillary Clinton

CARSON

Giving nature a voice, **Rachel Carson** *put man's destruction of resources on the century's agenda*

To an admiring friend, Rachel Carson was "a nun of nature, a votary of all outdoors." With a rare gift for transmuting scientific fact into lucid, lyrical language, she opened the eyes of millions of readers to the complex beauties of the natural world in a pair of best sellers. But her talent truly flourished when she harnessed it to a powerful social end: to sound an early warning of mankind's suicidal destruction of the natural world.

Carson's book *Silent Spring* was concerned mainly with the deadly effect of chemical pesticides, and its claims were intensely debated at the time. But seen in retrospect, its significance transcends the arguments about its specific claims. As Carson wrote, a disparate group of scientists, conservationists, naturalists and Sunday gardeners were becoming alarmed about the increasingly destructive effects of technology on the natural world. *Silent Spring* was a wake-up call that crystallized those concerns, firmly placed the issue of conserving natural resources on the century's agenda and planted the seeds of the environmental movement.

It was in 1951, after 15 years with the Fish and Wildlife Service—much of the time as editor in chief of its publications—that Carson published her second book, *The Sea Around Us.* Written in hypnotic, susurrant prose, it brimmed with intriguing knowledge; though intended for a popular audience, it was scientifically rigorous. *The Sea* stayed on the best-seller lists for 86 weeks and won for its author a worldwide reputation as a gentle spokeswoman for nature.

The Sea Around Us brought Carson fame and fortune; she resigned her Washington job; wrote another successful book, *The Edge of the Sea;* and overcame her painful shyness to lecture widely. Then, in the late 1950s, her old friends Stuart and Olga Huckins complained that antimosquito spraying had damaged birds in the two-acre nature sanctuary that they maintained near Duxbury, Massachusetts. Carson visited, investigated—and found a cause. Thus was born *Silent Spring.*

Published in 1962, the book became a runaway best seller and an extremely effective polemic that stirred fierce argument, from village councils to the halls of Congress. In its dramatic centerpiece, Carson pictured a time when the sprays, dusts and aerosols used to control insects would "still the song of birds and the leaping of fish in the streams," finally bringing on the silent spring of her title.

To its author, *Silent Spring* was more than a book; it was a crusade. Despite her scientific training, she rejected facts that weakened her case, and used some suspect material to support her thesis. Her critics, including many scientists, objected that the book was too exaggerated and emotional.

But crusaders operate on emotion. Early in her writing of *Silent Spring,* Carson learned that she had cancer. But she soldiered on until the book was completed. She died two years after the book was published, six years before the world celebrated the first Earth Day, and 24 years before TIME named Endangered Earth its "Planet of the Year." ∎

Carson in 1961

1907 Born in Springdale, Pennsylvania
1951 *The Sea Around Us,* her first book
1955 *The Edge of the Sea*
1962 *Silent Spring* arouses fierce debate
1964 Dies at 56

FIRST PERSON

"The history of life on earth has been a history of interaction between living things and their surroundings. To a large extent, the physical form and the habits of the earth's vegetation and its animal life have been molded by the environment. Considering the whole span of earthly time, the opposite effect, in which life actually modifies its surroundings, has been relatively slight. Only within ... the present century has one species—man—acquired significant power to alter the nature of his world.

Along with the possibility of ... nuclear war, the central problem of our age has therefore become the contamination of man's total environment with substances of incredible potential for harm."

—*Silent Spring,* 1962

FREUD

The mind was terra incognita, until **Sigmund Freud** *explored its secrets*

THE INTENSE YOUNG MAN AMBLING through the great arcaded court at the University of Vienna was deep in fantasy. He was still a student, a nobody, a Jew in Franz Josef's Austria. Yet as he admired the statues of great professors in the university's hall of fame, Sigmund Freud dreamed of a day when his own likeness would be there among the great; he even envisaged the inscription for it.

In 1996, some 120 years later, Freud's bronze image stands in that hall of fame, and below, just as he had conceived it, is the inscription he chose. It is from Sophocles: "Who divined the famed riddle and was a man most mighty?" The riddle that entranced Freud was the same one that had confronted Oedipus in Sophocles' play *Oedipus Rex*, and has challenged man through the ages—What am I? Freud did not divine the riddle. But he penetrated so deeply and so disturbingly into its dark recesses as to earn permanent membership in that small fraternity of men who, by thought alone, have shaken and shaped man's image of himself.

Freud's legacy is controversial: his specific findings are endlessly debated, his stock is continually rising and falling among students of the mind and the general public. He has entered the world's folk memory as a sort of exaggerated caricature of himself: just as Einstein is the personification of all that is intellectual, Freud is the avatar of the mind's dark recesses. To millions his name and the terms he has willed into the language have become shorthand and used, half in jest, to cover up a *lapsus linguae* ("a Freudian slip") or to explain a character defect ("Don't blame Johnny; it's just a defense mechanism"). His theories are a high-assay lode for the pickaxes of sitcom writers. And there are still many to whom Freud remains a spade-bearded Antichrist who debased mankind by insisting that all man's works, whether he desires it or not, are inspired by S-E-X.

But despite the caricatures, Freud's central contribution is clear: as the pioneer of psychoanalysis, the exploration of the unconscious mind, he toppled old taboos and blazed the path followed by modern psychiatry and medicine into the diagnosis and cure of mental illness. Freud was in essence less a scientist than a philosopher, perhaps less a healer than the

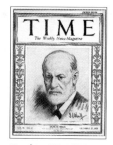

October 27, 1924

1856 Born in Moravia
1899 Writes *The Interpretation of Dreams*
1907 Attracts disciples
1923 Publishes *The Ego and the Id*
1938 Leaves Vienna after Nazi Anschluss
1939 Dies in London

maker of a system of thought—and a mythos—acceptable to his time. His ideas, defying harness and too soaring to rest within the confines of hospital wards and doctor's offices, flared out to all compartments of 20th century life—religion, morals, philosophy, the arts, even commerce and industry and the assembling of armies.

World of riddles. Freud was born in Freiberg, Moravia, the oldest of eight in his wool-merchant father's second brood of children. Jakob Freud was 41, his new wife 21. By his first marriage, Jakob had two sons. The eldest, Emanuel, had already made him a grandfather by the time Sigmund was born, so the new arrival had a nephew older than himself. And his other half brother, Philipp, was almost exactly his mother's age. The complex family circle has given Freud scholars much fodder for analysis. When Sigmund was four, the family moved to Vienna. A bookworm, he graduated from high school at 17. There is no clear explanation of his choice of medicine as a career. His own best version (one of several) is that "I felt an overpowering need to understand something of the riddles of the world in which we live, and perhaps even to contribute something to their solution."

At 25 Freud fell in love with Martha Bernays and plunged into the practice of neurology to make enough money to allow them to marry. A traveling fellowship to study in Paris under the famed Jean Martin Charcot in 1885 turned Freud's thoughts upon the inner workings of the human mind, and especially upon hysteria and the hypnosis that Charcot used in treating it. It was a long series of hesitant steps from there to the development of psychoanalysis.

The case of hysterical Anna O. gave Freud the first hint of how a troubled person may ease or banish symptoms by talking about them. From patient Emmy von N., Freud realized that a victim of hysteria becomes emotionally attached to her (or his) physician. It occurred to him that there was a sexual basis for emotional upsets, so they could be resolved by analysis with a laboratory-style emotional attachment. When Freud interrupted the "stream of consciousness" recital of patient Elisabeth von R., she said that it was better to let her ramble on, because one idea led to another in her mind. Thus another insight, free association,

FIELD OF DREAMS: Critics scoffed at it and his disciples venerated it: the couch in Freud's study became a lasting totem of psychoanalysis

Adler broke with Freud; then Jung, his heir apparent, followed. "The brain is viewed as an appendage of the genital glands," Jung once claimed of Freud's theories. The cult of psychoanalysis began to develop its schismatic sects and diametrically opposed dogmatists. But Freudian thought remained its core, and it began to win acceptance among the unhappy and emotionally distressed. Psychoanalytic institutes sprang up in Vienna and Geneva, Paris and London, New York City and Chicago.

As Freud's theories spread, he was superficially described as the greatest killjoy in the history of human thought, transforming man's jokes and gentle pleasures into dreary and mysterious repressions, discovering hatreds at the root of love, malice at the heart of tenderness, incest in filial affections, guilt in generosity and the repressed hatred of one's parents as a normal human inheritance. Unmoved, he continued to refine his theories. Having divided the mind into conscious and unconscious, he now divided it again into id, ego and superego. He repeatedly modified his theories about man's basic instincts and, in the 1920s he began to suspect that there may really be only two: a life-and-love instinct (Eros) and an equally strong death-and-aggression instinct (Thanatos).

came to Freud. The couch, with its comfortable invitation to talkativeness, became his workbench.

The world stirred only fitfully at first. When he began lecturing on the sexual basis of neuroses, in Vienna in 1896, his worldly colleagues regarded him with embarrassed annoyance. Lighthearted fin-de-siècle Vienna boasted of its sexual freedom, yet many shunned him. Prudish physicians complained that he made too much of sex, that he destroyed beautiful illusions (such as the innocence of childhood), that he invaded his patients' privacy. Freud's key book, *The Interpretation of Dreams*, in which he set forth his gospel, sold only 600 copies in the eight years after its publication in 1899.

Freud had the ear of only a small group of devoted admirers among Vienna's psychologists and psychiatrists, including Alfred Adler, whom he met weekly at his home. From Switzerland came better tidings. In Zurich, Carl Gustav Jung had learned Freud's methods from his writings and had begun to apply psychoanalysis to patients, including a few suffering from psychoses. Then, early in 1907, there came to Vienna in pilgrimage the first of the few disciples who were to remain loyal to Freud through all the storm and stress of later years: Karl Abraham, Hanns Sachs, Ernest Jones and others.

It was not surprising, in an adventure so heady, intense and trackless, that dissension developed among the explorers.

Shades of gray. Freud was a contradictory character. By nature both tolerant and reflective, he could also be both impatient and intolerant. A searching student of human nature who saw it in all its shades of gray, he still had a naive way of seeing all acquaintances as either black or white—and a white friend could turn into a black foe overnight. Freud could be charming, and his penetrating, attentive eyes inspired confidence. He was relatively short and slight, unaffected and simple in demeanor. Stricken with cancer of the jaw in later years, he bore the pain bravely and without complaint. He stuck it out in Vienna even after the Nazis took over in March 1938—until disciple Ernest Jones flew in and plucked him to the safety of London, where he died in 1939, at 83.

If Sigmund Freud were still alive, he might be surprised and even put out to discover how calmly the revelations that shocked Vienna in the 1900s have become absorbed into modern society. "They may abuse my doctrines by day," he once declared, "but I am sure they dream of them by night." In a sense he was right. Freud as philosopher and counselor to man will be the subject of arguments and doubts for years to come. But about Freud as the bold pioneer who explored the dark side of the mind there is no argument left. As the Swiss Catholic psychiatrist Charles Baudoin said, "Modern man cannot conceive of himself without Freud." ∎

JUNG

Master of sign and symbol, **Carl Gustav Jung**

deciphered the hieroglyphs of the unconscious

February 14, 1955

1875 Born in Kesswil, Switzerland
1907 Journeys to Vienna to meet Freud
1912 Parts with Freud
1921 *Psychological Types* defines introvert and extrovert types
1961 Dies at 86

WREATHED BY PIPE SMOKE THAT SWIRLED through his white hair and gave him the aspect of a medieval alchemist, Carl Gustav Jung was busy in the study of his old-fashioned, high-ceilinged house on Lake Zurich. The three-volume work on which he was dotting the last *i* seemed strange for a modern psychiatrist: *Representation of the Problems of Opposites in Medieval Natural Philosophy.* "Pretty abstruse, huh?" said Jung to a visitor. Then laughter rocked his heavy shoulders. "I must laugh! I have such a hell of a trouble to make people see what I mean."

Jung was a master of the abstruse. His explorations took him through yoga, alchemy, fairy tales, the tribal rites of the Pueblo Indians, Hindu mandalas, extrasensory perception, prehistoric cave drawings—and an estimated 100,000 dreams. But when Dr. Jung was accused of having left medicine for mysticism, he replied that psychiatry must reflect all of man's experiences, from the most intensely practical to the most ten-uously mystical. If the details of his work were sometimes foggy, his overall purpose was clear: to help man live at peace with his unconscious.

Sigmund Freud saw sexual energy, or libido, as the prime mover of the unconscious; his disciple Alfred Adler made it the drive for power to overcome inferiority feelings. To Jung, the systems constructed by his rivals were narrow-gauge, "nothing-but" explanations of human life, which reduced man's most numinous visions to sordid sex symbols and shrank the soul to a vanishing point. Jung posed bolder concepts. Man's unconscious, he argued, is a vast subterranean storehouse full of both good and evil. He divided the unconscious into two layers. Within one, relatively superficial, he perceived the libido and the power drive in less ambitious roles. In the second and far deeper stratum, he perceived the force of the primeval, collective unconscious of the human race.

Jung was the only son of a Reformed Church pastor. He had a lonely, bookish boyhood in Basel; his father began teaching him Latin at six, and later he read Greek and Sanskrit and steeped himself in philosophy. He took up medicine to please his father—and began digging into the minds of patients. Practicing in Zurich, young Dr. Jung was fired by Freud's descriptions of psychoanalysis. In 1907 he made the pilgrimage to Vienna, and Freud saw his heir apparent in the tall Teuton. But Jung broke with Freud in 1912, unable to accept his libido-driven system.

Continuing his own research, Jung began to unearth "archetypes"—patterns of experience and feeling that have reappeared down through the ages in dream symbols, as collective myths, or in the arts. Among the most significant: the "old wise man" and the "earth mother." In the persistence of religious movements throughout history, Jung saw an archetypal need for a religious attitude. A religion did not need to be formalized, he insisted, but to be emotionally healthy, a man must have made his peace with the unseen and perhaps unknowable power behind creation and the universe.

A sworn foe of organizations, Jung discouraged his followers from starting formal institutes to perpetuate his teachings. With advancing years, he withdrew more and more from the arena of battling psychologies, concentrating on his arcane studies. In the years before his death, living happily in his willow-shaded house, surrounded by grandchildren and great-grandchildren, the old wise man seemed to many of his admirers the most convincing case history in support of Jungian theory. ■

SARTRE

Finding philosophy in nausea and poetry in despair,

Jean-Paul Sartre *dressed the wounds of postwar Europe*

H E LOOKED LIKE A TOAD, AS HE SAID OF HIMSELF. HIS sexual life was more intricate than the plot of a Restoration comedy, and he once remarked, with a humor rare in his profession, that sex preoccupied him far more than philosophy. He did not write like a philosopher either, for he commanded a graceful prose style that could turn the subtlest concept into a memorable aphorism or a playable drama. But Jean-Paul Sartre managed to become an influential philosopher in a century when philosophers had ceased to influence almost anybody.

Sartre's moment was the bitter aftermath of World War II. Exhausted Europe, shaken by the absolute evil of Adolf Hitler and by the paralyzing fear of nuclear annihilation, had been delivered not into peace but into the ambiguous stalemate of the cold war. Looking for guidance when most moral values seemed questionable and all ideals suspect, the postwar generation found solace in the austere arms of existentialism. Sartre did not invent the term, and he owed an intellectual debt to other European thinkers, especially the German philosopher Martin Heidegger. But in Sartre's prose, abstract ideas were translated into demands for decision. "Man is free," he wrote. "The coward makes himself cowardly. The hero makes himself heroic."

Because God does not exist, said Sartre, man defines what he is, his essence, through his own actions. Each individual is responsible for choosing one course of action over another. It is the choice that gives value to the act, and nothing that is not acted upon has value. Lending a moral dimension to an otherwise indifferent universe, Sartre declared that a person cannot define himself by "disappointed dreams, miscarried hopes or vain expectations." Most people seek to evade responsibility by blaming something or somebody else for their fate; he regarded this as "bad faith."

Sartre expounded his ideas in nine plays, four novels, five major philosophical works and innumerable lectures and essays. He also led demonstrations, fired off protests and manned almost every political barricade raised by the left. Ironically, his most conspicuous disciples—the young, the bitter and the cynical—understood Sartre least. Had he not proclaimed life absurd, reality nauseating and man free of moral laws, religious dogma and restricting obligations, either to ideals or family?

This inadvertent guru was convinced of the corruption of the bourgeoisie, even though he was to the bourgeoisie born. His father was a naval officer who sickened and died when Jean-Paul was only two. Never in robust health, Sartre went blind in his right eye at age three. At the Ecole Normale Supérieure he studied philosophy and met Simone de Beauvoir, his lifelong love, intellectual alter ego and a pioneering feminist. In 1940, as a clerk in the army weather service, he was captured by the Nazis. But he wangled release by a clever ruse, returned to Paris and sweated out the Occupation, risking arrest and imprisonment by writing for the underground French press.

As a revolutionary, Sartre was drawn to communism. Reluctant to believe that communism could not tolerate dissent, he became an outspoken defender of the Soviet Union. Eventually disillusioned, he finally sought solace from the Maoists, who professed to take their leadership directly from the masses, and thus were the purest of revolutionaries.

Sartre has been called the conscience of his generation. Unquestionably he was too often wrong for that. In a lifetime of searching for a place where man could put his feet, he never found a place for his own—and he knew it, which is more than most people know or care to admit. He did care, and it is the eloquence and intensity of that caring—for himself and on behalf of others—that are his monument. ∎

Sartre in 1946

1905 Born in Paris
1938 Writes his first novel, *Nausea*
1943 Writes *Being and Nothingness,* his philosophical gem
1944 Writes *No Exit,* his most famous play
1980 Dies in Paris

ROBINSON

He was the most artful Dodger, but **Jackie Robinson** *never backed down*

BRANCH RICKEY, THE BEEFY, BUSHY-BROWED BOSS of the old Brooklyn Dodgers, was at his histrionic best. Scowling at the young black ballplayer seated in his office, he portrayed in turn a bigoted umpire deliberately making bad calls, a haughty railroad conductor pointing to the Jim Crow car and a hostile waiter snarling, "Nigger, you can't eat here." "Suppose they throw at your head?" Rickey demanded. "Suppose you're fielding a ground ball, and a white player charges into you and sneers, 'Next time get out of my way, you dirty black bastard.' What do you do then? Can you walk away from him?" Jack Roosevelt Robinson was puzzled. "Mr. Rickey," he said, "are you looking for a Negro who is afraid to fight back?" "On the contrary," said Rickey. "I'm looking for a ballplayer with guts enough not to fight back. They'll taunt you, goad you. Anything to make you fight. Anything to bring about a race riot in the ballpark. If they succeed, they'll be able to prove that having a Negro in baseball doesn't work."

It was no small task for Robinson to don what Rickey described as an "armor of humility." As a track, basketball, football and baseball star at UCLA, he was a belligerent competitor who always prided himself on "reacting spiritedly when insulted or scorned." As a lieutenant in the Army, he had, in fact, been threatened with a court-martial for refusing to sit in the back of a bus. The toughest task of his career, he once recalled, was learning "to conquer and control myself." But he succeeded, and in succeeding he became one of the great pioneers of civil rights in the United States.

When Rickey startled the sports world in 1945 by announcing that Robinson would join the Dodgers farm team in Montreal, his prophecies proved true. Minor league commissioner W.G. Bramham called Rickey a "carpetbagger." Said Bob Feller, the fireballing Cleveland Indians pitcher: "If he were a white man, I doubt if they would even consider him as big-league material."

At spring training, the slurs continued. Once, after watching Robinson pull off a dazzling play in the field, Rickey exclaimed to Montreal manager Clay Hopper, "That was a superhuman play!" Hopper, a Mississippian, drawled, "Mr. Rickey, do you really think a nigger's a human being?" Hopper's bias toward Robinson soon turned to open admiration. In the season's first game, Robinson collected four hits, including a three-run homer; stole two bases; and scored four runs. But the taunting cries of "Kill the jungle bunny!" still echoed from the bleachers, north and south of the Mason-Dixon line. During one game in Syracuse, New York, the opposing team turned a black cat loose on the field, shouting that it was the "black boy's cousin." Robin-son responded in classic fashion, drilling a double to left.

In 1946, after leading the International League in hitting, with a .349 average, Robinson moved up to the big leagues—and bigger troubles. First Rickey had to chew out some of the Southern members of the Dodgers, most notably Georgia-born Dixie Walker, for organizing a ban-the-black petition. Then National League president Ford Frick was forced to intercede with a tough play-or-else edict to put down a proposed boycott of the Dodgers by a group of St. Louis Cardinals.

The bigotry that was characteristic of so many big-league ballplayers was expressed in other, more painful ways. In the field, Robinson was frequently spiked; at bat, he had the dubious distinction of being hit by beanballing pitchers more times than any other player in the league. Through it all, though, he kept his temper and helped lead the Dodgers to the 1947 pennant with a team-high batting average of .297. He quieted his critics with a display of clutch hitting, bunting, slick fielding and flashy base running that won him Rookie of the Year honors. In one poll at season's end, he was runner-up to Bing Crosby as the most popular man in America.

Though his batting average through 10 seasons with the Dodgers was a formidable .311, Robinson's greatest gift was his daring, pigeon-toed base running. He stopped and started as though turned off and on with a toggle switch. He was not only jackrabbit fast, but about one thought and two steps ahead of every base runner in the business. He made a specialty of the game's most thrilling play: before he retired from baseball in 1956, the great infielder had stolen home 11 times, a feat that has not been equaled since.

Robinson spent his last years as a well-to-do businessman, a conspicuous Republican turned Democrat and a tireless, outspoken champion of civil rights and rehabilitation programs for drug addicts. (His eldest son Jack Jr., a reformed heroin addict, was killed in an auto accident in 1971.) In later years Robinson was slowed by a heart condition, arthritis and a case of diabetes that left him blind in one eye; he was only 53 when he died. When the 1972 World Series opened, only a few weeks before his death, he was presented with a plaque commemorating the 25th anniversary of his arrival in the big leagues. "I am extremely proud and pleased," he said, "but I will be more pleased the day I can look over at third base and see a black man as manager."

By the end of the century Robinson's dream had in large part become reality. There were black players and coaches in the dugout and a few black managers on third base. But the great Dodger would most likely have kept pushing to see more racial diversity in baseball, particularly among the executive ranks. The Hall of Fame second baseman was never satisfied with second best. ∎

September 22, 1947

1919 Born in Cairo, Georgia
1946 Plays on Dodgers farm team
1947 Joins Brooklyn Dodgers, wins Rookie of the Year honors
1956 Leaves baseball
1972 Dies at 53

DECEMBER 6, 1926 The principal pioneer of radio telegraphy, Guglielmo Marconi first sent radio messages across the Atlantic in 1901 and shared the Nobel Prize for Physics in 1909.

AUGUST 20, 1928 Pioneer of polar exploration by aircraft, Richard E. Byrd claimed to be first to fly over the North and South poles and mapped key features of Antarctica by air.

SEPTEMBER 30, 1957 The new technologies of broadcast TV and radio demanded a new kind of journalism; Edward R. Murrow helped establish the standards in both fields.

JANUARY 10, 1964 The novel ideas of designer and engineer R. Buckminster Fuller—like the geodesic dome—earned him a Harvard chair in poetry as the first "poet of technology."

NOVEMBER 28, 1932 Adviser to Prince Faisal as the Arabs revolted against the Turks in World War I, Briton T.E. Lawrence lived with the Bedouins as "Lawrence of Arabia."

AUGUST 24, 1953 Though his research methods have been attacked, Dr. Alfred Kinsey was a pioneer in applying scientific scrutiny to the once taboo field of human sexual behavior.

JULY 20, 1981 When U.S. President Ronald Reagan named Sandra Day O'Connor to the Supreme Court, the conservative jurist found herself in the unlikely role of feminist superstar.

SEPTEMBER 3, 1984 The first woman to run for national office on a major-party ticket in the United States was a Democrat, Congresswoman Geraldine Ferraro of New York City.

THE INN

Tom Watson Jr., 1957

OVATORS

Assembly kit for an innovator: take one part scientist, one part pioneer, one part creator—and lubricate with genius. Cranky, dream-haunted perfectionists, hardworking and hard to work for, innovators are inspired zealots—like Henry Ford—who tinker their daydreams into reality and then struggle to satisfy the demand they've created. Alert to the possibilities of technology and to the unspoken urges of the mass market, the century's great innovators prospered by anticipating the immense desire for the newfangled: automobiles and radios, television and the movies. Behind the Model T and Windows 95, behind Mickey Mouse and the table radio, behind CNN and NBC, stood a single person charged with the vision and drive to hot-wire the future—and make it real. ■

FORD

An inspired tinkerer who built an empire of Tin Lizzies, **Henry Ford** *jump-started the automotive age*

T HE FUNERAL OF HENRY FORD CAUSED A TRAFFIC jam. After the church service, Ford's body was carried in a Packard hearse to the small family cemetery beside a four-lane highway. Henry Ford wouldn't have approved; he had never ridden comfortably in any car but one of his own make. They lowered the coffin into a hole in the wet, clayey mud. The rain came down in buckets while the police hustled 20,000 sightseers on their way and opened the highway again to traffic. The cars rushed past, filling the night with the smell of gasoline.

To Henry Ford, the smell of gasoline had been like perfume. It was gasoline that fueled the Model T, and it was with the Model T that Ford, the master of mass production, put the U.S. on wheels. More than any man in the 20th century, Ford changed the way people lived. He did so by originating a means of getting a useful instrument in many people's hands at lower and lower cost, and in so doing had shown the way to distribute many other useful instruments to the millions.

In his lifetime, Ford was damned as a communist, an anarchist and an anti-Semite; he was also praised as the greatest living American, whose diverse interests made him seem a kind of machine-age Leonardo. A lean Midwesterner with a farmer's flair for opinionating and a mechanic's scorn for words, Ford was always two men. He was a cantankerous, stubborn, cracker-box philosopher who could not bear to be contradicted, and he was a maker, a maker of machines that work.

Axing the shed. He was born a tinker, not a farmer, which was what his farmer father had wanted him to be. He was also born stubborn, so he quit the farm, married Clara Bryant and ended up tinkering with a gasoline contraption in a red brick shed in back of his house in Detroit. He lavished the hours he could spare from his job at Detroit Electric Co. working on a "horseless carriage." One day in 1896 he took an ax to the wall of the shed (the door was too small) and drove the contraption out into the world. That was the start. He persuaded 11 businessmen to finance him and went into production.

A lot of other men had built autos,

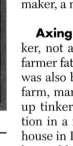

March 17, 1941

1863 Born near Dearborn, Michigan
1903 Founds Ford Motor Co.
1908 Model T debuts
1915 Sails to Europe on peace mission
1927 Model A debuts
1947 Dies at 83

EARLY DAYS At age 30 in 1893, Ford—in the center of the top row, above—was a young engineer with the Detroit Edison Co., and a new father. In earlier years he had repaired steam engines for Westinghouse.

GET A HORSE! This rare photo shows Ford with his first car, a light carriage powered by a two-cylinder engine, which he completed building in his backyard shed in June 1896.

ROLLING Ford's assembly-line building process allowed him to keep prices low: the Model T debuted in 1908 at $825 for a roadster and $850 for a touring car. When this 1913 photo was taken, Ford cars made up nearly 50% of the U.S. market for autos.

but Ford had a special theory. Build cars cheaply, he said, so everyone could own one. Make them simple, he said. His first Model T had only 5,000 parts, counting every last nut. Standardize the parts, he said, so that anyone could buy a new carburetor in any one of the thousands of garages that he visualized springing up across the country. From a crude assembly line in Detroit, Model Ts began to jerk. He turned out 10,607 in 1909. In 19 years Ford made 15 million of them.

High-slung, narrow-wheeled and homely, the Model T became a legend. Said Ford: "Customers can have it painted any color they want so long as it's black." The Tin Lizzie rattled across the country, leaving in its wake a spoor of fruit skins, pop bottles, flat tires. Ford's flivver had to have roads. Roads were built. It had to have gas. Gas pumps sprouted. It paid taxes. It made jobs. It made modern America and the modern age.

Ford built an industrial empire of coal mines, rubber plantations, iron mines, timberland, sawmills, hydroelectric works, companies in a dozen other nations. The empire's capital was the plant on Dearborn's River Rouge, where the cantankerous Henry Ford ruled the roost. He had opinions on everything, and particularly about labor. In 1914 the country was flabbergasted when he established an unheard-of minimum $5-a-day wage and a profit-sharing scheme. Good pay makes good workers, he said. Good workmen, like good steel and rubber, resulted in better Model Ts. And well-paid workmen could buy more products of industry—including more Model Ts. So many thousands stormed his gates for jobs that fire hoses were used for crowd control. But there were moral strings attached to the profit sharing. He appointed the dean of Detroit's St. Paul's Cathedral to see that the money went into

sensible food and Ford cars—not into liquor and riotous living.

Ford was a teetotaler and a pacifist. During World War I he chartered a ship, the *Oscar II*, and sailed for Europe, determined to confront the Continental leaders and argue them out of their senseless conflicts. He returned home sickened by ridicule and disillusion. He ran for the U.S. Senate and was beaten. He sued the Chicago *Tribune* for calling him an anarchist; he won and collected 6¢. He made a fetish of raw carrots and soybeans. He fought so-called "international Jewry" in the pages of his Dearborn *Independent* newspaper with the faked *Protocols of Zion*, until he was forced into a retraction in 1927.

Ruler in overalls. As the car crowded out the horse and his company became the No. 1 carmaker, Ford quarreled so bitterly with his stockholders that in 1919 he paid them off with $105 million. Now he ruled his empire alone. He went everywhere, met everyone, became such a national hero that millions urged him to run for President. When he refused in 1923, Calvin Coolidge, who wanted the job, sent him a telegram of thanks. But by 1927, Ford's sales were slipping: the Model T was out of fashion, and Ford shifted to the snappier, more powerful Model A in time to avert disaster. In 1932, when early attempts at casting its new V-8 engine were a failure, Ford, now 69, went down to the foundry, put on a pair of overalls and went to work, tinkering until the job was done.

Years before, his $5-a-day wage had made him a hero, but now his labor policies were as antiquated as his Tin Lizzie. The unions tried to move in, and he fought them. He assigned his bodyguard, Harry Bennett, a hard-faced ex-sailor and boxer, to guard his empire. Heads were cracked. In 1932 four jobless

SHIP OF FOOLS In 1915 Ford and a group of fellow isolationists took the steamship *Oscar II* to Europe to wage peace. The mission met with derision and utterly failed.

LIKE MINDS Ford shakes hands with his hero—a great man of the 19th century—Thomas A. Edison. Ford wound up buying Edison's lab for his museum.

"A car for the masses ... One in every family ... Nothing will do as much to make good roads as a car in every family."

—Ford's early notes on automobiles, found after his death

"If you will study the history of almost any criminal, you will find he is an inveterate cigarette smoker ... I do nothing because it gives me pleasure ... An army or navy is a tool for the protection of misguided, inefficient, destructive Wall Street ... Most of the ailments of people come from eating too much ... There is something sacred about wages ... Reading can become a dope habit ... To say it plainly, the great majority of women who work do so in order to buy fancy clothes ... A man learns something even by being hanged."

—Selected aphorisms

marchers were killed outside the Rouge plant. But in 1941, when the unions had ringed the Rouge plant with pickets and barricaded the entrances, the unpredictable Ford suddenly sent word that he would not only deal with the union but give it everything it wanted—closed shop and all. Said a friend: "His wife Clara refused to let him fight it out. She didn't want to see a lot of rioting and bloodshed because of the strike."

The arsenal. The strike was resolved just in time, for the world faced larger battles. At the Rouge plant, men were already beating plowshares into swords. Like Charles Lindbergh, Ford had been an ardent member of the isolationist organization America First. But the pacifism in Ford's soul was bombed away at Pearl Harbor. He called in his executives and said, "We might as well quit making cars now." The gigantic engineering and production problems of retooling to make tanks and bombers took him back to his early days, when mass-production was just a bright gleam in his eye. Ford—79 in 1942—threw himself into the battle: striding along the great assembly lines, prowling through the

LONER: Ford was a brilliant auto man, and a bullying autocrat

engineering labs, sitting birdlike and domineering among his reverent executives. With characteristic energy, he turned Ford into an arsenal of democracy. By 1945, his plants had built 8,800 bombers, 278,000 jeeps, 57,000 airplane engines.

But before the war ended, Ford's beloved only son Edsel—his right-hand man at the company—died suddenly at only 50. And some of the spirit died in the old man. Edsel's son, Henry II, came home from the Navy to run the empire. Henry spent more and more time puttering around his pet project, the Greenfield Village and museum, where he collected the relics of the age he had helped destroy: buggy whips and butter churns, the courthouse where Lincoln started practicing law.

One day in 1947 the River Rouge swelled with rain and flooded the cellar of Ford's mansion. The house was without electricity or phone service, heated only by open fires, as Clara and Henry retired. Hearing her husband in distress, Clara Ford sent the chauffeur off to the nearest telephone to call the doctor. But death arrived first. In the cold, hushed room, the master of the machine age passed away by the light of old-fashioned kerosene lamps and flickering candles. ■

RICKENBACKER

*Flying legend **Eddie Rickenbacker** got commercial aviation off the ground*

H E WAS AMERICA'S "ACE OF ACES," THE MOST decorated pilot of World War I. He was a daredevil auto racer who at one time held the world speed record. He was a pioneer of commercial aviation and the last of the early flyers to run one of the nation's great airlines. But of all the stirring stories that trailed him throughout his long lifetime, none seemed to please Eddie Rickenbacker so much as the legend of his invincibility. "I've cheated the Grim Reaper more times than anyone I know," he liked to boast. "And I'll fight like a wildcat until they nail the lid of my pine box down on me."

He was by any measure a remarkable, many-faceted man who represented some of the best attributes of an earlier America. A product of McGuffey's *Readers*, he had a fierce faith in God and in the attitudes and platitudes (an honest day's work for an honest day's pay) of the 19th century. He was driven by pride, rather than narrow acquisitiveness. He had a Spartan sense of duty, discipline and self-control—and a hell raiser's humor. And at his core—steely, stainless and incorruptible—was a gladiator's indomitability.

Born Oct. 8, 1890, in Columbus, Ohio, of immigrant parents (his father was German Swiss), he left school at 13, after his father's death. He was all sorts of things in the next three years: a foundry worker, a monument polisher, a brewery hand, a railroad roustabout. But in 1905 he got a job in a garage and fell in love with the internal-combustion engine. He took a correspondence course in mechanical engineering and became a racing driver in the early days of the automobile. Grease-stained, speed-mad and thirsting for glory, he had won seven national championships by the time he was 21. When the U.S. entered World War I Rickenbacker was making $40,000 a year, was one of the three top U.S. drivers and a prime celebrity.

In 1916 Rickenbacker sailed to England to buy engines for a racing team. Sportswriters had dubbed him "the Happy Heinie" and "the wild Teuton," so suspicious British officials took no chances with him. They detained him on arrival, tore his shoes apart looking for messages and scrubbed his chest with lemon juice in the hope of finding secret writing. He was, of course, both completely clean and completely loyal.

When the U.S. entered the war, Rickenbacker joined the Army. Properly enough, he was assigned as chauffeur to General John J. Pershing, commander in chief of the American Expeditionary Forces. As soon as he could, Rickenbacker transferred to the fledgling Air Corps. "If you're as dangerous to the Germans as you are to me," Pershing told the former racing driver, "you'll be an ace in no time."

So he was. Rickenbacker learned to fly in 17 days, joined the 94th Aero Pursuit Squadron under Captain James Norman Hall (later the co-author of *Mutiny on the Bounty*) and soon was diving his fighter to within 150 yds. of enemy planes before opening fire. The race tracks had given him a marvelous judgment of speed and distances and a chilled steel nerve. When Hall was shot down and captured, Rickenbacker took over Hall's group—and later the entire squadron—in the battle against the Flying Circus of "Red Baron" Manfred von Richthofen. By the end of the war, Rickenbacker had shot down 26 German planes and blimps and had been awarded 56 decorations, including the Congressional Medal of Honor.

After the war, the famous ace helped manufacture an automobile that bore his name, but the company failed in 1927, leaving him $250,000 in debt. Rickenbacker paid his bills and bought the Indianapolis Motor Speedway, which he continued to run until 1945. His press parties at Indianapolis on the eve of each Memorial Day 500 race were notorious; liquor flowed until dawn, and "Captain Eddie" customarily called for order by hammering the table with a baseball bat.

In 1934 General Motors asked him to take over the management of a money-losing subsidiary, Eastern Air Lines. Red ink was hardly unusual in the aviation business in those days; no airline, in fact, had ever operated in the black. Within a year, the tightfisted Rickenbacker made Eastern profitable, and in 1938 he raised $3.5 million and took control of the line. Every year from 1935 to 1960 Eastern turned a profit under Rickenbacker's management, thereby disproving the prevailing theory that airlines inevitably needed federal subsidies to survive. Rickenbacker worked hard as a salesman for Eastern and for commercial aviation; among his innovations was Eastern's shuttle service between Boston, New York City and Washington. As Eastern's boss, he was a stern taskmaster as always, using a microphone at management

TIME

April 17, 1950

1890 Born in Columbus, Ohio
1918 Becomes famous U.S. air ace in WW I
1938 He takes over Eastern Air Lines
1942 Survives ordeal in Pacific Ocean
1973 Dies at 82

meetings to heckle subordinates with withering sarcasm. "You're not managers!" he would snap. "You're leeches!"

In February 1941, Eddie Rickenbacker was aboard Eastern's Mexico City–bound *Silver Sleeper* when the DC-3 crashed as it approached Atlanta. Rickenbacker was badly injured. In the hospital, he heard the radio voice of famed commentator Walter Winchell announce that he was dying. "I began to fight," Rickenbacker recalled later. "They had me under an oxygen tent. I tore it apart and picked up a pitcher. I heaved it at the radio and scored a direct hit. The radio fell apart and Winchell's voice stopped. Then I got well."

Only 16 months later, while making an inspection tour of wartime bases in a B-17, Rickenbacker crash-landed in the South Pacific. For 24 days, he and six other men survived on three rafts; an eighth man died of injuries. Though he was the only civilian in the group, Rickenbacker took charge: he carefully divided four oranges and made them last six days.

One day a sea gull landed on his head. He captured it, apportioned its flesh and used its entrails as bait for fish. He cursed one man who prayed for death, and dragged back another who tried to drown himself to make more room for the others. His comrades later credited Rickenbacker with taunting them into staying alive.

"The sensation of dying is sweet, sensuous, placid," he once said. "It is the easiest thing in the world to die. The hardest is to live." Rickenbacker's will endured, but his strength finally faltered: he died in 1973 of a heart ailment at 82. In his final years he had remained spry, cantankerous and active. A TIME correspondent saw the aging ace disembark from a jetliner at an airport a year before his death: Rickenbacker gruffly rejected an offer to help him with his crutches. "Hell no, thanks, I can make it down on my own," he said. Then, leaning the crutches against the stairs, he stopped to give autographs to a swarm of admirers, a hero to the end. ■

HEARST

EXTRA! William Randolph Hearst

in sensational newsprint escapade!

ALMOST TO THE MOMENT OF HIS DEATH in his 89th year, his fertile, facile brain kept tabs on all his outposts of empire. In his great house atop one of the lushest of the Beverly Hills, he still spread his papers on the floor, turning the pages with one slipper and bending down to scrawl his piercing critiques, giving his editors lessons in journalism, William Randolph Hearst–style. Deskmen at the Los Angeles *Examiner*, nerve center of the chain, received commands as late as 3 a.m. Whether they called for an editorial blast against the President or for a box of Kleenex, they got action. It would be a long time before his editors got used to doing business without the edicts that began "The Chief suggests …"

The gaunt, wasted old man with the haunted eyes had given journalism entirely new techniques. But in the minds of many, he had often misused those techniques to sensationalize journalism, seduce its public and debauch its practitioners. For good or bad, Hearst left his brand on four generations of U.S. life in a multiple career as politician, publisher and plutocrat that at his death stretched back beyond the memory of all but the oldest living Americans. At the end of it all, his earthly holdings added up to some $200 million, including:

• 16 daily newspapers; the world's largest Sunday paper, the *American Weekly*, and eight magazines, including *Cosmopolitan* and *Good Housekeeping*.

• Property, including the fabulous California castle San Simeon and the Homestake Mine, rich gold producer at Lead, South Dakota, and font of his fortune.

• Incidentals: fabulous collections of armor, Georgian silver, paintings, sculptures, tapestries, antique furniture.

March 13, 1939

1863 Born in San Francisco
1887 Boss of the San Francisco *Examiner*
1895 Buys Manhattan's *Morning Journal*
1922 Fails in last bid for public office
1951 Dies at 88

Chamber pots and newspapers.

Hearst was a complex child of simple, ambitious parents. His mother Phoebe Appleton married a rough and rowdy Missourian named George Hearst, who lost two fortunes but won three in gold and silver. Their son William was born in San Francisco in 1863. Like his bustling, newly rich hometown, Willie Hearst grew up fast. He was 10 when his mother took him off to Europe for his first grand tour. At Harvard, he studied Joseph Pulitzer's sensational New York *World*, sold ads for the *Lampoon*—and still had time for pranks. For Christmas 1885, he sent each of his professors a chamber pot and was promptly expelled. He had lost interest in school anyway; he had his eye on the puny San Francisco *Examiner*, which his politicking father had taken over to get himself a Democratic Party mouthpiece.

The lanky, blond-mustached 23-year-old took over the *Examiner* on March 4, 1987. He subtitled his little sheet "Monarch of the Dailies," and set out, as one editor put it, "to arouse the 'gee whiz' emotion." The *Examiner's* boss rushed special trains to cover out-of-town fires, and he wrote boob-catching headlines like A SUNDAY SUICIDE OF A LOVE-SICK LOAFER. He spent his father's money like a tipsy prospector—but made it back as circulation multiplied.

He gathered around him a brilliant, erratic crew of staff and contributors (Ambrose Bierce, Mark Twain, Edwin Markham), entertained them by dancing jigs in the office and strode

XANADUDE: Young Hearst, left, inherited wealth; his San Simeon castle, above, was "Xanadu" in Orson Welles' *Citizen Kane*

through the streets with a cane that whistled. He was great fun to work for; after a hard day's work he liked to gather the staff at his big house for lavish parties complete (said horrified gossip) with "abandoned dancing girls." After his father died in 1891, his mother heard a friend complain that William was wasting the family fortune at $1 million a year. "Too bad," said Phoebe Hearst sweetly. "Then he'll only last 30 years."

He'll take Manhattan. By 1895, having perfected his techniques of carnival journalism, Hearst felt ready to conquer Manhattan. He had $7.5 million with him, and he was ready to bet it all on his new paper, the *Morning Journal.* One day Hearst rocked Pulitzer by hiring away the entire Sunday staff of Pulitzer's *World*—and steered the blatant *American Weekly* toward the world's biggest circulation with such stories as NAILED HER FATHER'S HEAD TO THE FRONT DOOR. It was the Hearst-Pulitzer tug-of-war over Richard Outcault's forlorn *Yellow Kid* that brought on the day of the colored comic strip—and gave "yellow journalism" its name.

From there to jingo journalism was an easy step. Knowing nothing would boost circulation like war with Spain over Cuba, Hearst sent reporter Richard Harding Davis and artist Frederick Remington to Cuba in 1897 to "document" Spanish atrocities. When the artist complained that there were no signs of strife and asked leave to return home, Hearst sent him a supremely cynical cable: PLEASE REMAIN. YOU FURNISH THE PICTURES AND I'LL FURNISH THE WAR.

Hearst led other crusades: he muckraked the trusts, exposed Standard Oil for bribing Senators, campaigned for the eight-hour day (which Hearst properties ignored) and women's suffrage. In 1902 he was elected to a seat (rarely to be occupied) in Congress. He celebrated by marrying Millicent Willson, from the chorus of *The Girl from Paris.* Enamored of pol-

itics, Hearst poured out $1.5 million in an unsuccessful try for the 1904 Democratic nomination for President. He almost won the mayoralty of New York City in 1905, failed in a run for the governorship of New York State and was foiled in a bid to run for the U.S. Senate in 1922.

Citizen Hearst. All the while, like Orson Welles' Citizen Kane, for whom he was the model, Hearst grew in wealth, if not in stature. As his dailies crusaded against various "perils"—the yellow peril from Asia, the red peril from the Soviet Union, the dope peril and so on—Hearst added dozens of papers to his string. At the 240,000-acre San Simeon, where he rode with his father as a boy, Hearst decreed stately pleasure domes that would have awed Kublai Khan. He equipped the place with everything from giraffes to Roman baths to a lavish theater. He also acquired Miss Marion Davies, who was a bubbly chorus girl in the Ziegfeld Follies when W.R. met her during World War I. Soon she was a star of Hearst's Cosmopolitan pictures and its president. She was to be the aging press lord's companion until his death.

In 1932 Hearst helped cut the cards for the New Deal by supporting Franklin Roosevelt's nomination, but when he realized F.D.R. was opposed to everything he now stood for, Hearst ordered his papers to call it the "Raw Deal." The 1936 landslide against his candidate, Alf Landon, was a measure of the decline of his papers' clout. With money troubles as well, he turned over financial control of his overextended empire to a board of regents. But the World War II boom restored his empire to health. Once he had summed up his credo: "All nature strives and vies, not to attain tranquillity but a more effective degree of activity … Whatever begins to be tranquil is gobbled up by something which is not tranquil." In 1951, at long last, contentious, vigorous William Randolph Hearst found tranquillity. ■

DISNEY

Visionary handyman **Walt Disney** *built an industry out of daydreams*

THE MYTHMAKER IS A PRIMITIVE. HE molds his fantasies out of primordial impulses that are common to all people. In an age of stern realities, he is a rarity, for he celebrates an innocence that does not mix well with the times. Walt Disney was such a man, molding myths and spinning fantasies in which innocence always reigned. Literally billions of people responded out of some deeply atavistic well of recognition, and they lavished their gratitude on him. Soldiers carried the cartoon-figure emblems of his creations on their uniforms and their war planes. Kings and dictators saw them as symbols of some mysterious quality of the American character. Harvard and Yale gave him honorary degrees in the same year; at his death in 1966 his shelves groaned with the weight of an unprecedented 30 Oscars.

Eternal cream puffs. Walt Disney made myths—and so potent was the power of his art that he seemed to defy death. After his demise, the vast assembly lines of his corporation produced ever slicker products to dream on, most of them bearing his name and the unmistakable stamp of his vision. By 1996, 30 years after his death, the Walt Disney Co. was one of the world's largest media and entertainment concerns, fat with the 1995 acquisition of the Cap. Cities/ABC TV empire. The essential Disney creations— the full-length animated films, the cartoon characters, the fantasy-filled cream puffs called Disneyland and Walt Disney World—were definitive components of 20th century culture.

December 27, 1954

1901 Born in Chicago
1928 Mickey Mouse makes his film debut
1937 Releases *Snow White,* the first full-length animated film
1955 Disneyland opens in California
1966 Dies at 65

Measured by his social impact, Disney was one of the most influential men of his time. He appropriated the bedtime stories of yesteryear, the myths that all former races of men teethed on, the brightest creations of the best children's writers, and amalgamated them into a kind of mechanical folklore. It's Disney's Snow White now and Disney's Little Mermaid, Disney's Winnie-the-Pooh and Disney's Mary Poppins, even Disney's Hunchback of Notre Dame. In the world's nurseries, the hand that rocks the cradle belongs to Disney.

Disney's success was plain to see, but the secret of it, like the motive force in a Rube Goldberg invention, was hidden in the depths of an astonishing psychological contraption. For all his millions, Disney was not a businessman, and though he produced fine folk art, he was not an "artist." He was a genuine, hand-hewn American original, a garage-type inventor with a wild guess in his eye and a hard pinch on his penny, a grass-roots genius in the tradition of Thomas A. Edison and Henry Ford.

Like most self-educated men, Disney pulled himself up from nowhere by grabbing the tail of a runaway idea and hanging on for dear life. He was a hard-working monomaniac, and a hard man to work for; his chief strength was his deep, instinctive identification with the common impulses of common people. A friend described him as "a sort of visionary handyman who has built a whole industry out of daydreams. He has that rarest of qualities, the courage of his doodles."

Critics charge that Disney refused to see life in the raw, to accept the end of innocence. They are scandalized by the artificiality of his theme parks. But Disney knew what he was doing: he came from the Midwest—born in Chicago, reared there and in Missouri—and stubbornly adhered to the idea that wickedness was no subject for entertainment. In his work, children and animals were naturally good; nature, at least in his animated films, was not so red in tooth and claw as it was cuddly in fur and paw.

Here's Mickey! It was in the early days of film animation—1928—that Disney labored and brought forth his Mouse. Mickey first hove into public sight at the wheel of *Steamboat Willie.* But the big news was the music: sound films were just coming in, and Mickey was tootling a tune on his signal whistles, which suddenly had faces that scrooged up as they blew. Audiences loved it. In the next few years Walt made a Mickey Mouse cartoon every month. His staff quickly grew from 20 to 50 to 150 employees. With a foresight remarkable in a man only 28 years old, he set about strengthening his

BIG WHEELS: Disney and friend, this page; opposite, the hardworking fantasy master's only relaxation was captaining the miniature train in his backyard

organization for the long creative haul. He started the *Silly Symphonies*, even though they showed little promise of popularity, because he felt that he and his staff, weary of drudging away at Mickey, needed "something to grow on." And grow they did. *Three Little Pigs* (1933) proved that Disney was ready at last for his goal: to make a full-length cartoon feature. He borrowed $1.5 million and made 1937's *Snow White*, which became a gigantic hit at the box office; produced seven top tunes; won eight Oscars (one for each dwarf and one for their creator); and sold $10 million worth of merchandise.

Heigh-ho! Disney was on his way, and despite some setbacks in the 1940s—a debilitating studio strike, the flop of the ambitious Mickey-goes-classical *Fantasia* on its first release—he never looked back. As money flowed in, he and his gifted collaborators explored new canvases for their art. Disney

conquered television, creating a sensation in the 1950s with his Davey Crockett series. He launched a series of landmark "real-life" nature documentaries. Above all, he and his "imagineers" reinvented the idea of the amusement park, first with Disneyland in California, then with the far larger Walt Disney World in Florida, which opened five years after Walt's death.

The theme parks were the apotheosis of the Disney style: highly stylized environments from which litter, vice and reality were banished by the maker's fiat. Phony? From top to bottom. But the world came, and the world loved them. When Soviet boss Nikita Khrushchev toured the U.S. in 1959, he asked to see only one place: Disneyland. The "magic kingdoms" are Disney's monuments, the children of his unique marriage of fantasy and commerce, proof that the man who wished upon a star could make not only his dreams but also *your* dreams come true. And make a buck in the process. ∎

AUGUST 27, 1934 Choosing the obscure Los Angeles suburb of Hollywood to make the 1914 film *The Squaw Man,* director of spectaculars Cecil B. DeMille gave the movies a home.

JUNE 12, 1950 The movie industry flourished under moguls who bossed studios and stars. One of the last of the breed was the co-founder of 20th Century Fox, Darryl F. Zanuck.

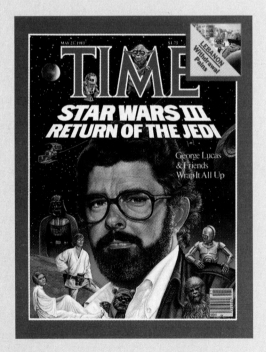

MAY 23, 1983 The force was with him: writer-director-producer George Lucas reinvented the Hollywood spectacular for a new generation in his sweeping *Star Wars* trilogy.

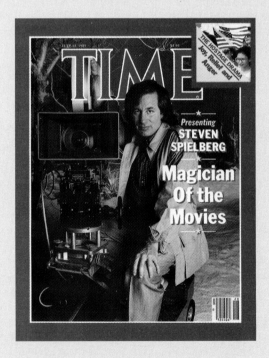

JULY 15, 1985 With a string of box-office hits—*Jaws, E.T.* and the *Indiana Jones* series—Steven Spielberg invented a new Hollywood genre: the summer special-effects blockbuster.

KEYNES

Spend your way to prosperity? The radical theories of
John Maynard Keynes *turned economics upside-down*

ECONOMICS, SAID THE ESSAYIST THOMAS CARLYLE, IS A "dismal science," and the greatest economist of the century, John Maynard Keynes, once remarked that economists should be humble, like dentists. Yet Keynes enjoyed trouncing countesses at bridge and Prime Ministers at lunch-table debates. He became a leader of the Bloomsbury set of avant-garde writers and painters, married a ballerina from Diaghilev's Russian ballet, and shortly before he died, announced that his only regret in life was that he had not drunk more champagne.

Yet the thrust of Keynes' personality, however strong, was vastly less important than the force of his ideas, which give him rank with Adam Smith and Karl Marx as one of history's most significant economists. Keynes was born the year Marx died (1883) and died in the first full year of capitalism's lengthy postwar boom (1946). The son of a noted Cambridge political economist, he whizzed through Eton and Cambridge—getting his lowest mark in economics—then joined the civil service. He entered the India Office, and soon after became a Cambridge don. Later, he was the British Treasury's representative to the Versailles Conference, and felt it would ensure nothing but the inevitability of another disaster. He resigned in protest and wrote a book, *The Economic Consequences of the Peace*, that clearly foretold the crisis to come. Keynes went back to teaching at Cambridge, but at the same time he operated with dash in a host of arenas: he chaired an insurance company, edited economic journals, became a director of the Bank of England and earned a fortune on the markets.

As a precursor of macroeconomics, Keynes' approach measured all the myriad forces that tug and pull at economies—production, prices, profits, incomes, interest rates, government policies. Confronted with the disaster of the Depression, he responded in 1936 with his magnum opus, *The General Theory of Employment, Interest and Money*, which became the foundation of modern economic theory.

Adam Smith had argued that capitalism's "invisible hand" always brought economic forces into balance. But Keynes claimed that a market economy can operate at less than full employment and that market processes can be ineffective and even perverse in eliminating unemployment. His conclusion: governments should actively intervene to correct economic imbalances through fiscal and monetary policies.

December 31, 1965

1883 Born in Cambridge, England
1919 Rejects Versailles Conference
1925 Marries ballerina Lydia Lopokova
1936 Publishes *The General Theory*
1946 Dies at 62

Keynes transformed economics from a descriptive and analytic tool into a policy-oriented discipline that would manage, not simply study, economies. In the '30s, he cried out that the only way to revive aggregate demand was for governments to cut taxes, reduce interest rates, spend heavily—and deficits be damned. Nations could "spend their way back to prosperity," he said, and he made an early convert of Franklin Roosevelt. Yet he insisted that governments had no right to tamper with an individual's freedom to choose jobs, to buy or sell goods and to earn respectable profits.

Critics charged that Keynes' theories made spenders seem virtuous and savers wicked. But even his detractors bowed to his brilliance, used the macroeconomic framework he devised, and conceded that his main theories have largely worked out in practice. As Milton Friedman, the conservative U.S. economist, once said, "We are all Keynesians now." ∎

SWITCHED-ON: Left, in 1912 Sarnoff reported the *Titanic* tragedy in Morse code; by 1965, right, he was watching color TV

SARNOFF

The father of mass media, **David Sarnoff** *opened the door to radio and TV with a telegraph key*

AS A NEW CENTURY DAWNED IN 1900, A SCRAWNY nine-year-old from Minsk clambered out of steerage class and onto the hardscrabble streets of Manhattan—and got to work. His name was David Sarnoff, and in the next 70 years he never stopped working. Though Sarnoff was neither a scientist nor inventor, he did more than any other person to bring the new technologies of the communication age to the masses. He was the man who put radio and television in just about every home—and he never forgot it for a waking moment. He liked to boast that he was born about the same time the electron was discovered, as if they were somehow twins. With considerable justification, he cast himself as the father of the entire electronic-communications industry. "In a big ship sailing in an uncharted sea," he would say, "one fellow needs to be on the bridge. I happen to be that fellow."

Sarnoff's special gift was that he was not only a visionary but also a hustling salesman who could persuade scientists and capitalists to invest their brainpower and money to make his own dreams of the future come true. As a teenager, he taught himself telegraphy and talked his way into an operator's job at the Marconi Wireless Telegraph Co. of America. There he noted that the company's wireless operators knew nothing about the business, and the business staff knew nothing about wireless. He decided to learn both. A classic tragedy gave him a big break: when the *Titanic* sank in 1912, Sarnoff stayed at his telegraph key in New York for 72 hours, providing the only news of the disaster and its survivors. The *Titanic* brought much attention to the possibilities of radio communication—

July 23, 1951

1891 Born in Minsk, then White Russia
1900 Arrives destitute in America
1912 Relays details of *Titanic* disaster
1921 Begins to develop commercial radio
1971 Dies at 80

and to Sarnoff, who soon became commercial manager of American Marconi.

The company was bought from its British owners after World War I by General Electric, which changed its name to Radio Corp. of America. Sarnoff became general manager and, during the 1920s, persuaded its reluctant owners to invest in a series of chancy schemes. He pushed for the development of radio, predicting in 1921 that $75 million in radios could be sold in three years. Actual sales: $83 million. Sarnoff, a prophet with honor, was soon radio's wonder boy. By 1932, when the trustbusters forced the company to spin off RCA, Sarnoff had been president for two years. Restless, driven and forward-looking, Sarnoff led RCA to set up a broadcasting network (NBC), spent millions in research to develop television and then color television. He led by sheer force of personality; he owned only one-third of 1% of the stock—though by the time of his death that small stake was worth $7.4 million.

With his big cigars and his hard-boiled manner, Sarnoff sometimes seemed to be trying to prove his own aphorism that "competition brings out the best in products and the worst in men." Critics charged that he should have taken more interest in the quality of the programming on his NBC television network. His retort: "Basically, we're the delivery boys." Sarnoff also ran RCA with a messianic but too simplistic belief in technology's ability to advance the frontiers of society. He once predicted that color TV would bring "a new era of art appreciation." Still, what made Sarnoff one of the great innovators of the century was his willingness, as he phrased it, to put "more faith in scientists than they have in themselves." ∎

TURNER

*Skeptics scoffed at **Ted Turner**, but his Cable*

News Network rewrote journalism—and history

THE LIFE OF TYCOON TED TURNER MAY BEST BE SEEN AS a series of disasters transformed into triumphs. When he skippered his yacht in Britain's prestigious Fastnet race in 1979, he was so absorbed in victory that he did not know a gale was killing 15 yachtsmen in the boats behind him. The Atlanta Braves, the baseball team he bought in 1976, shuffled along in the gutter for years, until in the 1990s they became the sport's most consistent winners. Above all, there was his visionary creation, the 24-hour all-news Cable News Network. At first derided as the "Chicken Noodle Network" for its amateurish presentation, CNN became the world's video medium of record after only a decade on the air.

With CNN, Turner changed the very definition of news—from something that *has happened* to something that *is happening* at the very moment you are hearing of it. When Turner launched the channel in 1980, it had a staff of 300 and a newsroom tucked into the basement of a converted country club. Technical flubs were common. But the all-news network soon turned more professional, and eventually it became the common frame of reference for the world. From the White House to the Kremlin to Main Street, CNN gave everyone around the globe the same information at the same instant.

CNN's crowning moment as the world's most widely heeded news organization occurred on Jan. 16, 1991, when U.S. bombs began to drop on Saddam Hussein's Baghdad. The entire world tuned in to watch CNN's exclusive live coverage. Seven months later, the world again turned to CNN, to see Russian President Boris Yeltsin climb aboard a tank and defy the hard-line plotters who were detaining Soviet leader Mikhail Gorbachev and staging a coup. The image of a defiant Yeltsin sent the signal to the world that the battle for freedom was not lost. Thus CNN not only reported events; it changed the dynamic of the events it reported. Ted Turner had made good on the prophecy of information-age guru Marshall McLuhan: he had turned the world into a global village.

Turner's personal life is another example of triumph snatched from disaster. A streak of wild unpredictability underlay his driving vision: one minute he was the overly boisterous cheerleader of the Braves or the over-the-top "Captain Outrageous" of the yacht-racing world; the next he was the impresario of the Goodwill Games, happily losing millions to advance world peace. After two failed marriages he vowed to settle down, and he did so, Ted Turner–style. In 1991 he married a woman whose personal legend equaled his own: Hollywood star, activist and fitness guru Jane Fonda. Turner and Fonda now devote themselves to their home where the buffalo roam, a huge ranch in Montana. And Turner has a new enthusiasm: environmentalism. Like all his favorite projects, it's a tall order. But if he does manage to save the world's resources, he knows one network will carry the story live. ■

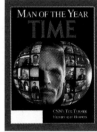

January 6, 1992

1938 Born in Cincinnati, Ohio
1977 Triumphs in the America's Cup
1980 Launches CNN
1986 Sponsors first Goodwill Games
1991 Marries actress Jane Fonda

WATSON

*With a one-word gospel—think—*the Watsons of IBM *automated an age*

FEW COMPANIES HAVE PIONEERED AND DOMINATED an industry with the overpowering force of International Business Machines. For some 60 years, from its birth in the 1920s until the mid-1980s, IBM established the standards for the new age of electronic automation that revolutionized the conduct of business around the world. IBM— "Big Blue"—and the revolution it sparked were both logical extensions of a famous slogan: Think. That slogan was coined by Thomas J. Watson Sr., the man whose driving vision helped automate an era. His son Thomas Jr. was his father's equal: taking over the reins of IBM in the early 1950s, when electronic technology was in its infancy, he spurred Big Blue to even greater dominance in its field. Together, the

Watson dynasty ran IBM and its predecessor, C-T-R, for a total of 57 years, and in that time they nurtured the computer into the pre-eminent tool of a new age—and their company into a widely imitated model for other corporations.

Knocking on the door. Tom Watson Sr. believed that "opportunity never knocks on the door. You have to knock on opportunity's doors, and they are all around us." He also said that "nobody really gets started until he's 40," and he spoke from personal experience. He had joined the National Cash Register Co. in Dayton, Ohio, in 1898, and had worked his way up to become the company's general sales manager. Then, at 41, he suddenly pulled up stakes. Going east to Manhattan, he went to work for the Computing-Tabulating-Recording Co.,

which in 1911 had begun making new kinds of time clocks, butcher's scales and accounting machines. Tall and spare with a kindly, canny Scots face, Watson was his own best salesman. Carefully he designed new machines to fit each customer's needs, and within a year he was president of C-T-R. Two years later, the company paid out it s first $3 dividend, and Watson was on his way.

A visionary salesman rather than a scientist or inventor, Watson still conjured up so many new ideas that he held in his own name more than a dozen patents for machines. Wherever he went, he drove his staff to do more, learn more—above all, to *think* more. By 1924 C-T-R had three plants in the U.S. and expanded abroad with branches in France, Britain, Canada and Germany—"developing Europe," as Watson called it. He changed C-T-R's name to International Business Machines and expanded still more.

Corporate culture. Watson's high, stiff collars, his aversion to smoking and drinking, his vast store of aphorisms became trademarks of IBM to the outside world. Inside the organization, he operated as a benign patriarch. At company banquets, Watson liked to lead his employees in singing company songs like his *Hail to IBM* anthem. Every executive, both big and little, became a polished speechmaker, and every one dressed like Watson—dark suit, white shirt, polished shoes. To some, Watson's

THINKERS: Above, Thomas Watson Jr. escorts Nikita Khrushchev on a plant tour; opposite, Tom Watson Sr. and his watchword

concern with everything that had to do with his employees appeared paternalistic, even overbearing. Yet Watson was convinced that the fuller he made his employees' lives, the faster IBM would forge ahead. IBM never had a union; it never needed one. Watson refused to lay off people, even during the depths of the Depression. In a typically pioneering move, IBM put large chunks of its payroll into employee benefits such as free country clubs, bowling alleys and extracurricular activities, including bands and choirs and classes in everything from art appreciation to home repairs.

Through the '20s and '30s, no fewer than 45 new business machines appeared under the IBM label. In 1933 Watson bought Electromatic Typewriters, Inc., a Rochester, New York, firm that had built the first completely electric typewriter, and put the first such mass-produced machine into U.S. business offices. By the time Watson handed over the leadership of the company to Thomas Jr. in 1952, IBM had become the ultimate blue-chip stock. By 1955, an investor who had bought 100 shares of C-T-R in 1914 for $2,750 and spent another $3,614 to take advantage of all options would have owned 3,893 shares of IBM—worth $1,492,965.

The son also rises. Tom Jr. was trained in the IBM spirit as soon as he was old enough to toddle. He went on his first plant inspection at five, his first overseas tour at nine, and made a speech before IBM's star salesmen at 12. Joining the company after college, he started as a junior salesman in Manhattan's financial district and hit 231%

March 28, 1955

1874 Tom Sr. is born
1914 Tom Jr.is born;
Tom Sr. is named
president of C-T-R
1924 C-T-R named IBM
1952 Tom Jr. becomes
president of IBM
1971 Tom Jr. retires
1993 Tom Jr. dies

of his sales quota, a record. Said his father: "He had to make his own records. Otherwise, people might feel that he had some special help, which he did not have." After serving as a pilot during World War II, Tom Jr. quickly rose to become vice president of sales. As president, he led a group of younger executives and technicians at the company who recognized the importance of the new electronic technologies, and accelerated the corporation's transition from electromechanical calculators to electronic computers, ensuring IBM's dominance of the new field.

If the Watsons had only been corporate titans, they would have been famous enough. But the father and son represented a new breed of U.S. businessmen who realized that their social responsibilities extended far beyond their own companies. Both were committed social reformers who dedicated much time and money to medical research, education and charitable activities. They were also passionate internationalists. Tom Sr. mandated that every envelope dispatched from IBM carry the message SUPPORT THE UNITED NATIONS. After retiring from IBM in 1971, Tom Jr. served as ambassador to the Soviet Union from 1979 to 1981.

In the 1980s IBM watched its lead in the computer industry slip. Failing to keep abreast of the personal computer revolution, it let the microchip miracles of younger companies undermine its core business in large mainframe computers. Without a Watson at the helm, the legendary company was no longer singing *Hail to IBM*. For the first time, Big Blue was singing the blues. ∎

GATES

Charismatic hacker—or the robber baron of bytes? **Bill Gates** *is both*

ASK BILL GATES, THE CO-FOUNDER AND chairman of the giant software company Microsoft, about something he wants to talk about—like a new software system or his futuristic house outside Seattle—and he acts like the teenage boy that he still resembles. He grins. His voice breaks. He rocks back and forth as if to contain his excitement. But press Gates on a subject he doesn't want to talk about—like the charges of anticompetitive business practices that have dogged his company—and he is liable to throw a tantrum. "I challenge your facts!" he shouts when confronted with one such allegation. "That's a lie! I mean, it's just not true. What a bunch of nonsense!"

It is a curiously revealing moment. Bill Gates is a contradictory character, a man-child brimming with vision and enthusiasm one moment, a tyrannical mogul the next. Though he is famous for his lack of pretension, his habit of flying in coach class and his easy accessibility, he can also be brash, imperious and brutally blunt. A visionary who helped put powerful computers into a sizable number of the offices, schools and homes in the U.S., he also has a reputation as a fierce—some say ruthless—competitive businessman. One thing *is* certain: he is very, very rich and so powerful that even his enemies are eager to cut deals with him.

How powerful is Microsoft? In 1995, eight out of 10 of the world's personal computers could not boot up (that is to say, start) if it were not for Microsoft's operating-system software. The company also dominates the market for almost every big-ticket software application program, like word processing, electronic spreadsheets, scheduling. In some respects, the power Microsoft wields over the computer industry may exceed that of IBM in the heyday of the Watsons. How rich is Microsoft? Thousands of current and former employees have become millionaires, at least on paper, and three became billionaires.

Gates was one of them. A billionaire at 31, in 1995 he was worth more than $10 billion, making him either the richest or the second richest man in America, depending on the closing price of his shares. He was married in 1994 in Hawaii, and he and

his wife, former Microsoft executive Melinda French, had a daughter in April 1996. His $40 million-plus home on suburban Seattle's Lake Washington will have video "walls" to display an ever changing collection of electronic art, a trampoline room with a 25-ft. vaulted ceiling, a 20-car underground garage and a trout stream. In 1995 Microsoft launched the hugely successful Windows 95 software program—and Gates launched his book on the information age, *The Road Ahead*, to the top of the best-seller lists.

The road behind Gates is equally impressive. At 13 the math whiz wrote his first program, to make a computer play ticktacktoe. At 14, he became the president of a company called Traf-O-Data that used computers to measure traffic patterns; it earned $20,000 in its first year. As a senior in high school he worked as a computer programmer at the software firm TRW; as a 19-year-old at Harvard he joined boyhood friend and fellow hacker Paul Allen to write the software for the world's first home computer, the Altair 8800. Working day and night, the driven hackers succeeded: the new program worked on the first try—even though they didn't have an Altair machine to work with, only a book that described it.

June 5, 1995

1955 Born in Seattle
1975 Drops out of Harvard to found Microsoft
1980 Creates MS-DOS for IBM computers
1995 Launches highly successful Windows 95 program

Flush with this triumph, Gates dropped out of Harvard in his sophomore year. He and Allen founded Microsoft in 1975 and began developing software. When they heard that IBM was building a new personal computer but needed an operating system—the program that directs the machine's internal operations—they bought some software from a small Seattle company, modified it and licensed it to IBM. Big Blue's clout made the program, MS-DOS, the world standard.

The race was on: Microsoft's staff grew from 15 in 1978 to 125 in 1981, and its sales mushroomed from $4 million in 1980 to $16 million in 1981 to $140 million in 1985. But all along, the firm's soaring success has been accompanied by allegations that it used its superior position in operating-systems software to squelch competition in other areas, especially applications software. It is these charges that Gates denies—and that make him so complex a character, a man who seems to straddle the centuries. For the visionary who is blazing the path into the digital frontiers of the information age can often resemble an overbearing robber baron of the Gilded Age. ∎

MARCH 31, 1924 Founder of the modern photographic industry, George Eastman made Everyman a cameraman with his breakthrough inventions, flexible film and the box camera.

DECEMBER 27, 1926 Pioneer of the modern principles of marketing and management, Alfred P. Sloan Jr. put General Motors ahead of Ford by giving customers what they wanted.

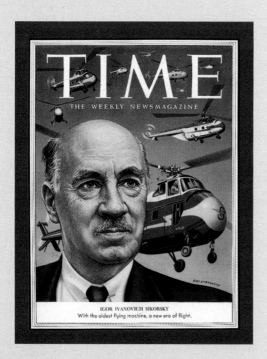

NOVEMBER 16, 1953 Aircraft designer Igor Sikorsky made bombers for the Russian military, then immigrated to the U.S. to craft the first commercially successful helicopter.

APRIL 17, 1964 Savvy automan Lee Iacocca restored Ford's zip with the sporty Mustang in the '60s, restored failing Chrysler in the '80s, then led the restoration of the Statue of Liberty.

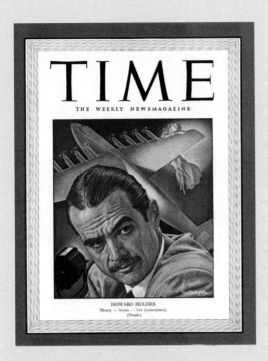

JULY 19, 1948 Industrialist Howard Hughes used his inherited wealth to become a film producer and pioneer aviator but ended his colorful life as an obsessive, paranoid recluse.

OCTOBER 31, 1949 Father of streamlining, engineer and designer Raymond Loewy influenced countless imitators and pioneered much of the functional look of the century.

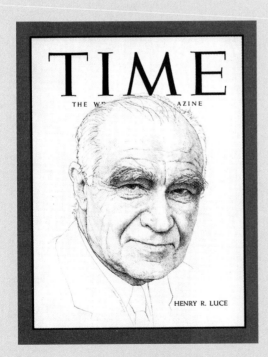

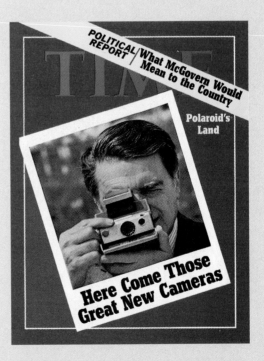

MARCH 10, 1967 Pioneer magazine man Henry Luce invented the weekly newsmagazine with TIME in the 1920s, then fostered the development of photojournalism with LIFE in the '30s.

JUNE 26, 1972 After creating a new polarizing filter that found wide use in sunglasses and optical devices, Edwin Land developed instant photography with the Polaroid camera.

THE SCI

The most significant scientist of the century didn't wear a lab coat. Albert Einstein's laboratory was in his mind, where he conducted his "thought experiments." Yet more than any scientist since Charles Darwin, Einstein altered mankind's place in the cosmos. His dynamic universe—in which light was bent by gravity and even time was not an absolute—shattered certainty. Aided by giant strides in technology, scientists now explored—even harnessed— forces of nature that were fluid, complex, unstable. The universe, astronomers told us, was older and vaster than we had thought. Heredity, biologists told us, had a local habitation and a name —the double helix of DNA. Most unnerving of all, the operating principle of all matter, physicists told us, is uncertainty. ■

ENTISTS

James Watson, 1957

EINSTEIN

Architect of a dynamic cosmos, **Albert Einstein** *redrafted our view of nature*

A LMOST EVERY MORNING FOR 22 years, a self-effacing little man, carelessly clad in baggy pants and a blue stocking cap, stepped down from the front porch of a modest frame house at 112 Mercer Street, Princeton, New Jersey, and trudged off to the Institute for Advanced Study. At a glance, the little man could have been the gardener. He puffed meekly at his pipe, he sidled into his office quietly, he seldom spoke unless spoken to. But on a second look, a rare quality glowed in that sad and wizened face, with its disordered halo of white hair and its soulful brown eyes. The quality was genius, a compound of soaring intellect and wide-ranging imagination that had carried Albert Einstein past the confines of man's old scientific certitudes and deeper into the material mysteries of the universe than any man before him.

Einstein was a modern Merlin, conjuring up astonishing new notions of space and time, changing forever man's perception of his universe—and of himself. He fathered relativity and heralded the atomic age with his famed formula $E=mc^2$. His only instruments were a pencil and scratch pad; his laboratory was under his cap. Yet he saw farther than a telescope, deeper than a microscope. Traveling in lonely splendor to the crossroads of the visible and the invisible, he came close to his goal: proving that the laws that move the tini-

July 1, 1946

1879 Born in Ulm, Germany
1905 Publishes four papers that redefine the study of physics
1933 In America as Hitler comes to power, he decides to stay
1955 Dies in Princeton

est unseen electrons must also govern the macrocosms of intergalactic space.

Scientists idolize him, for Einstein was the most eminent among them in this century, and in some eyes, the greatest scientist of all time. In person he was diffident, almost childlike. But as a man of scientific thought, he strode with history's handful: Pythagoras and Archimedes, Copernicus and Newton. Yet he was so opposed to posthumous veneration that he willed his ashes to be scattered at an undisclosed place. Constantly called upon to pose for photographers, painters and sculptors, he once gave his occupation as "artist's model."

For all his scientific wisdom, Einstein was a worldly innocent who charmed everyone with his simplicity. He loved to play his violin and sail. He also loved children, lost his shyness with them and could send them into gales of laughter. The prototypical absent-minded genius, he once walked into the salon of an ocean liner in his pajamas. Unconcerned about money, he used a $1,500 check for a bookmark, then lost the book. Asked why he used one soap for washing as well as shaving, he replied, "Two soaps? Too complicated." Stymied by a thorny problem, he would tell his colleagues in his accented English, "Now I will a little tink," pace slowly up and down while twirling a lock of his unruly hair, suddenly erupt in a smile and announce a solution.

Holy geometry. In his earliest years in Germany, Einstein showed no obvious sign of genius; he did not begin talking until the age of three. He went through a deeply religious period as a teenager, but this phase passed soon after he began studying science, math and philosophy on his own. He was especially enamored of a basic math text—his "holy geometry booklet." At 16, he devised one of his first "thought experiments," procedures that can only be done in the mind, not in a laboratory. In this case, he imagined what a light wave would look like to an observer riding along with it.

When his father's business failed and the family moved to northern Italy, Einstein dropped out of school. He spent a year traveling, then applied to the famed Swiss Federal Institute of Technology in Zurich. But he failed the entrance exam and was admitted only after a year's further study. At university he cut lectures and read what he pleased; one teacher called him a "lazy dog." He managed to graduate but failed to obtain a university teaching post, and at 23 he settled for a job as an examiner with the Swiss Patent Office in Bern. His title: technical expert, third class. His pay: a modest $675 a year. But the post enabled him to marry a fellow student, Mileva Maric, a Serb, and gave him time to think about physics.

There was plenty to ponder. For more than two centuries, the basic laws of motion and gravitation postulated by Sir Isaac

GENIUS Einstein in 1905, the annus mirabilis in which he revolutionized modern physics with four breakthrough papers.

CELEBRITY With fellow physicist Charles Steinmetz in New Jersey in 1921. In 1919 observations had proved Einstein's theory that gravity would bend light; now renowned around the world, he traveled and lectured widely.

REFUGEE Reviled by the Nazis for his "Jew physics," Einstein became a U.S. citizen in 1940. Later he rejected David Ben-Gurion's offer to become President of the young state of Israel.

TRAGEDY The bomb at Nagasaki. Einstein later said: "Had I known that the Germans would not succeed … I would have done nothing for the bomb."

MUSIC OF THE SPHERES Einstein's favorite pastimes were sailing and playing the violin (his favorite composers: Mozart and Bach). Ever unconventional, in his later years he seldom wore socks or neckties.

Newton had prevailed. They were more than adequate to describe planetary movements, the behavior of gases and other everyday physical phenomena. But in the 1880s, more sensitive instruments were uncovering awkward phenomena, particularly in the physics of light, that operated in open violation of Newton's laws. It appeared that light was not a particle, as Newton had said, but a wave. To make Newtonian physics work, scientists presumed the existence of a substance called ether, which they thought was necessary to carry light waves through space. But experiments proved that ether did not exist. Scientists were plunged into a paralyzing dilemma, caught between their reliance on the old

Newtonian concepts and the results of their experiments. For close to 20 years they floated in an etherless void.

In the year 1905, Einstein published four papers that filled the void; in one simple two-page paper, he concluded that if a body emits energy (E) as radiation, it would lose mass equivalent to E/c^2, where c is the speed of light. Later he refashioned this insight into a brief, daring equation that tripped off the tongue with the doomful simplicity of the first few notes of Beethoven's *Fifth*—$E=mc^2$—the equation that ultimately produced the atom bomb. Einstein went on to demonstrate mathematically that there can be no absolute measure of time or space because all spatial bodies are in perpetual motion, relative to one another. He showed that increasing the speed of mass, whether in a railroad train or a whole whirling galaxy, not only changes the mass but also alters the very yardsticks by which men seek to measure it. His conclusion: "Mass is merely another form of energy."

In his 1905 work, Einstein also delved into the mechanics of matter, introducing the revolutionary idea that light at times has the characteristics of particles (later named photons) and at other times those of a wave. Another paper accounted for Brownian motion—the random movements of microscopic particles within liquids noted by botanist Robert Brown in 1827—by suggesting that the specks were being jostled by molecules in the fluid, an idea that finally convinced many skeptics of the atomic nature of matter.

Bending minds. Almost overnight, the Swiss patent clerk became the world's most famous scientist. Universities competed for him, and he became a professor at the famed Kaiser Wilhelm Institute in Berlin. In 1915 he expanded his ideas into the general theory of relativity; among its mind-bending conclusions, the theory asserted that the force of gravity would curve light. The first practical proof of Einstein's new cosmic concepts came on May 29, 1919. During a total solar eclipse, British astronomer Arthur Eddington found deflections in starlight that almost matched Einstein's prediction. Later, when Einstein was asked what he would have concluded if no bending had been detected, he replied, "Then I would have been sorry for the dear Lord—the theory is correct."

In Einstein's universe, the only absolute remaining was the speed of light. His theories on the relationship between space, time, mass and gravity led to some seemingly bizarre conclusions about the effect of so-called relativistic speeds, those near the velocity of light. In one famous example, Einstein postulated a pair of imaginary twins, one of whom departs on a spacecraft whose speed approaches that of light. On returning to earth, the traveling twin would be younger than his earthbound sibling.

The idealistic Einstein was a socialist and a pacifist, and when World War I broke out, he signed a manifesto condemning it. His wife and their two sons had returned to Switzerland; within a few years the separation led to divorce. Shortly after the divorce, Einstein married his widowed cousin Elsa. World famous now, he found himself embroiled in controversy. His revolutionary ideas collided directly with ancient prejudices and seemed to contradict everyday experience. More important, in Germany Jews were being made scapegoats for the loss of World War I, and he was the target of scurrilous attacks. Shortly after Hitler took over in 1933, Einstein, who was in America at the time, accepted a post at the new Institute for Advanced Study in Princeton. He would never return to Germany.

Einstein's work contributed significantly to the rebirth of cosmology, the study of the origin, history and shape of the universe. But here he committed a rare blunder: some scientists claimed his work pointed to an unstable, possibly expanding universe. But Einstein opted for a stable, unchanging universe, managing the feat with a mathematical sleight of hand that involved what he called the cosmological constant. After the American astronomer Edwin Hubble showed that the distant galaxies were all receding from one another and that the universe was indeed expanding, Einstein reversed himself and accepted Hubble's work. The cosmological constant, he allowed, was the worst mistake of his career.

Einstein was just as stubborn on other scientific issues. He objected to what had become the basic conceptual tool for studying atomic structure: quantum mechanics, a statistical way of looking at the atom that Einstein himself had helped develop by using German physicist Max Planck's theories to explain the nature of light. Einstein was troubled by the theory's uncertainty principle, which says, for example, that it is impossible to tell both the exact position and the momentum of a single atomic particle, because the very act of observing disturbs it. Only by statistical means (like those used to determine probability in dice throwing or poker) can a scientist predict the results of such an experiment. The universe, Einstein insisted, could not operate on chance. Again and again, he would say such things as "God does not play dice with the cosmos." Exasperated, the Danish physicist Niels Bohr, Einstein's friendly adversary, finally replied, "Stop telling God what to do."

Einstein, however, was determined to go his own way: he spent much of the second half of his life pursuing the development of what scientists call a unified field theory—an all-encompassing construct that would unite under a single set of equations the basic forces in the universe. Most physicists thought Einstein's lonely quest was hopeless, and in fact he never succeeded.

ON THE BEACH: Like Gandhi, Einstein saw the forces he had unleashed operate in direct conflict to his ideals

Bombshell. In 1939 Einstein's fellow refugees Leo Szilard and Eugene Wigner learned that German scientists had managed to split the atom, and the two sought his help. He agreed to write a letter to President Roosevelt alerting him to the possibility that the Nazis might try to make an atom bomb. That letter is popularly credited (though its precise effect remains unclear) with helping to persuade Roosevelt to fund the Manhattan Project, which produced the first atomic weapons. Later, when A-bombs devastated Japan, Einstein expressed deep regret. In his last public act before his death in 1955, he joined other scholars in a desperate plea for a ban on warfare.

British science writer Niger Calder has claimed that "the Einstein honored in later generations expired … in 1919." There is truth in that statement. But Einstein remains a towering figure, a 20th century Newton who set physics aflame with insights whose depths remain a source of wonder and discovery. If the mushroom clouds of atomic fission are his unwanted monuments, humanity's chance to turn earthshaking force into good is also his legacy. ∎

CURIE

Digging deep into nature's secrets,

Marie Curie *gave her life to science*

THE YEAR WAS 1898; THE MONTH, DECEMBER; the place, Paris. A woman with blue eyes and blond hair and a dark, bearded man worked in taut silence in a place described as a "cross between a horse stable and a potato cellar." The walls were of rough planks; the glass roof, patched in places, leaked when it rained. There were three battered deal tables covered with apparatuses, a few chairs, a pot-bellied stove. On the asphalt floor lay coarse mats. Suddenly the woman turned off the gas lights. The darkness was complete except for a faint luminescence, a glow emanating from something in a tube she held in her hand. A few days later Marie Sklodowska Curie and her husband Pierre announced they had discovered a radioactive element. They called it radium.

Marie Sklodowska was born in Warsaw in 1867; her father had been a physics professor, her mother the principal of a girls' school. Their daughter Marie joined her older sister in France when Russian officials frowned on her efforts to stimulate interest in the Polish language. While studying in Paris she lived in a bare garret and ate meals that cost half a franc a day. She met a brooding, handsome young physics instructor, Pierre Curie, and she twitted him for expressing astonishment at her learning. But they shared an interest in magnetism: Marie had begun her career in science by investigating the magnetic properties of different kinds of steel, and Pierre had already made significant contributions to the study of magnetism. They married in 1895.

French scientist Antoine Henri Becquerel's accidental discovery in 1896 of the radioactivity of uranium compounds excited the couple greatly. They tested a number of elements in their search for this curious attribute, and soon they found that thorium was also radioactive. Suspecting pitchblende shared the property, they obtained a ton of the mineral from the Austrian government and began a long series of crushings, pulverizations, leachings and crystallizations, trying to isolate the radioactive components of pitchblende with equipment at which a modern physicist would sneer.

The shed at the School of Physics was suffocating in the summertime, freezing in the winter. Much of the time Mme. Curie spent stirring a cauldron with an iron rod as thick as one of her thin arms. "It was in this miserable old shed," she later wrote, "that the best and happiest years of our life were spent, entirely consecrated to work ... In the evening I was broken with fatigue ... [Yet] in spite of the difficulties of our working conditions, we

felt very happy." She lost 14 pounds, began to walk in her sleep and lost a child after it was born prematurely. At last, from the ton of pitchblende they had extracted a thimbleful of a white salt. In it they first found polonium—named for Marie's homeland—and finally radium.

The discovery rocked the world of science. Radioactivity—Marie coined the term—seemed to contradict the principle of the conservation of energy; it forced scientists to reconsider the nature of matter and inaugurated the era of particle physics. Medicine was revolutionized as well: the effect that radium treatments had on cancer, first known as Curie-therapy, seemed almost miraculous. In 1903 the Curies were awarded the Nobel Prize, along with Becquerel, and Pierre was named to the chair of physics at the Sorbonne. In 1905 he was elected to the French Academy of Sciences. But the following year, Pierre Curie was run over in the street by a horse-drawn dray and died instantly. Marie was appointed to her late husband's position, thus becoming the first woman to hold a Sorbonne professorship.

For her first lecture, two years after Pierre's death, Mme. Curie appeared in a plain black working dress. The President of France, the entire French Cabinet, the president of the University of Paris and scientists of three continents joined her students for the occasion. The self-effacing scientist bowed politely, waited for the applause to stop and turned to her class: "Pierre Curie has prepared the following lesson for you," she said, and from a notebook she began to read.

In 1911 Marie Curie became the first person to win the Nobel Prize in both Physics and Chemistry, when she was honored with the prize in Chemistry for her research into the chemical properties of radium. She was now the most famous woman scientist in history, and honors were showered upon her. Yet the chauvinistic French Academy of Sciences, which had welcomed her husband, refused her entry by a single vote—besmirching its name rather than hers.

In the years that followed, Curie continued her research and her teaching, and managed the Institut du Radium's

Marie Curie c. 1895

1867 Born in Warsaw
1903 Awarded Nobel Prize for discovery of radium
1906 Her husband Pierre is killed
1934 Dies of cancer induced by exposure to radioactivity

Curie Laboratory, which she founded in 1912. In 1921 her admirers in the U.S. presented her with one gram of radium, then worth $100,000. She also came to preside over a dynasty: her daughter Irène and her son-in-law Frédéric Joliot continued her work and discovered artificial radioactivity, which led to the creation of thousands of new radioactive isotopes. Frédéric became the head of the French Atomic Energy Commission, but was ousted in 1950 for his leftist political views, thus ending a 50-year period in which the Curie family kept France in the vanguard of nuclear science.

Marie Curie lived long enough, barely, to see Irène's success with artificial radioactivity. In 1934 Mme. Curie became a patient at a sanatorium in the French Alps under the shadow of Mount Blanc. A racking cough had settled in her chest; pernicious anemia was in her blood. The pitchblende had done its work. Magnetically drawn to the power of radium, Marie Curie died a victim of the substance that had brought her immortality. ∎

APRIL 25, 1927 The electron was first identified by J.J. Thomson in 1897. In a series of experiments in 1909, Robert A. Millikan determined the magnitude of its charge.

NOVEMBER 1, 1937 With the building of his first cyclotron in 1929, Ernest O. Lawrence pioneered the development of a potent new research tool, the nuclear particle accelerator.

NOVEMBER 8, 1948 Director of the Los Alamos laboratory, which developed the atom bomb, J. Robert Oppenheimer was later deemed a security risk by the U.S. government.

NOVEMBER 10, 1961 A pioneer of nuclear chemistry, Glenn T. Seaborg was a co-discoverer of the transuranium elements and head of the U.S. Atomic Energy Commission.

FLEMING

When 20 years of research resolved into a flash of insight, **Alexander Fleming** *molded a miracle*

THE MOST EXCITING STORIES IN SCIENCE INVOLVE THE sudden spark when mundane observation meets sudden inspiration. The tradition includes Galileo's watching the swing of a lamp in the Cathedral of Pisa and deducing from it the law of the pendulum, and Sir Isaac Newton's watching the fall of an apple and deducing from it the law of gravity. In like fashion, for thousands of years men looked at the everyday cryptogamic mold called *Penicillium notatum,* but Dr. Alexander Fleming, a bristle-haired Scottish microbe hunter, was the first to see its hidden meaning. His discernment, restoring to science the miraculous flash of inspiration it sometimes seemed to lack in the regimented laboratories of the 20th century, also restored health to millions of humans, living and unborn.

To more colorful colleagues, Fleming's research in a cluttered laboratory at London's St. Mary's Hospital seemed downright dull. But he was nothing if not dogged. In 1928 he was 47 years old, and he had spent 20 years trying to find something to kill the microbes that cause infections in man, especially in wounds—to no avail. He found a substance in human tears that killed some germs, but not the important ones. It seemed just another minor setback when, on a Sep-

tember morning of that year, Fleming looked at a little glass dish in which he had been growing some staphylococci (the germs that flourish in boils) and saw that the culture was "spoiled." A kind of claim-jumping mold had moved in and started its own colonies among the staph. A less observant scientist, or one more fussy about keeping a tidy laboratory, would have thrown out the adulterated growth. But Fleming's keen blue eye noticed a peculiarity: around each patch of mold growth was a bare ring where the staph had not been overgrown or crowded out but had nevertheless been killed. He deduced that the mold secreted a substance that killed this breed of staphylococci, at least.

Fleming scraped off some of the mold with a loop of platinum wire and grew the stuff by itself. In the fluid in which it multiplied was a something that killed several kinds of microbes. The mold was a variety of penicillium, and Fleming called the unseen but magical substance penicillin. When he wrote about it in a British medical journal, one man paid close heed: chemist Harold Raistrick extracted a crude form of penicillin, but concluded it had no future as a medicine for humans—it was too unstable. Fleming's mold was forgotten.

May 15, 1944

1881 Born in Lochfield, Scotland
1914-17 In war, observes infected wounds
1928 Discovers antibiotic nature of penicillin
1945 Wins Nobel Prize for Medicine
1952 Dies at 71

Then, in the mid-1930s, came the sulfa drugs and a revival of interest in germ-killing chemicals. An Oxford research team composed of pathologist Howard Florey and chemist Ernst Chain dug up Fleming's old paper and did the tests all over again. By 1941 they had obtained enough penicillin to prolong the lives of two patients. World War II hastened research; money and materials speeded the perfection and manufacture of the "wonder drug," and thousands of lives were saved.

Penicillin was technically not the first of the antibiotics, but it was the first to make medical sense, let alone history. While Fleming went on puttering in his littered laboratory, interrupted often to accept awards—including a Nobel Prize, with Florey and Chain—other antibiotics appeared, but penicillin remained the most widely applicable of them.

Fleming's discovery marked an epoch in medicine. Untold millions of all ages who formerly would have died of infectious diseases have been spared—including Fleming, who, in 1953, made a quick recovery from pneumonia with penicillin's aid. When the great microbe hunter died at 73 in 1955, the cause of death was a heart attack. ∎

WATSON & CRICK

*Meet **James Watson** & **Francis Crick**—the double dads of the double helix*

ILD WITH EXCITEMENT, TWO men dashed out of a side door of Cambridge University's Cavendish Laboratory and ducked into the Eagle, a pub where generations of Cambridge scientists have met to gossip about experiments and celebrate triumphs. Over drinks, James D. Watson, then 24, and Francis Crick, 36, talked excitedly, Crick's booming voice damping out conversations among other Eagle patrons. When friends stopped to ask what the commotion was all about, Crick did not mince words. "We," he announced exultantly, "have discovered the secret of life!"

Brave words—and in a sense, incredibly true. On that late winter day in 1953, the two unknown scientists had finally worked out the double-helical shape of deoxyribonucleic acid, or DNA. In DNA's famed spiral-staircase structure are hidden the mysteries of heredity, of growth, of disease and of

aging—and in higher creatures like man, intelligence and memory. As the basic ingredient of the genes in the cells of all living organisms, DNA is truly the master molecule of life.

The unraveling of the DNA double helix was one of the great events in science, comparable to the splitting of the atom or the publication of Darwin's *Origin of Species.* It also marked the maturation of a bold new science: molecular biology. Under this probing discipline, man could at last explore—and understand—living things at their most fundamental level: that of their atoms and molecules. Following Watson and Crick's great discovery, molecular biology became one of science's most active, exciting and productive arenas.

Peas and destiny. Ever since Cro-Magnon man, parents have probably wondered why their children resemble them. But not until an obscure Austrian monk named Gregor Mendel began planting peas in his monastery's garden in the mid-19th century were the universal laws of heredity worked out. By tallying up the variations in the offspring peas, Mendel determined that traits are passed from generation to generation with mathematical precision in small, separate packets. These packets subsequently became known as genes (from the Greek word for race).

Mendel's ideas were so unorthodox that they were ignored for 35 years. But by the time the Mendelian concept was rediscovered at the turn of the century, scientists were better prepared for it. They already suspected that genetic information was hidden inside pairs of tiny, threadlike strands in cell nuclei called chromosomes, or "colored bodies" (for their ability to pick up dyes). During cell division, chromosomes always split lengthwise, thereby giving each daughter cell a full share of what was presumed to be hereditary material.

A few years later, the pioneering U.S. geneticist Thomas Hunt Morgan mapped the relative positions of genes in the chromosomes of the fruit fly. Still, the gene's physical nature remained as great a mystery as ever. DNA had been discovered in the nuclei of cells by the Swiss biochemist Friedrich Miescher a few years after Mendel did his work on peas. But since the chromosomes in which the DNA was found also contained proteins, the basic building blocks of life, it was not yet clear that DNA might play an even more central role.

In 1944 U.S. bacteriologist Oswald T. Avery demonstrated that it was DNA, and not protein, that carried the genetic message. Gradually, scientists probed deeper into the molecule, using such new technologies as X-ray crystallography, a technique for deducing a crystallized molecule's structure by taking X-ray photographs of it from different angles.

Toying with fate. Inspired by these experiments, Watson, then a young Ph.D. in zoology from Indiana University, decided to take a crack at the complex structure of DNA itself. The same thought struck Crick, a physicist turned biologist who was preparing for his doctorate at Cambridge. Neither man was particularly well equipped to undertake a task so formidable that it had stymied one of the world's most celebrated chemists, Linus Pauling. Watson, for his part, was deficient in chemistry, crystallography and mathematics. Crick, on the other hand, was almost totally ignorant of genetics. But together, in less than two years of work at Cambridge, these two spirited young scientists solved the mystery.

Out of Pauling's work, Watson and Crick got the idea that the extremely long and complicated DNA molecule might take the shape of a helix, or spiral. From the X-ray crystallography laboratory at King's College in London, where biochemist Maurice Wilkins was also investigating the molecule's structure, they quietly obtained unpublished X-ray data on DNA. Working in a shabby shack sandwiched between the imposing academic buildings on the flower-bordered lawns of Cambridge, they had a magpie's nest of old books and model molecules strung like mobiles from the ceiling. Relying as much on luck as logic, they constructed Tinkertoy-like molecular models out of wire and other metal parts. To their astonishment, they suddenly produced a DNA model that not only satisfied the

FIRST PERSON

"In contrast to the popular conception ... a goodly number of scientists are not only narrow-minded and dull, but also just stupid."

"Each night for a week [at a conference] there were receptions, dinners and midnight trips to waterfront bars ... An important truth was slowly entering my head: a scientist's life might be interesting socially as well as intellectually."

—From *The Double Helix*, James Watson, 1968

crystallographic evidence but also conformed to the chemical rules for fitting its many atoms together. Within weeks, they published their findings in an understated 900-word article in *Nature*, a scientific weekly published in Britain. In a follow-up letter, they described how the DNA molecule copied itself by unzipping right down the middle during cell division.

How do we see? Their names had become inextricably linked, but Watson and Crick drifted apart after their epochal discovery. In 1968 Watson produced a highly irreverent, gossipy best seller, *The Double Helix*, which revealed the human story behind the triumph: the bickering, the academic rivalries, even the deceits that were practiced to become the first to identify the structure. Its first sentence: "I have never seen Francis Crick in a modest mood."

Watson studied and taught at Caltech and Harvard before becoming director of a famed biological research facility, the Cold Spring Harbor Laboratory on Long Island, New York. He lobbied vigorously for the creation of the Human Genome Project, an enormous study that seeks to identify each gene in the genetic chain, and guided it through its first four years before resigning over political issues.

Crick continued his work on the cell, then studied developmental biology. In 1976 he moved to California to work at the Salk Institute for the Biological Studies, where he has devoted a good deal of time to studying the brain and its visual system, because "I want to know how we see something."

Watson and Crick have lived long enough to see their epochal discovery transform biology; create the biotechnology industry; change the practice of medicine; and begin to affect business, industry, agriculture and food processing. And prove you can build a Nobel Prize from Tinkertoys. ■

Watson in 1957

1916 Crick is born in Northampton, England
1928 Watson is born in Chicago
1953 They identify the structure of DNA
1962 They share the Nobel Prize with Maurice Wilkins

SALK

Heroes didn't wear lab coats, until **Jonas Salk** *stopped polio in its tracks*

ONE GOOD WAY TO ASSESS THE GREATEST figures of medicine is by how completely they make us forget what we owe them. By that measure, Dr. Jonas E. Salk ranks very high. Partly because of the vaccine he introduced in the mid-1950s, it is hard now to recall the sheer terror that was once connected to the word polio. The incidence of the disease had risen sharply in the early part of this century, and every year brought the threat of another outbreak. Parents were haunted by the stories of children stricken suddenly by the telltale cramps and fever. Public swimming pools were deserted for fear of contagion. And year after year polio delivered thousands of people to hospitals and into wheelchairs, or into the nightmarish canisters called iron lungs. Or into the grave. In the worst year of the epidemic, 1952, when nearly 58,000 cases were reported in the U.S. alone, more than 3,000 Americans died of the disease.

Yet by the time of Salk's death in 1995, polio was virtually gone from the U.S. and was nearing extinction throughout the world. The beginning of the end for the virus can be dated precisely. On April 12, 1955, a Salk colleague announced that a vaccine developed by Salk and tested on more than 1 million schoolchildren had proved "safe, effective and potent." As a result of the mass inoculation that followed, new cases in the U.S. dropped to fewer than 1,000 per year by 1962.

Superman of science. The triumph over polio made Salk one of the most celebrated men of his time. Streets and schools were named for him; in polls he ranked with Gandhi and Churchill as a hero of modern history. Though his fame was expertly fostered by the public relations machinery of the National Foundation for Infantile Paralysis and its March of Dimes campaign, which helped finance Salk's work,

national adulation was still an unexpected fate for a dedicated scientist in an unglamorous field.

The son of a manufacturer of women's wear, Salk was introduced to viral research as a first-year medical student at New York University in the 1930s. He became so interested in research that he took a year out to work on protein chemistry. Asked later why he devoted his life to research, Salk countered, "Why did Mozart compose music?" The research bug was in his blood to stay. After receiving his degree, he moved to the University of Michigan to work with Dr. Thomas Francis Jr., one of his former professors. There he helped to develop commercial vaccines against influenza that were used by American troops during World War II.

TEST-TUBE MOZART: Salk in 1952, at right; opposite, with wife Françoise Gilot at the Salk Institute, where he ended his years seeking an AIDS vaccine

After the war Salk headed the viral-research program at the University of Pittsburgh. A quick and logical thinker and a quick, incisive speaker, he plunged into his work with boundless energy. He began by sticking to his first love, the influenza viruses. But soon he decided to "look into this polio problem to see what it was about." The time was exactly ripe for a man with a passion for plotting knowns and unknowns in schematic diagrams and an ability to stick to it day and night. Salk was prepared to work: it was not unusual for him to work a 16-hour day six days a week.

The virus of fame. The first breakthrough in polio research came in 1949. A team of Harvard researchers headed by the brilliant virologist John F. Enders reported that they had succeeded in growing polio viruses in tissue cultures taken from the kidneys of the rhesus monkey. At last researchers had a method of mass-producing a safe starting material for a vaccine. Salk's first chance to contribute to the search for a vaccine came in the same year. The National Foundation for Infantile Paralysis commissioned four university laboratories, including Salk's, to classify 100 strains of polio. In the next three years, Salk and his associates typed 74 strains, and along the way, he learned the new Enders technique for cultivating strains of polio in living tissue cultures.

At the time, medical wisdom held that vaccines, to be effective, should use live viruses that had been rendered harmless in the laboratory. Salk believed it would be possible to make a vaccine using killed viruses; this method, he thought, was preferable since it carried less risk of actually causing the disease the vaccine was meant to prevent. Step by painstaking step, Salk made experimental vaccines and tested them in monkeys. The goal: to kill or inactivate the virus and still leave it with the power to stimulate the human system to produce protective antibodies.

In June 1952 Salk was satisfied that he had a vaccine safe enough to be given to human beings. Still, for utmost safety, he decided that the first subjects should be those who had already recovered from polio. Thus they should be immune to further disease, but he could measure a rise in their antibody level if the vaccine produced, as he expected, a booster effect. It did. Salk saw to it that he and his family were among the first healthy subjects to be injected. The vaccine was released to the public in 1955, following massive field tests in 1954.

That America's greatest hero was for a time a man in a white lab coat might have delighted Salk's peers in medical research. Instead many of them resented him as a man who claimed success to a radio audience before he had properly published his findings, and reaped the glory for work that had been pioneered by less celebrated scientists. By 1962 Dr. Albert Sabin's oral vaccine, derived from live viruses, had become the preferred method of inoculation in the U.S., and Sabin was bitter about Salk's earlier triumph. Just a few years before his own death in 1993, Sabin claimed that "Salk didn't discover anything." Salk himself came to be uncom-

fortable with the fuss surrounding him. He made a point of crediting the contributions of other scientists and tried to discourage use of the term "Salk vaccine."

Co-authors of destiny. In 1963 Salk was able to realize a lifelong dream when he became director of the Salk Institute for Biological Studies at a magnificent compound designed by the prominent architect Louis Kahn on an oceanfront promontory in La Jolla, California. It attracted researchers from many fields to pursue biomedical research. In 1970, two years after divorcing his first wife, Salk married Françoise Gilot, the onetime companion and muse of Pablo Picasso and mother of two of Picasso's children.

When AIDS emerged in the 1980s, Salk plunged into the effort to find a vaccine—but success eluded him. The greatest pleasure of his later years was to reflect on the large questions of human evolution and people's roles as "co-authors" with nature in their own destiny—such as, for instance, his own. "I could have studied the immunological properties of, say, tobacco mosaic virus," he once reflected, "published my findings, and they would have been of some interest. But the fact that I chose to work on the polio virus, which brought control of a dreaded disease, made all the difference." All the difference for him. And for hundreds of thousands of others too. ∎

March 29, 1954

1914 Born in New York City
1952 Tests of the new vaccine begin
1955 Vaccine is released
1963 Salk Institute opens in California
1995 Dies at 80

PAULING

Linus Pauling—*an "unreasonable man"—was science's Renaissance man*

THE ALCHEMISTS OF THE MIDDLE AGES WERE THE first chemists. They were acquainted with chemical reactions, but had no rational theories about them. Early chemists developed general principles to explain what happened in their test tubes. The most useful of these was the concept of "chemical bonds": the forces that make atoms stick together as the molecules that form nearly everything on earth. But chemists knew little about this mysterious process—until Linus Pauling illuminated the microscopic world of the chemical bond in the 1930s.

Pauling's vision was broad as well as deep. A true Renaissance man, he won the Nobel Prize for Peace in 1962 for his work to limit nuclear testing in the atmosphere. He claimed his philosophy was captured in a quote from George Bernard Shaw a fan sent him: "The reasonable man adapts himself to the world. The unreasonable one persists in trying to adapt the world to himself. Therefore, all progress depends upon the unreasonable man."

Born in Oswego, Oregon, Pauling grew up collecting insects and minerals and conducting experiments with chemicals from an abandoned iron and steel smelter. Fascinated with the properties of materials, he studied chemical engineering in college, then headed off to the California Institute of Technology to do graduate work. In 1926-27 he traveled in Europe, meeting many of the most prominent physicists of the time and gaining an indispensable understanding of the new field of quantum mechanics. As he later said, at the time he was "the only person in the world who had a good understanding of quantum mechanics and an extensive knowledge about chemistry."

In 1928 Pauling published his theory that the "resonance" of the atoms in a molecule—their internal vibration—holds the molecule together. He collected his findings in a book still considered a classic, *The Nature of the Chemical Bond* (1939). A host of applications sprang from his work: in drugs, in plastics, in synthetic fibers.

Pauling also fertilized the nascent field of molecular biology with his work on proteins. In 1942 he and his team produced the first synthetic antibodies, and in the early 1950s Pauling and a colleague were the first to describe the molecular structure of proteins in three-dimensional terms. He was the first to suggest that the structure of DNA might be arranged in a twisted spiral; later his friendly rivals, James Watson and Francis Crick, identified it as a double helix.

Pauling joined Albert Einstein's Emergency Committee of Atomic Scientists, a group that called for a ban on atmospheric testing of nuclear weapons, in 1946. When he was given the Nobel Prize for Chemistry in 1954 for his work on the chemical bond, he used his new fame to promote his antitesting efforts, denying McCarthy-era insinuations that he was a communist sympathizer. His Nobel Peace Prize was announced on the day the nuclear test-ban treaty was signed by the U.S., the Soviet Union and Britain.

In his later years, Pauling again took the spotlight with his advocacy of large doses of vitamin C to prevent and cure the common cold. His claims sparked enormous controversy, and Pauling was accused of having insufficient scientific findings for his opinions. An exuberant humanist, cocky and obstinate, reveling in debate, Pauling lived to 93, his own best advertisement for his 1986 book, *How to Live Longer and Feel Better*. Famous with the public for his activism, the "unreasonable man" was admired by other scientists for his wide-ranging mind. When Albert Einstein was asked about Pauling, he replied: "Ah, there's *true* genius." ∎

Pauling in 1927

1901 Born in Oswego, Oregon
1939 *The Nature of the Chemical Bond*
1954 Wins Nobel Prize for Chemistry
1962 Wins Nobel Prize for Peace
1994 Dies at 93

HAWKING

An iron wheelchair is his prison, but the mind of **Stephen Hawking** *roams free*

Hawking in 1988

DARKNESS HAS FALLEN ON CAMBRIDGE, ENGLAND, when down the crowded King's Parade comes the university's most distinguished vehicle, a motorized wheelchair, bearing its most distinguished citizen. The wheelchair's occupant is a man who is able to move only his facial muscles and two fingers on his left hand, who cannot dress or feed himself, who communicates only through a voice synthesizer that he operates by laboriously tapping out words on a computer keyboard attached to the wheelchair. Disease has made the man a virtual prisoner in his own body. But it has left his courage and humor intact, his intellect free to roam. And roam it does, from the infinitesimal to the infinite, from the subatomic realm to the far reaches of the universe. The man in the wheelchair is Stephen William Hawking, one of the world's greatest physicists.

Rejecting the urging of his father, a biologist, to study medicine, Stephen Hawking chose instead to concentrate on math and theoretical physics, first at Oxford and then at Cambridge. But at age 21 he developed the first symptoms of amyotrophic lateral sclerosis (ALS)—also known as Lou Gehrig's disease—a disorder that would inevitably render him paralyzed and incapable of performing most kinds of work. Fortunately, as Albert Einstein had shown, the work of the theoretical physicist requires only one tool: the mind.

Hawking has used that tool with consummate skill. While still a graduate student, he became fascinated by black holes, the bizarre objects created during the death throes of large stars. Working with mathematician Roger Penrose, he developed new techniques to prove mathematically that at the heart of black holes were singularities—infinitely dense, dimensionless points with irresistible gravity—and he went on to calculate that the entire universe could have sprung from a singularity. This Big Bang that gave birth to the universe, he later asserted, must have created tiny black holes, each about the

1942 Born in Oxford, England
1966 His Ph.D. thesis posits origin of universe in a singularity
1974 Claims black holes emit radiation
1988 *A Brief History of Time* is a best seller

size of a proton but with the mass of a mountain. Then, upsetting the universal belief that nothing, not even light, can escape from a black hole, Hawking argued that these miniholes (and larger ones too) emit radiation. Other scientists eventually conceded that he was correct, and the black-hole emissions are now known as Hawking radiation.

Hawking does not dwell on his handicap. His succinct, synthesized-voice comments are often laced with humor, but he can also be stubborn, abrasive and quick to anger. Without his wife Jane, Hawking used to emphasize, his career might never have soared. She married him shortly after he was diagnosed with ALS, fully aware of the dreadful, progressive nature of the disease, giving him hope and the will to carry on with his studies. They had three children early in the marriage, and as Hawking became increasingly incapacitated, she devoted herself to catering to his every need. Friends were shocked in 1990 when Hawking abruptly ended their 25-year marriage; he wed one of his former nurses in 1995.

With his 1988 best seller, *A Brief History of Time*, Hawking became perhaps the best-known scientist in the world. Why the rush to buy a dense volume of mind-bending physics? Ever wry, Hawking insists, "No one can resist the idea of a crippled genius." ∎

HUBBLE

Following the stars, **Edwin Hubble** *peered deeply into time and space*

O F ALL THE SCIENCES, ASTRONOMY IS IN many ways the most pleasant. There are no dead animals (as in biology), no horrible smells (as in chemistry); there are no terrible teenagers (as in sociology) or terrible food (as in anthropology). Astronomers work on clear-aired mountaintops with clean and beautiful instruments. Their experimental material—light—filters down unbidden out of the far reaches of the cold, dark sky.

Perhaps it was the lure of the mountains that drew Edwin Hubble to astronomy. He found the law dull, and he passed up a somewhat more exciting opportunity—boxing Jack Johnson for the heavyweight championship of the world—to study the stars. Hubble claimed to believe that astronomy is something like the ministry. No one should go into it without a genuine "call." And the only way to test a call, he believed, is to have another calling to be called away from.

Hubble followed the call. He was born in Marshfield, Missouri, in 1889, and took his bachelor's degree in 1910 at the University of Chicago, where he was a boxing standout. He knew by then that he wanted to be an astronomer, but he took time out for a Rhodes scholarship and two years of law at Oxford. After one year of law practice in the U.S. (very dull), astronomy called with unmistakable loudness, and Hubble went to the Yerkes Observatory in Wisconsin to make friends with the sky. After serving in France in World War I, he took a long-promised job at the observatory at Mount Wilson in California. The story he found there in the faint traces of light on photographic film revolutionized our understanding of the universe. The whole visible universe, Hubble's data told him, is apparently expanding. The matter in space appeared to be flying apart far faster than the white-hot gases of detonating TNT. And the universe into which it was flying was far vaster and far older than anyone had previously believed.

Even as an apprentice astronomer, Hubble concentrated on the nebulae—the faint patches of light scattered among the stars. Some had been proved mere wraiths, irregular clouds of dust that shined with reflected starlight. Others, more interesting, were globes, ellipses, open spirals like patterns of fire from great spinning pinwheels. When the brightest of these were photographed with powerful telescopes, they dissolved into vast congregations of faint stars, whose dimness suggested that they might be very far away—perhaps even outside our own Milky Way galaxy. But astronomers, lacking a proper

February 9, 1948

1889 Born in Marshfield, Missouri
1919 Begins working at Mount Wilson
1930 Puts forth his theory of the expansion of the universe
1953 Dies in San Marino, California

measuring stick, were not agreed. Some thought that the nebulae were comparatively near and small. Hubble's first step at Mount Wilson was to find out how far away they were.

His general method was to determine the intrinsic brightness of objects in a nebula and then gauge its distance (the fainter it was, the farther away). Variable stars called Cepheids told him that the bright nebula called Messier 31 was 680,000 light-years away. Messier 31 was therefore no mere part of the Milky Way galaxy, but an isolated star system far out in space, and as big as our entire galaxy. Other, longer-range measuring sticks carried him farther on his march into space. There seemed to be no end to the swarming nebulae. The most distant showed as tiny, dim blobs. By a complex statistical method, Hubble proved after years of work that these dimmest glimmers were so far away that their light took 500 million years to reach Mount Wilson. His success in measuring the distance of dimmer and dimmer nebulae led to his crowning discovery—the theory of the expanding universe.

Astronomers have a speedometer to clock the motions of skittish heavenly bodies. They take spectrographs: photographs of the body's light spread out by a prism into a band of colors. If the band is "shifted toward the red" (i.e., if it is redder than normal), it shows that the body is moving away from the earth. Studying the light of the distant nebulae, Hubble found in every case a red shift. The farther off a nebula was, the faster it appeared to be rushing away, and the enormous speeds (thousands of miles per second) were new, strange and startling.

Hubble reached a momentous conclusion: that the speed of recession of the nebulae is directly proportional to their distance. This meant that each of the large units of matter in the universe (nebulae) is moving away from every other unit. The Milky Way galaxy is not the center of the explosion. Every other nebula is equally an explosion center. Casting around for a layman's analogy, Hubble compared the expanding universe to a rubber balloon with small dots (representing nebulae) spaced equally far apart on its surface. When the balloon is blown up larger, each dot becomes more distant from every other dot. Place an observer on any dot, and he will see the same picture. Every other dot-nebula will be moving away from him.

The announcement of Hubble's theory caused an uproar: the idea of an expanding universe gave some sober scientists goose pimples. But Hubble's theory prevailed, and he went on to use the linear relationship between the velocity of the receding galaxies and their distance from the earth—ultimately to become known as Hubble's law—to measure the size and age of the universe. He assigned to the knowable universe a radius of about 18 billion light-years and an age of about 2 billion years. Both figures have been altered by the advances in measuring tools since his day, but the principles he laid down remain unchanged. Hubble died in 1953, and if you seek his monument, look up: America's Hubble telescope orbits the earth, probing ever deeper into the universe that called a young lawyer to chart its depths. ∎

LEAKEY

How the first family of fossils—the Leakeys—found the first families of mankind

November 7, 1977

1903 Louis Leakey is born in Kenya
1913 Mary is born
1944 Richard is born
1960 Louis and Mary discover *Homo habilis*
1972 Richard discovers skull ER-1470
1972 Louis dies

E FOUND HIS FIRST FOSSIL, THE INTACT JAW OF AN extinct giant pig, when he was six years old. Yet Richard Leakey was initially reluctant to follow in the footsteps of his parents. Louis and Mary Leakey's excavations at Tanzania's Olduvai Gorge had transformed paleoanthropology—the study of human origins—from a superficial examination of stones and bones into a rigorous discipline intent on reconstructing the life-style of early man and pinpointing the crucial steps on the evolutionary pathway to modern humans. Instead, young Richard ran a successful safari company and learned to fly. "I just wanted to get out—to go away and look at animals," he once said. "But it passed. The time came."

Richard's parents had set the standard high. Louis, born in Kenya the son of missionaries, was attending Cambridge when he joined his first expedition. At Lake Victoria in 1948 he discovered a skull of *Proconsul africanus,* an apelike ancestor of modern primates that lived 25 million to 40 million years ago. He and his wife Mary took their search for fossils to east Africa's Olduvai Gorge, in what is now northern Tanzania. There, in 1959, Mary discovered jaw fragments of a 1.75 million-year-old hominid, which they named *Zinjanthropus.* This apelike prehuman that first evolved some 4 million years ago is now called *Australophithecus boisei.* In 1960 the Leakeys and their eldest son Jonathan unearthed fragments of another hominid, *Homo habilis* ("handy man"), which had a larger brain than the australopithecines. They believed *Homo habilis* was the first tool-using hominid.

Richard broke free of his parents' considerable shadow in 1968 when, without warning his father, he asked the National Geographic Society for a grant to explore some promising sediments on the eastern shore of Kenya's Lake Turkana. Like his parents' site at Olduvai, Turkana is part of the Rift Valley system, a giant fissure that runs north to south in eastern Africa for about 6,000 miles. It soon became clear that Richard was blessed with the fabled "Leakey's luck": the first hominid fossil, a weathered jaw from *A. boisei,* turned up after just three weeks. Over the next 20 years—before Richard gave up hunting fossils in 1989 to save Kenya's animals as head of the National Wildlife Service—the wealth of fossils of early man that he and his colleagues found in the region eclipsed his parents' discoveries. Among them:

• ER-1470, a 1.8 million-year-old skull that is one of the best-preserved specimens ever found of *Homo habilis.*

• "Turkana boy," the nearly intact skeleton of a strapping youth who lived at least 1.6 million years ago. Discovered in 1984, Turkana Boy is the oldest and most complete fossil to date of a close relative of *Homo erectus,* the first human ancestor to establish campsites and master the use of fire.

• The "Black Skull," a 2.5 million-year-old cranium that is now thought to resemble the common ancestor of the southern and western species of *A. boisei.*

Unhappily, Louis Leakey did not take kindly to the acclaim that greeted Richard's early work, and their intense conflict threatened to split the family. The feud ended in 1972 when the elder Leakey flew to visit his son's camp; by the harsh light of a gas lamp they examined fossils late into the night. That night Louis predicted that Richard would find evidence of three hominid species at Turkana. A few weeks later Louis died, unaware that events would prove him right. ■

THE DIGGERS: Above, Louis and Mary Leakey in Olduvai Gorge, 1961; right, Richard holds skull "ER-1470" in his left hand

MEAD

From the South Seas to North America, **Margaret Mead**
became the watchful grandmother of the global village

A REPORTER TURNING UP AT ONE OF HER LECTURES
noted that the speaker had somehow managed to
discuss museums, stones, stuffed birds, cave
painting, Cro-Magnon man, dinosaurs, whales,
the possibility of life in outer space, education,
the oneness of the human species, pollution, evolution, growing up in New Guinea, relations between the sexes, communes and the fragmentation of communities.

The list was typical: Margaret Mead got around. Her studies—and the two dozen books that resulted from them—revolutionized her chosen field of anthropology. Long before her colleagues recognized the validity of her approach, she studied the biological, psychological and sociological forces that shaped personality in primitive cultures, then used her findings to explain how individuals learn adult roles in modern societies. Her application of this approach to other areas

and her willingness to speak out on almost any subject made her ideas—and her smallish but somehow imposing figure topped by its Buster Brown hairdo—famous around the world. By the time of her death at 76, Margaret Mead had become the grandmother of the global village, an all-wise matriarch whose often provocatively put, commonsense opinions were sought by millions.

Both observation and involvement came naturally to Mead, who was born in 1901 to parents who quite literally raised her to be a social scientist. She was only eight when she was assigned to observe and record her younger sisters' speech patterns. After training at New York's Barnard College and Columbia University, she sailed for Samoa in 1925 and spent nine months observing the adolescent girls of three small coastal villages in the Manua Islands. The result of her study was published three years later as *Coming of Age in Samoa.*

The book, which described the easygoing, neurosis-free island way of life and suggested that the Western attitude toward sex could be relaxed without endorsing promiscuity, was an instant success. Many of the young researcher's colleagues condemned her way of reaching conclusions from observed evidence, which Mead called "disciplined subjectivity." But students snapped it up, partly because its ideas interested them, often because, as the author briskly explained, "I wrote it in English."

Mead wrote her other books in the same easily understood idiom. But anthropology alone could not satisfy her. A fluent speaker who rarely needed notes, she also carried a heavy teaching schedule. She established a Hall of the Peoples of the Pacific at the American Museum of Natural History, where she was curator of ethnology. She brought her keen mind and anthropological insights to bear on her own society, and with a confidence that made clear she would brook no arguments, she spoke out frequently on social problems that many of her colleagues preferred to avoid.

Mead in 1974

When Mead appeared on TV talk shows to endorse women's liberation or other causes, envious colleagues said she was "overexposed"; conservative academicians called Mead, who served on more committees than anyone could remember, an "international busybody."

Mead carried on. She had survived malaria, three marriages and years of native foods, but in 1978 she succumbed to cancer. Characteristically, she turned her trained eye upon herself and recorded her own progress of aging. Her attention was appropriate. Of all the people she studied, few were as interesting as Margaret Mead herself. ■

1901 Born in
Philadelphia
1925 First trip to the
South Pacific
1928 Publishes *Coming of Age in Samoa*
1930 Publishes *Growing Up in New Guinea*
1978 Dies at 76

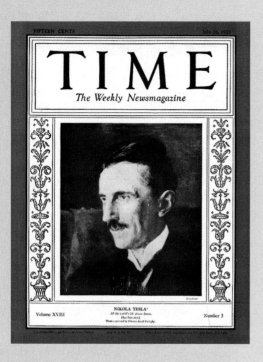

JULY 20, 1931 Electrician and inventor Nikola Tesla was the first to make practical use of alternating current and did key research on transformers, telephone and telegraph systems.

APRIL 16, 1934 Observing a total eclipse in 1919, astronomer Arthur Eddington confirmed Einstein's theory of relativity. His major area of study was the internal constitution of stars.

MAY 28, 1965 A pioneer in the development of surgical techniques that have saved thousands of lives, Dr. Michael DeBakey was one of the first to conduct heart-bypass surgery.

DECEMBER 15, 1967 Although his 1967 operation to transplant a human heart failed, Dr. Christiaan Barnard led the way toward the development of heart-transplant surgery.

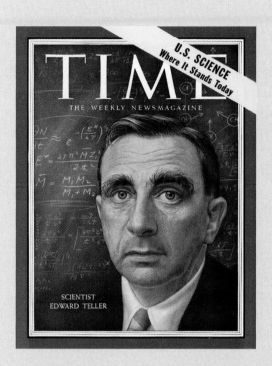

NOVEMBER 18, 1957 A physicist caught up in cold-war politics, Edward Teller helped develop the hydrogen bomb and later advocated the proposed "Star Wars" defense shield.

MAY 4, 1959 Mounting Geiger counters on early satellites, astronomer James Van Allen discovered the two belts of radiation that encircle the globe; they now bear his name.

SEPTEMBER 20, 1971 His work on the learning process in animals was valuable, but when psychologist B.F. Skinner proposed using his behaviorist tools on humans, critics balked.

OCTOBER 20, 1980 A respected planetary astronomer who helped NASA design exploratory probes, Carl Sagan won fame as the TV host who extolled the "billions and billions" of stars.

THE CR

As science undermined certainty, as politics tainted ideals and language, creative artists channeled the century's passions into radical new forms. Audiences and critics revolted: Picasso, they said, couldn't paint. Stravinsky, they said, was out of key. Joyce, they said, was obscene. But, in Ezra Pound's phrase, "the age demanded an image of its accelerated grimace." Artists wrought that new image by divesting old forms of their outworn trappings to reveal classic simplicities: Balanchine stripped dance to its purest essentials, Mies van der Rohe found less was more, Picasso refracted painting into its raw components. "History is a nightmare from which I am trying to awake," said Joyce's hero, Stephen Dedalus. In casting off history's spell, the creators awakened us all. ∎

EATORS

Georgia O'Keeffe, 1948

PICASSO

With protean virtuosity, **Pablo Picasso** *held the mirror up to the century*

H E WAS THOUGHT TO BE DEAD AT birth in Málaga on Oct. 25, 1881. Then his uncle Salvador Ruiz, a celebrated Spanish physician who had delivered the boy, calmly puffed cigar smoke up the baby's nose, provoking howls of protest. Thus did Pablo Ruiz Picasso embark on his 91 years of rugged life. In those nine decades, he became the century's most significant artist, the man who created new ways of seeing and expressing reality that shaped the times as much as the work of Einstein, Freud or Henry Ford. Picasso's art was distinguished by a passionate omnivorousness, a refusal to accept received ideas of what painting or sculpture could express, an energetic and Mediterranean humanism. His life sprang from his appetites, and the art from both; he lived and worked full tilt, in grand, sweeping style.

Picasso's virtuosity in every field is the one fact of modern art that everybody knows something about. Indeed, the full sweep of his effect on modern art is difficult to document simply because it so pervasive. His co-invention of Cubism, with Georges Braque, proved to be the first workable alternative to Renaissance perspective in modern art. He established collage as a formal device. His Cubist constructions steered the course of modern sculpture away from mass and toward open forms and rigging. His sheet metal *Guitar* of 1912 was as prophetic of future sculpture as his breakthrough work *Les Demoiselles d'Avignon* was to later painting. His combination of found objects with metal, wood or string provided cues to later junk assemblers. He was the most influential artist of his time; for many lesser figures a catastrophic influence, and for those who could deal with him—from Braque through Giacometti to de Kooning and Arshile Gorky—an indescribably fruitful one.

The prodigy. Not all great painters are precocious, but Picasso was. His father was a painter named Jose Ruiz Blasco, and by 13 the young artist was so good at drawing that his father is said to have handed over his own brushes and paints to the boy and given up painting. If the story is true, it goes some way to

June 26, 1950

1881 Born in Málaga, Spain
1900 Arrives in Paris
1900-07 Paints in his Rose and Blue modes
1910 Cubist style reaches full maturity
1937 *Guernica*
1973 Dies at 91

WHAT, NO BERET? Picasso as—yes—a struggling young artist in Montparnasse, Paris

explain the mediumistic confidence with which Picasso worked. "Painting is stronger than I am," he once remarked. "It makes me do what it wants."

It was not merely that Picasso—first as an art student in Barcelona and, after the autumn of 1900, as a young artist in Paris—was markedly better at imitating Toulouse-Lautrec than other Spanish artists were, but that he could run through the influences so quickly, with such nimble digestion. What he needed he kept. Living in poverty in the little Spanish artists' colony in Montparnasse, he identified himself in a sentimental way with the wretched and down-and-out of Paris, the waifs and strays. This wistful *misérabilisme*, verging on allegory, was the keynote of his so-called Blue Period, in which a blue boundary line he had found in the work of Gauguin spread to become the dominant hue of his paintings. The blue had a symbolic value; it spoke of melancholy, of the "blues." But it also enabled Picasso to take color out of his work, so that he could make a compromise between decorative flatness and sculptural volume in terms of pure tone.

By the age of 25 Picasso was an able and gifted artist, but not yet a modern one. He had managed to tame the mannerism of the Blue Period, with its wistful elongations and neurotic passivity of form, by studying Degas. His new paintings—the Rose Period—featured beggars, circus players and street singers; they were less melancholy, more removed. He could have kept painting in the manner he had acquired for the rest of his life and died with honor. What happened was very different: he refused to stand still. The detachment of expression in his Rose Period hardened; through 1906 the faces took on an increasingly blank, masklike air. He stressed the sculptural instead of the linear and atmospheric.

The breakthrough. Having brought solid form to such density, what choice did Picasso have but to break it all down again? *Les Demoiselles d'Avignon,* 1907, the painting that provoked Cubism, is one of the most astounding feats of ideation in the history of art. No painting has ever looked more convulsive and contradictory. It is a brothel scene, freighted with aggression, carefully wrought. The five nudes are cut up

SELF-PORTRAIT (1901) This work was painted shortly after Picasso arrived in Paris. He had already achieved technical mastery and was absorbing the influence of such painters as Gauguin, Toulouse-Lautrec and Puvis de Chavannes.

LES DEMOISELLES D'AVIGNON (1907) The brutal painting is set in a Barcelona brothel on the Carrer d'Avinyo, or Avignon Street.

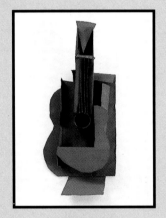

GUITAR (1912) From a few unpromising-looking shards of metal, Picasso invented an entirely new direction for sculpture.

THREE MUSICIANS (1921) Over time, Picasso moved beyond the muted palette of early Cubism into a more colorful style known as Synthetic Cubism that drew on his work with collage.

GUERNICA (1937) The work reflects Picasso's rage at the bombing of a Basque town by Francisco Franco's troops during the Spanish Civil War.

SCULPTOR, MODEL AND FISHBOWL (1933) This favorite Picasso theme employs classical Mediterranean motifs.

into segments, as though the brush were a butcher knife. Their look, eyes glaring from African-mask faces, is accusatory, not inviting. The space between the figures is flattened, like a crumpled box; it was in this play of code between solid and void that the formal prophecies of the painting lay.

No *Demoiselles*, no Cubism. But there was a long stretch between them while Picasso crossed from an art of paroxysm to one of exquisitely nuanced analysis. He now worked closely with Georges Braque, whom he met in 1907, in a supreme effort of teamwork. By 1910 they reached the Cubist surface: objects were sunk in a twinkling field of vectors and shadows, solid lapping into transparency, things penetrating and turning away, leaving behind the merest signs for themselves—the bowl of a pipe, the sound hole of a guitar.

This sense of multiple relationships was the core of Cubism's modernity. It was painting's unconscious answer to the theory of relativity or to the principles of narrative that would emerge in the work of James Joyce. The supremacy of the fixed viewpoint, embodied for 500 years in Renaissance perspective, was challenged by the new mode of describing space. As with painting, so with sculpture: Picasso's *Guitar* of 1912, an array of cut and folded metal sheets that opened to let space in, was the first constructed sculpture in the history of art. It abolished the solidity, the continuous surface that had been, until then, the basic narrative of sculpture. From that piece of rusty metal, a 60-year tradition of open-form sculpture was born.

As Picasso moved forward, he found in collage a way of linking Cubism back to the world. Collage, which simply means gluing, brought fragments of modern life—newspaper headlines, printed labels —directly into the painting. Cubism *was* news: it was art's first response to the torrent of change unleashed by startling new technology. Picasso inscribed "Our future is in the air" on several of his Cubist still lifes, and his nickname for Braque was "Wilbur," after Wilbur Wright.

SUN KING: Picasso clowns with Françoise Gilot, the mother of two of his four children

The maestro. The sense of being at the frontiers of history began to evaporate from Picasso's work before the end of World War I. It left behind a residue, however: his virtuosity. From 1918 to 1924 Picasso threw himself with ebullience into the role of the maestro, designing sets and costumes for Diaghilev's Ballets Russes, marrying one of its dancers, and allowing a conventional style of portraiture to alternate with a highly decorative form of Cubism. As solitary virtuoso, Picasso would from now on depend wholly on himself and his feelings. There would be no more collaborations. The corollary was that Picasso gave feeling itself an extraordinary, self-regarding intensity, so that the most vivid images of braggadocio and rage, castration fear and sexual appetite in modern art belong to the Spaniard. The frankness—allied with Picasso's power of metamorphosis, which linked every image together in a ravenous, animalistic vitality—explains his importance to a movement he never joined, Surrealism.

Picasso admired, and tried to embody, the child and the savage, both prodigies of appetite. To feel, to seize, to penetrate, to abandon; these were the verbs of his art, as they were of his cruelly narcissistic relationships with his string of "goddesses or doormats," as he categorized the women in his life. He had seven major liaisons in his life, and was married twice. Some of his more frightening images of women project fears that no French artist would even admit to. One needs colossal self-confidence to expose such insecurities.

On the other side of these appetites lay some of the most haunting images of erotic fulfillment in Western art. They were provided by his affair with Marie-Thérèse Walter, a young woman whom Picasso picked up outside a Paris department store in 1927. He was 45, feeling trapped in his sour marriage to the Russian dancer Olga Koklova; Marie-Thérèse was 17, a placid, ill-educated and wholly compliant person, who had never heard of him or his work. She offered nothing that even Picasso's egotism could interpret as competition.

In the 1930s Picasso turned to exploring visions of the classic Mediterranean. He felt the Greeks in the ground and was the last modern artist to raise them. But his river gods, nymphs, Minotaurs and classical heads are more than the conventional décor of antiquity: they are emblems of autobiography, acts of passionate self-identification.

Picasso's climactic work of the 1930s—*Guernica*, 1937—was inspired by the terrors of the Spanish Civil War. In its way it is a classicizing painting, not only in its friezelike effect, but also in its details. The only modern image in it is a light bulb; but for its presence, the mural would scarcely seem to belong to the world of Heinkel bombers and incendiary bombs. *Guernica*'s power flows from the contrast between its formal system and the terrible vocabulary of pain that Picasso locked into it. To view those hieroglyphs of anguish— the horse, the weeping woman, the screaming head, the clenched hand on the sword—is to witness one of the supreme dramas of the injection of feeling into conventional subject matter that the century has to offer. Picasso could saturate a motif with meaning, until it could hold no more truth. This free passage from feeling into meaning was the essence of his genius.

Picasso was 55 when he finished *Guernica*, and up to his 60th birthday or so he remained an artist of great power. Yet the inventions of necessity slowly gave way to the needs of mere performance. His sculpture retained its intensity almost to the end, but his painting did not. In the last quarter-century of his life, he became the subject of the most sustained exercise in mythmaking ever to be visited on a painter. In the end he was trapped by his own reputation, the idol and prisoner of his court of toadies and dealers. It showed in the work. But do the irresolutions of his old age really matter? Picasso shaped his century when it, and he, were younger, and all its possibilities were open to his ravening eye, in those three decades between 1907 and 1937. If ever a man created his own historical role and was not a pawn of circumstance, it was that Nietzschean monster from Málaga. ∎

MIES VAN DER ROHE

Master simplifier **Ludwig Mies van der Rohe** *found divinity in details*

LOOK UP—AND IN ANY CITY IN THE WORLD, THE building you see, if it is relatively new, and certainly if it is of steel, will bear traces of Ludwig Mies van der Rohe. In a time of confusion, he was a purist. In an era of innovation, he was a disciplinarian. He found office buildings of concrete masonry and transformed them into soaring towers of glass and steel—and the architecture of the world has not been the same since. Mies van der Rohe laid down a fundamental creed of honest structure. He called his work skin-and-bones architecture: "less is more" became his famous creed.

Born in 1886 in Aachen, Germany, Mies received no formal architectural education. But he learned from his father, a master stonemason, to value the distinctive heft and quality of pure materials. One of Mies' first jobs consisted of designing stucco ornaments for a local architect. The experience left him with a lasting disdain for the falseness of decoration and

a lasting relish for the honesty of materials. Mies considered glass, and in 1919 he designed a 20-story, all-glass office tower for Berlin that, although never built, is the admitted prototype of all the great glass-and-metal skyscrapers that followed. He considered concrete, and in 1922 he designed an office building with the continuous strip windows that eventually became a cliché. He considered the room as the basic unit of planning and concluded that it could be dispensed with, proving his contention in his famed German Pavilion for the 1929 International Exposition in Barcelona.

The pavilion in Barcelona, a low-slung one-story jewel brilliantly combining such elegant materials as travertine, Tinian marble, gray glass, onyx and steel, was Mies' first major public building to demonstrate many of his concepts. It immediately established its designer as a master. The following year he replaced Walter Gropius as the director of the seminal architectural school the Dessau Bauhaus, only to

Mies in 1954

1886 Born in Aachen, Germany
1929 Barcelona pavilion completed
1930 Heads Bauhaus
1938 Settles in U.S.
1958 Seagram Building completed
1969 Dies at 83

close up the experimental workshop three years later in protest against Nazi restrictions. In 1938 an invitation to head the school of architecture at the Armour Institute (later renamed the Illinois Institute of Technology) led Mies to Chicago and the full flowering of his genius. In the years that followed, he designed dozens of landmark structures in cities around the world, each distinguished by structural economy, elegant materials and an absolute perfection of detail. "God is in the details," Mies believed.

When no existing furniture quite matched the modern grandeur of his German Pavilion in Barcelona, he designed his own spare, geometrically curved pieces in leather, steel and glass— which became classics. In New York City's majestic Seagram Building, he set the ceiling lights to turn on automatically at a given intensity so that the building would stand against Manhattan's evening skyline, just as he had planned that it should. As one of his friends later said, Mies insisted on simplicity, no matter what it cost.

By the time of his death in 1969, the lessons Mies taught had been so absorbed into architectural thought that the young began to be impatient with him. The Mies formulas, the "less is more," the constant quest to produce something more spare, more pure, became restricting. In the 1970s and 1980s a new wave of architects would move beyond the modernism of Mies to a more vernacular vocabulary, one that paid more attention to entire cityscapes and to the heritage of the past.

Yet Mies' legacy is secure. Along with Frank Lloyd Wright, the arch individualist who pioneered an organic approach to space; Le Corbusier, the daring gambler with expressive form; and Walter Gropius, the dogged exponent of functionalism, Mies shaped the buildings of the 20th century. Whomever future architects may emulate, they must take his work into account. He set down principles and raised standards for construction from which there can be no retreat. ■

LESS IS MORE: Above, the 1958 Seagram Building, a template for the future of the skyscraper; opposite top, the classic furniture Mies designed for the Barcelona pavilion is still in production; below, Mies with the model for an office complex

STIEGLITZ

Photographs were little more than a novelty, until **Alfred Stieglitz** *developed them into a fine art*

A S A YOUNG AMERICAN STUDENT IN BERLIN IN 1883, Alfred Stieglitz paid $7.50 for his first camera. The purchase paid off: in the decades that followed, Stieglitz did more than anyone else to elevate photography from a curiosity to a respectable member of the visual arts. He did so both by example (his pictures were instantly recognized as transcendent) and by precept (he lectured, hectored and lobbied constantly on behalf of the camera). He also established and ran galleries and magazines and took up the task of forcing fellow Americans to look at 20th century art and like it.

Stieglitz's parents were German immigrants grown wealthy in America, allowing him a small private income. He became a professional photographer when there was, strictly speaking, no such job. In the 1890s he emerged as a leading practitioner and theorist of this new technology, noted for many firsts. He was the first to photograph moving objects at night. His imaginative eye made him a pioneer in picturing airplanes, snowstorms, skyscrapers, clouds.

In 1893 Stieglitz entered into a socially acceptable marriage to a woman who

CITYSCAPE: Winter, Fifth Avenue, 1893

had money and little interest in anything else. By then he was embroiled in the controversies that would occupy his career. Flamboyant and talkative, he battled with those who held photography in contempt, using his power as the editor of *Camera Work*, an influential quarterly, as a weapon. He was generous to those who struck him as talented; his protégés included Edward Steichen and Ansel Adams. Meanwhile, at his small gallery on Fifth Avenue, he staged the first one-man shows for both Henri Rousseau and Picasso. He also introduced American gallerygoers to a *Who's Who* of modern artists, including Cézanne, Matisse, Rodin and Georgia O'Keeffe. Stieglitz's affair with O'Keeffe, 23 years his junior, broke up his marriage of 25 years. The happy couple eventually married in 1924, and his portraits of her are among his finest work.

Stieglitz's photographs are deceptively simple; his art called for understatement. He never fell back on gimmickry, never allowed ingenuity or cleverness to distort his steady gaze. If his images seem familiar now, and photography routinely considered a fine art, that is because Stieglitz taught the century to open its eyes. ∎

O'KEEFFE

Fusing sweep and intimacy, **Georgia O'Keeffe**
painted images of hallucinatory intenstity

O'Keeffe in 1976

1888 Born in Sun
Prairie, Wisconsin
1916 Meets Stieglitz,
her future husband
1919 First exhibits
flower paintings
1970 A retrospective
confirms her stature
1986 Dies at 98

ONE OF HER EARLIEST MEMORIES WAS OF "THE brightness of light—light all around." Georgia O'Keeffe spent her life trying to recapture that elemental radiance on paper and canvas. The quest began obscurely on the loam of Sun Prairie, Wisconsin, in 1888 and ended in the desert of Abiquiu, New Mexico, 98 years later. Her career embraced the whole history of modernism in America, and her tenaciously original work—with its sharp focus on clear, emblematic shapes—was a reminder that major art is more apt to spring from deep allegiances to specific experience than from "isms."

The most important influence in her life was Alfred Stieglitz. Their relationship began with his passionate interest in O'Keeffe's drawings; it progressed to his passionate interest in O'Keeffe. The portraits he shot of her constitute the greatest love poem in the history of photography. They also make a statement far beyond the pleasure principle: the nude torso takes on the authority and bulk of sculpture. Before the onlooker, the model is gradually transformed into a work of art.

But O'Keeffe was a painter first, not simply another's model. In 1919 she exhibited the first of the bold flower paintings that inflamed her reputation. When the overripe irises and hollyhocks first appeared, the critics were intrigued, the public scandalized, the artist discomfited. When an interviewer remarked that the blossoms resembled female genitalia, O'Keeffe refused to speak about "such rubbish."

But it was the later artist who won more valid celebrity as the solitary poet of the desert, interpreter of bleached bone and sand and light—light all around. O'Keeffe was an archetypal individualist who knew about styles other than her own, who delved back to the roots of modernism (such as Oriental art) to discover her own direction, found it, and moved on. Above all, her paintings were clean: clean as a bone, clean as a desert rock, clean as a haiku. Her visions were Shaker-plain, lean and resilient, the forms reduced to their simplest and most mysterious denominators, not an ounce of fat left.

Wrinkled and spry, fiercely committed to her work and the solitude of her isolated New Mexico ranch, O'Keeffe lived to be 98. In her long old age she was venerated as an exemplar of feminine independence. "I am not a woman painter," she once declared in a famous statement; her life's work was a sustained manifesto against second-class aesthetic citizenship. Few other artists have fused their inner and outer worlds with such spare grace. Her life and work were one. ∎

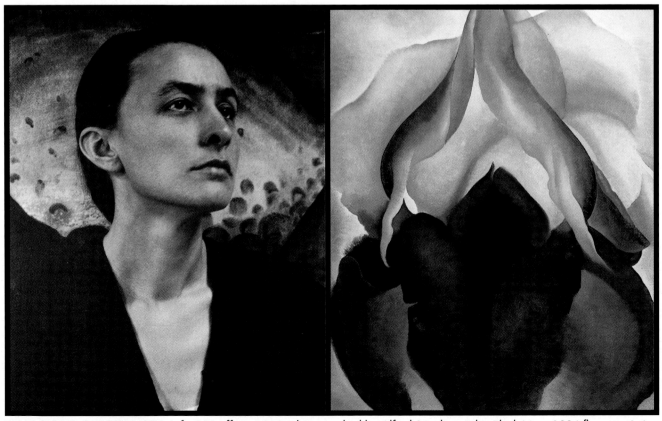

TENACIOUS ORIGINALITY: Left, O'Keeffe in 1918, photographed by Alfred Stieglitz; right, *Black Iris*, a 1926 flower painting

JOYCE

James Joyce *spun the unheard music of the mind into singing word-webs*

TATELY, SLIM, JAMES JOYCE LEFT IRELAND AS A young man of 22 in 1904. Describing his native land as "an old sow who eats her farrow," he resolved to live by "silence, exile and cunning." Yet whether he was living in Paris or Trieste, he kept his unparalleled knowledge of his native land green by subscribing to Dublin newspapers and poring over their gossip. Joyce had set forth his goal in his autobiographical classic, *A Portrait of the Artist as a Young Man:* to articulate the conscience of the Irish people. In realizing that ambition, Joyce achieved a larger one: he revolutionized literature, creating a radical new fiction that caught the pulse of the century by shattering old forms of narrative and diction. In Joyce's hands, character, language and consciousness were fused into a new vocabulary, a shimmering flow of words packed with jokes and puns,

obscure allusions and the mind's unpredictable monologue.

In a life plagued by near blindness and poverty, this erudite and fanciful Irishman, from homes in exile all over Europe, wrote the most influential works of his time: *A Portrait of the Artist,* the best of bildungsromans; *Ulysses,* first considered obscure and obscene but now accepted as the century's masterwork of fiction; and *Finnegans Wake,* his final, most complex novel, an attempt to re-create the language of dreams.

Epiphanies. James Joyce was born in Dublin and educated by Jesuits. Gifted, proud and rebellious, he chafed against the parochial constraints of Irish culture: the dominance of the church; the conformity of the middle class; and, in the arts, the celebration of the past urged by the poet W.B. Yeats and other artists of the Celtic Revival. Joyce had no interest in reviving the old; his urge was to forge the new. After his mother's death in 1903 he began the initial draft of *A Portrait of the Artist* and wrote the first short stories of his collection *Dubliners.* In these probing tales he aimed to create "epiphanies," moments of manifestation that illuminated a character's inner life.

Spurred to his own epiphany by his work, Joyce came to feel that his genius could only flourish away from Ireland. In October 1904 he left Dublin's "little brown bog" and headed to the sun in Trieste. He was accompanied by Nora Barnacle, a young woman from Galway; they had met in June of that year and had fallen in love. The rebellious exiles would not marry until 1931.

Joyce spent 10 years in Trieste, then resettled in Zurich when World War I began. He supported himself by teaching languages; Nora Joyce remembered poverty and small apartments "long on mice, short on kitchen utensils." But Joyce was happy: he worked hard on his new project, *Ulysses,* and drank wine in the same café Lenin used to frequent, though the literary and proletarian revolutionists never met. After the war the couple settled in Paris; a grant from Harriet Weaver, a U.S. expatriate publisher who considered Joyce "an authentic but difficult saint," enabled him to devote himself to his writing.

The wanderings of *Ulysses* proved to be longer, if less arduous, than those of its eponym. Joyce labored on the book

January 29, 1934

for seven years and finished it in Paris in 1921, but could find no publisher. Frank in its treatment of sexuality, the book was mistakenly labeled obscene. Excerpts printed in a literary magazine were promptly suppressed by the U.S. postal authorities. Finally, Sylvia Beach, an American who ran a bookshop in Paris, had *Ulysses* printed by a French press and presented the first copy to Joyce on his 40th birthday. Ten small editions were printed in the following 12 years; the forbidden text became an underground sensation. At last, in 1934, Random House was able to publish the first legal edition of the book in America on the strength of Federal Judge John Munro Woolsey's enlightened decision that it was not obscene.

Everyman's odyssey. Joyce first conceived the tale of Leopold Bloom, the hero of his novel, as a short story, only to discover too many possibilities in it. In his strolls down the beaches of literature, he stumbled on the *Odyssey*, an archaic old bottle but still stout, and decided it was just the thing for his 20th century wine. Joyce set his story on a single day, June 16, 1904, and recast Ulysses as Bloom, a wandering Irish Jew in search of home, wife and son. Writing each of the 18 episodes of the novel in a specific manner, Joyce gave free rein to his inventive wordplay, employing a stream-of-consciousness technique that sketched in words the internal dialogue of the mind. The result was a dazzling work whose breadth, density and variety of form radically enlarged the sense of what fiction could achieve.

Joyce next set himself a greater challenge: to articulate in prose the wordless world of sleep. For 17 years he labored on his "Work in Progress," and when he finally published *Finnegans Wake* in 1939, TIME called it "perhaps the most consciously obscure work that a man of acknowledged genius has produced." Reversing *Ulysses*, it is cast as a long Dublin night filtered through the dreaming mind of the central character, H.C. Earwicker. Stammering, incoherent, thronged with shape-shifting characters and allusions that span language, history and culture, *Finnegans Wake* has the torrential eloquence of the flow of a river to the sea. Joyce called his work an "extravagant excursion into forbidden territory," and this extravagant novel has proved too difficult for most readers.

Joyce was an aesthete who dressed with conservative elegance and favored a walking stick. Frail, with a thin, fine face, he looked as if a strong wind could blow him down. But he was iron-tough: over the years he endured 11 operations on his eyes, all without anesthetics. When World War II came, just after the publication of *Finnegans Wake*, the Joyces moved from Paris to a village near Vichy in unoccupied France. Joyce was unwell with a perforated ulcer. He died of peritonitis in 1941. The artist who forged his art in exile was buried in exile: literary pilgrims seeking the grave of the greatest of Irish writers buy tickets for Zurich. ■

FIRST PERSON

Welcome, O Life! I go … to forge in the smithy of my soul the uncreated conscience of my race.

—A Portrait of the Artist as a Young Man

The grainy sand had gone from under his feet. His boots trod again a damp crackling mast, razorshells, squeaking pebbles, that on the unnumbered pebbles beats, wood sieved by the shipworm, lost Armada. Unwholesome sandflats waiting to suck his treading soles, breathing upward sewage breath. He coasted them, walking warily. A porterbottle stood up, stogged to its waist, in the cakey sand dough. A sentinel: isle of dreadful thirst. Broken hoops on the shore; at the land a maze of dark cunning nets; farther away chalkscrawled backdoors and on the higher beach a dryingline with two crucified shirts … He turned his face over a shoulder, rere regardant. Moving through the air high spars of a threemaster, her sails brailed up on the crosstrees, homing, upstream, silently moving, a silent ship.

—Ulysses

—History, Stephen said, is a nightmare from which I am trying to awake.

—Ulysses

*Ladies and gents, you are here assembled
To hear why earth and heaven trembled
Because of the black and sinister arts
Of an Irish writer in foreign parts …*

*But I owe a duty to Ireland:
I hold her honor in my hand,
This lovely land that always sent
Her writers and artists to banishment
And in a spirit of Irish fun
Betrayed her leaders, one by one.*

—"Gas from a Burner"

WOOLF

Virginia Woolf shattered conventions of fiction and gender but lost her long struggle for sanity

O N THAT MORNING IN MARCH 1941, THE GREAT British novelist sat down at her writing desk as usual. But instead of revising her new novel, she wrote a note to her sister Vanessa saying "Farewell to the world." She also wrote a note to her husband Leonard Woolf, editor of the *Political Quarterly.* Then she took a walking stick and went for her favorite tramp across the rolling Sussex Downs to the River Ouse. What passed in her stream of consciousness beside the water no one else knew. But when her husband, following her footprints across the fields, rushed up in panic, only her stick was lying on the bank. Virginia Woolf was a suicide at 59.

Woolf was a delicate child who suffered her first breakdowns after her parents' deaths. Her mother Julia died when she was only 13; her father Sir Leslie Stephen, an eminent man of letters, followed nine years later. Two years before World War I, Virginia Stephen married Leonard Sidney Woolf, a liberal journalist and literary critic. Their tall house in Bloomsbury soon became the nucleus of England's smartest artistic

April 12, 1937

1882 Born in London
1895 Death of her mother; Virginia is 13
1912 Marries L. Woolf
1915 *The Voyage Out*
1925 *Mrs. Dalloway*
1929 *A Room of One's Own*
1941 Suicide at 59

set, the Bloomsbury group, which included critic Clive Bell, novelist E.M. Forster, biographer Lytton Strachey and economist John Maynard Keynes. The Woolfs housed their Hogarth Press under the same roof. There, in an "immense, half-subterranean room, piled with books, parcels, packets of unbound volumes," Virginia Woolf wrote.

Her first novel, the comparatively conventional and autobiographical *The Voyage Out*, appeared in 1915. Those that followed—including *Jacob's Room* (1922), *Mrs. Dalloway* (1925) and *To the Lighthouse* (1927)—were more impressionistic and formally inventive, as Woolf grappled to express "the arrows of sensation striking strangely through the envelope of personality which shelters us so conveniently from our fellows."

Woolf's critical essays were more direct, denouncing the materialism of the times and confronting issues of gender relations. In a classic essay she stated the requisite of modern women who want independence: "500 [pounds] a year and a room of one's own." She entered into a lesbian relationship with the writer Vita Sackville-West, believing that "it is fatal to be a man or woman pure and simple; one must be woman-manly or man-womanly."

Woolf's sheltering envelope of personality was paper-thin—just how thin was revealed only with the publication of Leonard's autobiography, beginning in 1960. Perhaps, as she stood beside the Ouse, she remembered the suicide of Septimus Smith from *Mrs. Dalloway:* "Human nature ... was on him—the repulsive brute with the blood-red nostrils ... The whole world was clamoring: kill yourself, kill yourself ..." ∎

FIRST PERSON

"It would have been impossible, completely and entirely, for any woman to have written the plays of Shakespeare in the age of Shakespeare. Let me imagine ... what would have happened had Shakespeare had a wonderfully gifted sister, called Judith ... Shakespeare ... [went] to seek his fortune in London ... Very soon he got work in the theater, became a successful actor, and lived at the hub of the universe, meeting everybody, knowing everybody, practising his art on the boards, exercising his wits in the streets, and even getting access to the palace of the queen. Meanwhile his extraordinarily gifted sister ... remained at home ... She was not sent to school ... She picked up a book now and then ... But then her parents came in and told her to mend the stockings or mind the stew and not moon about with books and papers."

—A Room of One's Own, 1929

SHAW

First came Man. Then Superman. Then **George Bernard Shaw**

W HEN GEORGE BERNARD SHAW DIED AT 95, he had become such a fixture in the public mind it seemed that Methuselah had passed away. Shaw was a great man of the 20th century, but he was also a great man of the 19th century. Truth to tell, he was also something of a great man of the 18th century, for he was always closer in spirit to Voltaire and Swift than to Marx and Tennyson. When he died, Shaw was as sweet and prim as any character out of Oliver Goldsmith. Inside this prosaic moral crust, his unique stage personality remained sharp, sagacious and dazzling; the delightful vanity of his genius kept the limelight till the last.

For some 65 years—from his days as a critic in the London newspapers in the 1880s through his long years of success as the most scintillating of playwrights, up to his final role as a crotchety prophet—Shaw harangued the world with his gospel of sanity, socialism and vegetarianism. His weapons were eloquent attack, irony, laughter, bounce, the intrigue of words and a wit that could cut everything to ribbons. In a prose so clear, fast and pure that it was like a charmer's music to the snake, Shaw hypnotized his audience. This immigrant Irishman knew his Englishman, as the stinging fly loves the thick hide it chooses as a safe home for its eggs.

Shaw had come to England as a young man, eager to escape Irish melancholy and cynicism. But the shocking Lon-

don of the 1870s was too much for the genteel and moral Irish Protestant, who had worked as an office clerk. He joined the Fabian Society, Britain's foremost group of socialists, and became one of its leaders. He wrote novels, but they failed; he was nearly 40 before he began to earn a decent living writing reviews of books and music. In 1895 he became the drama critic for the *Saturday Review,* and for 3½ years he attacked convention in the theater. He had already begun to write for the stage himself: his gift for satirical comedy first appeared fully in *Arms and the Man* (1894), a send-up of the romanticizing of war.

Shaw had a penetrating comic genius. His plays are alive with the love of ideas, and his prose is fresh with a vivid effrontery that often travels away from the point, like the words of an incurable but dazzling talker who is intoxicated by his own flow. In such classics as *Candida, Major Barbara* and *Pygmalion,* the agnostic and rationalistic Shaw skewered hypocrisy, punctured vanity, argued for the liberation of minds from cant and outworn creeds. In such plays as *Man and Superman* (1905) and the epic *Back to Methuselah* (1921), he put forth his own creed, a belief in a sort of evolutionary "Life Force" that perfects itself as man progresses ever upward.

For a time, after the disillusionment of World War I, Shaw admired Mussolini, even exalted Stalin; he thought he saw the Life Force in them. But he outgrew this infatuation, as, in his lively, lingering old age, he outgrew all his contemporaries. At the end, only one figure remained: the ever quotable, often petulant, always contrarian figure known as "G.B.S." His great age was his last great turn, which could hardly conceal an appalling loneliness: Charlotte, his wife of 45 years, died in 1943.

Shaw's art lay in the transmuting of disruptive dialogue into a kind of classical, Mozartean music. His plays date most seriously when they are debates, yet their verbal wit is perennially irresistible. There is no writer who so conspicuously and largely holds the whole social and political and intellectual life of a long, rich period of heresy and revolt in his hands. He was the indefatigable showman at the door for more than half a century, and his art still lives where it matters most; in theaters around the world, the stage lights never set on the Shavian empire. ∎

December 24, 1923

1856 Born in Dublin
1876 Leaves Ireland for London
1894 *Arms and the Man*
1905 *Man and Superman*
1913 *Pygmalion*
1950 Dies at 94

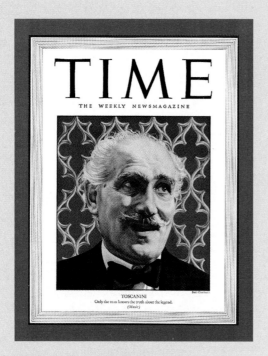

APRIL 26, 1948 Legendary conductor Arturo Toscanini enjoyed a lengthy career in both Europe and America. A specialist in opera, he often conducted from memory.

OCTOBER 29, 1956 Commanding an acting ability rarely seen on the operatic stage, Maria Callas was a reigning soprano from the early 1950s until her last *Tosca* in 1965.

APRIL 16, 1965 Following his defection from the Soviet Union in 1961, Rudolf Nureyev joined England's Royal Ballet and thrilled audiences with new partner Margot Fonteyn.

MAY 5, 1986 Russian piano virtuoso Vladimir Horowitz married Toscanini's daughter in 1933 and settled in the U.S. He finally returned to play in his native land in 1986.

OLIVIER

Shape shifter and scene stealer, **Laurence Olivier** *bestrode the world of acting like a colossus*

WHEN THE NEW BARON BRIGHTON gave his maiden speech to the House of Lords in 1971, the subject was not politics. "I believe in the theater," said the baron. "I believe in it as the first glamorizer of thought." That was the theater to Laurence Olivier, and that was Olivier to all who fell under the glamorous spell he wove. More immediately and lastingly than any other modern actor, Olivier picked words off the playscript page, flung them passionately into the dark and secured them in the minds of theatergoers. Director, producer, prime mover of Britain's National Theatre, Hollywood star and embodier of the most vital Shakespearean heroes, Olivier at his death in 1989 held undisputed claim to yet another title: the 20th century's most definitive man of the theater.

Like the century he almost spanned, Olivier displayed turbulent energy and embraced awesome excess; his genius and his folly fed each other. He was the son of a fifth-generation Anglican clergyman, yet he found his soul upon the wicked stage. The finest classical actor of his time, he attained his first fame as a West End matinee idol, and his second as a Hollywood dreamboat in *Wuthering Heights* (1939) and *Rebecca* (1940). Though he pored over scripts like a scholar, he was an irrepressibly physical stage performer, scaling balconies and executing dizzying falls. Like many men, Olivier housed a congeries of contradictions; uniquely, he transformed them into living art.

At the apex of his stage career, in the mid-1940s, Olivier could spread out the banquet of those contradictions in a single evening. The curtain would fall on his Oedipus, with its searing scream of self-revelation; after intermission he would mince on as Mr. Puff, the giddy paragraphist of Sheridan's *The Critic*. There was no Method to Olivier's masquerades: he worked from the outside in, often finding character in caricature, refusing only to err on the side of restraint. His most faithful theatrical aid was the makeup kit. A Proteus of the footlights, he bent, folded, spindled, mutilated himself to fit his role.

Olivier in this period often appeared with Vivien Leigh, Hollywood's Scarlett O'Hara in *Gone With the Wind;* they had fallen in love as co-stars of the 1937 film *Fire over England,* and married in 1940. By the mid-'50s this beautiful actress was tobogganing into mental illness. Olivier found a new challenge in the form of Archie Rice, the main character of John Osborne's *The Entertainer* (1957), in which he played a seedy music-hall comic in a tantalizing blend of parody and autobiography.

Late in his life Olivier might have retired on his laurels: a knighthood in 1946, the life peerage in 1970, the thanks of several nations and generations. But in 1974 he was struck with a crippling degeneration of skin and muscle tissue. He could no longer perform onstage eight times a week, but he could not stop working. Dozens of robust movie cartoons followed: Olivier as a mogul (*The Betsy*), a wily old Jew (*The Boys from Brazil*) a scheming Nazi (*Marathon Man*). In 1982 he answered a last call from Shakespeare, playing King Lear for TV, in a magnificent portrayal that left a record of his transcendence for ages to come. The greatest actor of the century knew how to leave them begging for more. ∎

April 8, 1946

1907 Born in Dorking, Surrey, England
1940 Marries Vivien Leigh; divorced 1960
1946 Stars and directs movie triumph *HenryV*
1963 First director of U.K.'s National Theatre
1989 Dies at 82

PROTEAN PLAYER: Olivier created roles from the outside in: from left, as Hamlet, 1948; as Othello, 1964; as King Lear, 1982

CHAPLIN

Tramping his way to immortality,

Charlie Chaplin *conquered time*

CRITIC EDMUND WILSON ONCE RHETORICALLY inquired, "Have we [Americans] ever turned out anything that was comparable artistically to the best German or Russian films?" Few disagreed with his answer: "I can think of nothing except Charlie Chaplin, who is his own producer and produces simply himself." But Chaplin's self was not so simple. It was first introduced to America as a vaudeville clown in 1910, and the country did not respond warmly. Charlie's comic flair failed to ignite enthusiasm until the epochal one-reeler in which he tried on Fatty Arbuckle's pants and Chester Conklin's jacket. In that moment the Tramp was born, and with him a long parabola of triumph and humiliation. The arc described a career bred of deprivation and encompassed nearly every cinematic skill, from acting, producing and directing to the writing of scenarios and scores, gags and tragedies. The Tramp has been called the most popular comic figure of the 20th century; with this breakthrough persona, Chaplin brought elements of pathos and comedy together for the first time on the screen and created enduring film classics whose appeal transcends age, geography, culture—and time.

A Tramp is born. Charles Spencer Chaplin had risen from the darkest of London slums. His father was an alcoholic; his mother sewed blouses for 1½ pence each. Charlie's great character was an echo of that Dickensian experience, a waif in the tradition of Oliver Twist and David Copperfield. Comedy derives from the Greek *komos*, a dance. And indeed, as the Tramp capered about with his unique sleight of foot, he created a choreography of the human condition. In classics like *The Gold Rush* (1925), *Modern Times* (1936) and *The Great Dictator* (1940), objects spoke out as never before: bread rolls became ballet slippers, a boot was transformed into a feast, a torn newspaper enjoyed a new career as a lace tablecloth. Such lyric moments lifted Chaplin into the pantheon of stars. He became the friend of kings and critics. Einstein sought him out; Churchill praised him. George Bernard Shaw called him "the one genius created by the cinema."

Chaplin's fame paralleled the explosive growth of Hollywood movies in the first decades of the century. His celebrity and his salary seemed to double every year: in 1913 he began making one-reel comedies for pioneering Hollywood producer Mack Sennet. He then signed with the Essanay studio in 1915 at 10 times his Sennet salary. In 1916 he was hired by the Mutual studio, again with a large salary increase, and by 1918 he had built his own studio and signed a $1 million contract with First National Films to produce eight motion pictures. He kept climbing: in 1923 he joined with three other Hollywood greats—Mary Pickford, Douglas Fairbanks Sr. and D.W. Griffith—to form the United Artists Corp., which produced the feature-length classics starring the Tramp.

A king in exile. But as Charles Lindbergh was also to learn, the celebrity-making machines of the 20th century followed predictable paths: a figure's rise to the heights was often followed by an evening of the Long Knives. For Chaplin, night came early and stayed late. He became embroiled in a series of affairs. He married and divorced two teenagers and earned a reputation as Hollywood's outstanding satyr. His dalliances shocked the nation and nearly ruined his career. But he always managed to rescue himself with new apologies and fresh performances.

In 1940 he was attacked by right-wingers for his satire of Adolf Hitler in *The Great Dictator*. Again he was rescued, this time by history. But after the war he could no longer be saved from his enemies. His leftist sentiments and continual womanizing were attacked in the press and in Congress. Chaplin had married his fourth wife, Oona—the daughter of Eugene O'Neill—in 1943 when he was 54 and she was 18. They were vacationing abroad in 1952 when he learned that he would be

TIME
The Weekly News-Magazine

July 6, 1925

1889 Born in London
1913 Hired by Mack Sennet to make movies
1923 Co-founds United Artists Corp.
1925 *The Gold Rush*
1936 *Modern Times*
1952 Exiled from U.S.
1977 Died at 88

detained if they re-entered the U.S. His new film, *Limelight*, was boycotted on the West Coast; the *Saturday Evening Post* announced that Charlie was a "pink Pierrot." He responded with *A King in New York* (1957), a humorless satire on America's obsession with political loyalty. By the time he published his autobiography in 1964, much of the anger and pain had subsided. But so had the inspiration.

Fadeout. Chaplin retired quietly to Switzerland, surrounded by his wife and their eight children, awaiting signs of nonbelligerence from old enemies. They came at last in 1972, when Hollywood finally recalled that the "disloyal" clown had paid millions in taxes, helped found United Artists and provided the aesthetic foundation for every film comedian since 1920. The evidence was an Academy Award for the "incalculable effect he has had in making motion pictures the art form of this century." When he received the Oscar, it was plain to see that the strange trick of celluloid relativity had done its work: the once wiry actor had become a fleshy, white-haired grandfather, but the little Tramp on the screen—now more than 50 years old—retained his perpetual youth and comic energy. Chaplin died five years later.

Chaplin was a poet of beginnings, not endings. It is the classic fadeout of the great Tramp films that stays longest in the mind's screen: the crumpled harlequin, twitching his shoulders, setting his head forward and skipping hopefully off on the unimproved road to Better Times. Chaplin may have encountered sadness along the road, but he will be remembered longest for his jaunty, indomitable celebration of life. ∎

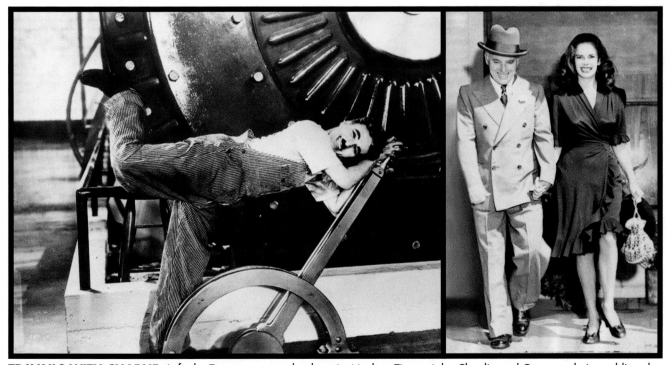

TRAVAILS WITH CHARLIE: Left, the Tramp versus technology in *Modern Times;* right, Chaplin and Oona on their wedding day

BALANCHINE

The prismatic genius of **George Balanchine** *refracted music into dance*

IS ENTHUSIASMS INCLUDED THE PAINTINGS of Braque, the writings of Pushkin, the politics of Eisenhower and the comedy of Jack Benny. But there was never any doubt about George Balanchine's greatest love. "I am a dancer," he once said, "body, soul and brain." But he was much more than that: he was the century's greatest choreographer, the master who brilliantly synthesized ballet's elegant classical heritage with the explosive athletic energy of modern dance and the show-biz turns of jazz and tap. His pared-down, neoclassical style liberated ballet from its dependence on theatrical trappings and gave primacy to the art's basic impulse: the beauty of the body in motion. A co-founder of the New York City Ballet, America's leading company, the Russian-born Balanchine wholeheartedly embraced all things American: clothes, attitudes and especially the American bodies that he idealized in his choreography.

In such revolutionary works as *Concerto Barocco* (1941) and *The Four Temperaments* (1946), Balanchine reveled in the joy of pure movement, unencumbered by sets, costumes or plot. "*Swan Lake* is a bore," he declared. For Balanchine, dance was really about motion, not tutus; the choreographer's intent, he felt, should be made explicit without panoply or program notes. Just as his company stressed dances and not stars, it was music, not pageantry, that catalyzed Balanchine's art. A conservatory-trained pianist who might have had a concert career, he possessed an understanding of musical tempo and structure that became fundamental to his work. Watching him rehearse, Martha Graham once observed, "It's like watching light pass through a prism. The music passes through him, and in the same natural yet marvelous way that a prism refracts light, he refracts music into dance."

Balanchine's musical acumen paid off, spectacularly, in an almost lifelong partnership with composer Igor Stravinsky, resulting in such landmarks as *Apollo* (1928), *Orpheus* (1948) and *Agon* (1957), in which the two great Russians worked side by side to create both score and choreography. For the City Ballet's 1972 Stravinsky Festival, following the composer's death, Balanchine choreographed a brilliant set of master-

SHOW AND TELL: Rehearsing with Arthur Mitchell; Balanchine's School of American Ballet has trained generations of U.S. dancers

January 25, 1954

1904 Born in St. Petersburg, Russia
1925 Joins Diaghilev's Ballets Russes
1933 Comes to U.S. to found a school
1948 Co-founds the New York City Ballet
1983 Dies at 79

works, including *Stravinsky Violin Concerto, Symphony in Three Movements* and *Duo Concertant.*

Born Georgi Melitonovich Balanchivadze in St. Petersburg, the son of a composer, young George got into ballet by accident. Accompanying his sister to a tryout at the Imperial School of Ballet, he found himself accepted after he walked across the floor in front of the judges, who were impressed by the nine-year-old's strength, posture and aquiline good looks. By his mid-teens he was choreographing. After leaving Russia in 1924, he made his way to Paris and at 21 became ballet master of Diaghilev's famed Ballets Russes.

In 1933 Balanchine formed his own company. One thunderstruck member of the audience was a young American balletomane named Lincoln Kirstein, an heir to a department-store fortune who dreamed of firmly establishing dance in the U.S. He and Balanchine founded the School of American Ballet in 1934; within six months, Balanchine created the ensemble masterpiece, *Serenade,* that exemplified his artistic philosophy: a plotless, continuously flowing tapestry of movement in which each dancer moves in and out of the ensemble to play an individual role.

Balanchine branched out to Broadway and Hollywood, racking up an impressive string of hits, including *On Your Toes* (1936), the first Broadway musical to integrate dance sequences with the plot. In 1948 Balanchine and Kirstein's company, then called Ballet Society, became the New York City Ballet. The new company grew to occupy a large home theater at Lincoln Center, tour the world and employ more than 100 dancers, but it remained what it was at the beginning: an instrument of one man's unique artistic vision.

A fast worker, Balanchine rarely began to choreograph a new piece until about three weeks before its premier. Unconcerned with wealth, he made money and spent it freely. Called "Mr. B." by the dancers who idolized him, Balanchine was married five times (once by common law), each time to a beautiful ballerina he had made famous: Tamara Geva, Alexandra Danilova, Vera Zorina, Maria Tallchief and Tanaquil LeClerq. He remained on good terms with them all.

Though Balanchine knew his worth, he refused to play the genius: he stressed that running a company and creating the ballets for its repertory demanded not only inspiration but also training, craftsmanship, endurance. He referred to himself as a "carpenter" of dances, and jokingly called the hardworking, highly disciplined women of his corps "racehorses." He loved women, and for him dance was feminine. "Ballet," he once said, "is the female thing. It is woman." The Balanchine ballerina was distinctive: long-legged, small-boned and high-breasted, with a small head and a strong back.

Though Balanchine forged his own unique neoclassical style, he experimented with and drew from all types of dance. He staged the Russian classics and a host of novelty pieces, and tried his hand at everything from avant-garde abstractions to Japanese court dance. His great legacy is the wealth of dances he left behind, dances that will serve as staples of the ballet repertory far into the future. In the breadth of his achievement, he invites comparison with the artist whose *Midsummer Night's Dream* he set dancing: George Balanchine is the Shakespeare of ballet. ∎

SERENADE, 1934 In his first U.S. work, Balanchine set a Tchaikovsky standard in neoclassical style.

AGON, 1957 This abstract masterpiece was set to an atonal score by longtime friend Igor Stravinsky.

UNION JACK, 1974 With fame came funds for décor—and a large theater to fill—so "Mr. B." staged spectaculars like *Union Jack* and *Vienna Waltzes.*

STRAVINSKY

Bonding modern discord to the harmonies of the past, **Igor Stravinsky** *scored the century*

TAKING THE MEASURE OF THE 27-YEAR-OLD IGOR Stravinsky, the ballet impresario Sergei Diaghilev said, "Mark him well. He is a man on the eve of celebrity." When celebrity came, Stravinsky had a long day of it: a stormy dawn of controversy, a high blaze of creative influence, a waning afternoon of waspish polemics. His death in 1971 ended six decades of dominance in which he shaped the musical thought of generations to come. It was the end, too, of what conductor Colin Davis called "a line of music that began with the early church music of the 14th century." For the 20th century, Stravinsky was the vital link with the music of both the future and the past.

The young Stravinsky's artistic calling card was a bombshell: *The Rite of Spring*, a sophisticated evocation of primitive myths and energies completed in 1913. Conductor Pierre Monteux recalled, when he first heard Stravinsky play it on the piano, "I was convinced that he was raving mad." Later, at the work's Paris premiere, many in the audience agreed: they booed, tussled and pelted the stage with programs.

Polytonal, polymodal, polyrhythmic, the *Rite* did not so much reject conventional harmony—which the 12-tone serialism of Stravinsky's contemporary, Arnold Schoenberg, did—as it brought contrasting tonalities crashing dangerously together. Its unexpected clustered stresses and pile-driving climaxes raised rhythm to a new pre-eminence. Like Joyce's *Ulysses* and Picasso's *Les Demoiselles d'Avignon*, it was a work that announced a new consciousness.

Stravinsky's earlier work had been marked by the colorful nationalistic flavor of his native Russian tradition. The son of famed St. Petersburg basso Feodor Stravinsky, he became a star pupil of Rimsky-Korsakov's, and his first orchestral fantasy, *Fireworks*, was written in 1908 as a wedding present for the composer's daughter. *Fireworks* dazzled Diaghilev, who commissioned Stravinsky to write a ballet. The result: *The Firebird* (1910), followed a year later by the even more brilliant *Petrouchka*, in which the solo piano projected a Pierrot-like puppet, portrayed onstage by the great Nijinsky. These works became popular favorites, identified Stravinsky with the dance and led to later collaborations with George Balanchine.

Stravinsky was never content to imitate himself: in the years following *The Rite*, works like *Oedipus Rex* (1927) and *Apollon Musagètes* (1928) eloquently confirmed his new allegiance to the Apollonian ideal of lucidity and order. He embraced the tonalities and modal styles of the past, yet always made them distinctively his own. It was not until 1953, two years after Schoenberg's death, that Stravinsky employed serialism in such classics as *Agon* (1957) and *Movements* (1960), for piano and orchestra.

Despite Stravinsky's fragile, birdlike appearance, he had indomitable physical zest. The features that had been caricatured by Cocteau and Picasso—bull-fiddle nose, guitar-like ears, pince-nez, natty mustache—remained mobile and alert in his later years. Characteristically, he planned his last rites. After his death in California, his body was flown to Venice for burial, where his *Requiem Canticles* (1966) was sung at a final service in a centuries-old church. The composer who had shocked the world with the Dionysian energy of his youth came to rest where his music had taken him: in the serene Apollonian sanctuary of the past. ∎

July 26, 1948

1882 Born near St. Petersburg, Russia
1910 *The Firebird*
1911 *Petrouchka*
1913 Riot at debut of *The Rite of Spring*
1957 *Agon*
1971 Dies at 89 and is buried in Venice

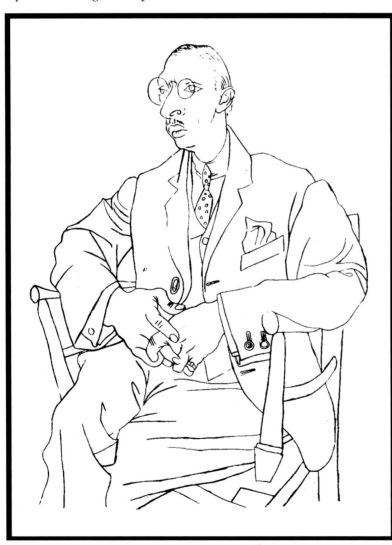

PORTRAIT OF THE ARTIST: A Picasso drawing of Stravinksy, circa 1920

JULY 25, 1938 Master conductor as well as master composer, Germany's Richard Strauss began his career in the 1880s, but his great operas date from the early 20th century.

JULY 20, 1942 Fancifully portrayed in a fireman's helmet, Russia's Dmitri Shostakovich finally satisfied Stalin's demand for patriotism in music with his *Leningrad Symphony* (1941).

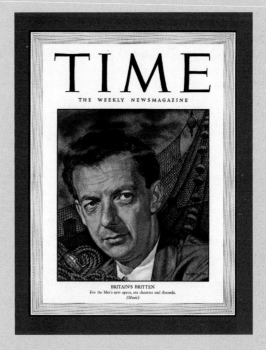

NOVEMBER 19, 1945 Russia's Sergei Prokofiev enhanced the modern repertoire with such classics as the suite *Peter and the Wolf* (1936) and the ballet *Romeo and Juliet* (1935).

FEBRUARY 16, 1948 Only a few composers created lasting operas in the modern idiom; England's Benjamin Britten scored with *Peter Grimes* (1945) and *Billy Budd* (1951).

ARMSTRONG

If you've got to ask what jazz is, you must not have heard **Louis Armstrong**

GABRIEL HIMSELF MIGHT HAVE envied his heaven-splitting, jubilant sound. His tone could be loud and lowdown. It could murmur suggestively or soar upward with an almost heraldic clarity. It had a sheer physical strength that amazed his rivals: he threw out high Cs like a Met soprano. And there was always a teasing syncopation and hint of heartbreak. Louis Armstrong was a remarkable technician of the trumpet who went on to even wider fame as a singer. The fact that his voice sounded like a wheelbarrow crunching its way up a gravel driveway made no difference. Legends don't need voices.

Armstrong's career spanned the life of jazz. He emerged during its early days, became the first big star to shine in front of a combo. He paved the road on which virtually every major jazzman would walk to fame thereafter. But he did have the luck to be born in the right place at the right time: in the bubbling melting pot of turn-of-the-century New Orleans, where a disreputable mix of musical influences—African, Spanish, French, Baptist—was shaping a unique new idiom. Around 1900, in the honky-tonks of New Orleans, it became jazz.

Armstrong was born near New Orleans' red-light district on July 4, 1900. Early on, his father decamped with another woman; his mother was left on her own. At five Armstrong discovered music; at 12 he was singing tenor in a strolling boys' quartet. An adolescent prank got him shipped off to the Colored Waifs' Home for Boys, where he took up the cornet. After a year, Armstrong, 14, got out and organized his own

February 21, 1949

1900 Born in New Orleans
1914 Leads his own band, on cornet
1922 His horn playing dazzles Chicago
1932 First trip abroad: he conquers U.K.
1971 Dies in New York City

band, playing lead cornet. Listening to and learning from other jazz artists, he worked on excursion boats up and down the Mississippi River in the early '20s, then was hired to join the band of his idol, trumpeter Joe Oliver. His debut with Oliver in Chicago in 1922 was sensational. Critics and audiences both fell before his horn like the walls of Jericho. Recording companies signed him up, and his best cuts—*Ain't Misbehavin', Basin Street Blues, Muskrat Ramble*—became classics. "Ain't nobody played nothing like it since," he said in 1970. "And can't nobody play nothing like it now." Legend says Armstrong invented scat singing in 1926: while recording a song, he dropped the sheet music and began ad-libbing nonsense syllables.

For more than five decades, "Satchmo" (a contraction of a boyhood nickname, "Satchel Mouth") led small combos and large bands, starred in movies, made 2,000 recordings and traveled frequently throughout the world; in his incarnation as "Ambassador Satch" he brought jazz to a huge international audience. A natural, swinging ebullience enlivened both his music and his persona. Asked to define jazz, he knew what to say: "Man, when you got to ask what it is, you'll never get to know." He survived adulation and wealth without losing his head, living in a modest house in a rundown neighborhood of New York City, "to be with my people." His death from a heart attack in 1971 was mourned around the globe, for his appeal crossed all barriers of language, race and culture. "A note's a note in any language," he used to say. "And if you hit it—beautiful!" Louis hit it. ∎

BLOWHARD: Left, Armstrong with his best small combo, the Hot Five, in the '20s; right, in the 1949 movie *A Song Is Born*

GERSHWIN

Strike up the band! From flappers to longhairs, everyone loved the fascinating rhythms of **George Gershwin**

WHEN HIS RUSSIAN IMMIGRANT parents moved from Brooklyn to Manhattan's overcrowded Jewish neighborhood on the Lower East Side, George Gershwin had just been born. The earliest sounds he heard were the clank of dishes in his father's restaurant, the clatter of the Second Avenue El, the confusion and bustle of the tenements. At 10, the aggressive, wild-haired little boy was the best roller skater on the block. Even then he would spend his pennies in a Grand Street arcade listening to a mechanical piano hammer out Rubinstein's *Melody in F.*

George was not much older when his mother bought a worn upright piano, chiefly to keep up with a relative who owned one. Older brother Ira was her first choice to play it. But George showed more musical zeal, and soon he was the pianist in the Gershwin family. By his death at the tragically young age of 38, the prodigy from the streets would

July 20, 1925

1898 Born in Brooklyn, New York
1920 His first hit song is *Swanee*
1924 *Rhapsody in Blue* is a triumph
1935 *Porgy and Bess* fails in its premiere
1937 Dies at 38

create a new kind of all-American, mixed-marriage sound, a hybrid that leavened "serious" music with the jangling energy of ragtime and jazz.

Gershwin was a child of Tin Pan Alley, the hustling New York City world of songwriters and publishers. At 16, he left school to plug songs for Jerome Remick & Sons, at $15 a week. He went into vaudeville as an accompanist, and soon was writing such songs as *You-oo Just You* and *There's More to a Kiss than the XXX.* He was only 20 when he wrote his first musical comedy, *La La Lucille.* The same year he scored his first success with *Swanee*, a huge hit for Al Jolson. He teamed up with Ira, who would develop into a first-rate lyricist: their first Broadway hit was 1924's *Lady, Be Good.* Just as the Beatles would later seem to distill the spirit of the '60s into their music, Gershwin bottled the headlong tempo and spritzy ebullience of the Prohibition-era '20s in such songs as *Fascinating Rhythm, Strike Up the Band* and *I Got Rhythm.* He became a rich man, filled his penthouse with expensive furniture, African sculpture, a fine collection of French modern paintings.

But Gershwin's ambitions transcended wealth and fame. He wanted to do serious work, and when he set his mind to something, he did it. Gershwin took three weeks away from his regular writing and produced 1924's *Rhapsody in Blue*, a 15-minute "jazz concerto" for Paul Whiteman's orchestra. It was an instantaneous success. Thereafter Gershwin wrote for two audiences. Concert audiences applauded *Concerto in F* for piano and orchestra (1925) and *Three Preludes for Piano* (1926) and loved the dazzling harmonies and crisp, slangy rhythms of his *An American in Paris* (1928). Meanwhile, Broadway audiences were dazzled by the classic musical comedies *Funny Face* (1927), *Strike Up the Band* (1930) and *Girl Crazy* (1930).

Having conquered the concert stage, Gershwin moved on to the ambitious *Porgy and Bess*, a "folk opera" based on black characters in Charleston, South Carolina, adapted from DuBose Heyward's novel. A failure on its first production in 1935, the work has since become a classic; it contains some of Gershwin's finest songs: the plangent *My Man's Gone Now*, the exuberant *I Got Plenty o' Nuttin'*, the raffish *It Ain't Necessarily So.* Its failure seemed a momentary setback in Gershwin's rocket-like ascent—until his life was cut short by an undiagnosed brain tumor at age 38.

In its 1937 obituary of Gershwin, TIME said, "If songs like *Somebody Loves Me, I Got Rhythm, Embraceable You, Let's Call the Whole Thing Off* were ephemeral, Gershwin at least had the satisfaction of hearing a nation sing them." Fifty-nine years after those words were written, those four songs are widely played, instantly recognizable classics. As the Tin Pan Alley crowd might have said, We should all be so ephemeral. ■

PRESLEY

Have you heard the news? If there's good rockin' tonight—you can thank **Elvis Presley**

Presley in 1958

1935 Born in Tupelo, Mississippi
1955 Cuts his first singles at Sun Studios
1958 Serves in Army
1968 Makes a "comeback" on TV special
1970s Plays Las Vegas
1977 Dies at 42

As the legend goes, Elvis Presley had only a year's passing familiarity with a recording studio when he cut his classic record in the winter of 1955. He had wandered into Sun Records in Memphis, Tennessee, two summers before, plunked down $4 to sing some tunes for his mom for a birthday present. Sun boss Sam Phillips had been looking for a "black sound inside a white boy" to make a national mark. Phillips called the 18-year-old truck driver back into the studio—after a year. That was the last time things would go slowly for Elvis Presley.

A song that came out of those first sessions, *That's All Right, Mama*, became a substantial local hit. When the next four singles did the same, Presley connected with a deadeye promoter named Colonel Tom Parker, who landed him a contract with RCA. In the winter of 1956 Elvis Presley released *Heartbreak Hotel* and sent American popular culture into a collective delirium. The rock-'n'-roll era had begun.

Time passed to a heavy back beat. In a giddy blur, Presley went on the *Ed Sullivan Show*, intimidated the adults of America and drove their kids into a frenzy. Parents said Elvis was suggestive, lewd, a greaser. To kids that was just the point.

Elvis used his music as an open invitation to release, and kids took him up on it. The lowered lids, the curling lip, the musky voice, the sensuous gyrations drove the girls crazy and inspired scores of imitators. He got drafted into the Army, served a tour of duty in Germany, sold millions of records. He went to Hollywood, appeared in 33 movies, sold millions of records. He played Vegas, married Priscilla Beaulieu, filled amphitheaters, got divorced. And he kept selling records, well over 500 million in all.

But the music got slicker, turned from rock toward sanctimonious spirituals and sound-track ditties from his string of brain-rotting movies. Elvis seemed increasingly bored with his own music and more absorbed in the lavish trappings of his celebrity. Only the pace remained the same. Elvis hewed to the rockers' code: live fast and die young—because it's better to burn out than fade away. At age 42, the overweight, paranoid drug abuser was found dead in the bathroom of his gaudy Memphis mansion, Graceland. Elvis Aron Presley, who had lived the legend, died right on schedule. But the eternally bright sound of those Sun sessions will not fade away. ■

THE BEATLES

With **John, Paul, George & Ringo,** *a splendid time was guaranteed for all*

AT THE HEIGHT OF THEIR FAME, the gifted young men seemed to be a four-way plug-in person—JohnPaulGeorge&Ringo—each lending his personal spark to the circuit of the larger creative entity. Bassist Paul McCartney, charming and outgoing, was as pleasingly facile at life as he was at composing melodies. Lead guitarist George Harrison was the quietly spiritual devotee of Indian music. Drummer Ringo Starr was the unpretentious Everyman with an innately comic temperament. And rhythm guitarist John Lennon was the creative mainspring: thoughtful, tough-minded, a voracious reader and born rebel. Together they were the Beatles, and together they managed to rise from the streets of Liverpool, England, to turn hand-me-down American rock 'n' roll into the most vital art form of the last decades of the century.

September 22, 1967

1962 Ringo Starr joins and completes group
1964 Beatlemania conquers America
1967 *Sgt. Pepper*
1968 *White Album*
1970 Group breaks up
1980 John Lennon killed in New York City

The Beatles began with John Lennon, who grew up on Liverpool's Penny Lane. Deserted by his father shortly after birth, he was sent to live with an aunt in the suburbs, and grew up with a rebellious streak. He was well into his teens when the rock 'n' roll of America's new hitmakers—Elvis Presley, Little Richard, Chuck Berry and Jerry Lee Lewis—shook him to his shoes. By his 16th year, he had formed his first band, the Quarrymen, and had enlisted Paul McCartney, the son of a cotton salesman and band leader, as a guitar player. They began to write songs together almost as soon as they had tuned up. Within two years, George Harrison, a bus driver's son, had joined the Quarrymen, and the band's members were actually earning some money.

Their growing reputation took them to club dates in the gritty seaport of Hamburg, West Germany, where they eventually changed their name to the Beatles and came to favor black leather jackets, pegged pants, stomper boots—and speed pills.

Just as American rockers hit a creative slump, the Beatles' music flourished. It was a peak-velocity transplant of U.S. rock, with its original blistering spirit not only restored but also exalted. Catching the local buzz, a Liverpool record-store owner named Brian Epstein signed on as the group's manager in 1961 and cleaned up its act. By the end of 1962, the boys had a producer, George Martin, then best known as a maker of novelty records. There was one final change of personnel: drummer Pete Best was replaced by Richard Starkey, a superior musician who went by the name Ringo Starr.

It took just a month for the second Beatles single, *Please Please Me*, to reach the top of the English charts. That was in January 1963. One year later, *I Want to Hold Your Hand* came out in the U.S., the Beatles played the *Ed Sullivan Show*, and it seemed for a while that both sides of the Atlantic were up for grabs. The Beatles' charm offensive was complete: they were witty and irreverent, "good copy" for the media with their long haircuts and nasal Liverpudlian accents—and their melodies and harmonies were catchy and distinctive.

Their future as pop stars seemed set: more *She Loves You*, more money, maybe a movie or two. But the "lads" surprised everyone by exercising a compulsion for growth and experimentation. Surprise: their first film, *A Hard Day's Night*, turned out to be a brilliant, cinema verité essay on pop stardom. Surprise: with the inspired aid of Martin, their music evolved; in just two years, *She Loves You* gave way to the eerie sitar sounds of *Norwegian Wood*, the haunting string quartet of *Eleanor Rigby*, the hilarious aural collage of *Yellow Submarine*. Surprise: their lyrics changed from "yeah-yeah-yeah" to become expressive, nuanced and provocative.

The Beatles retired from touring in 1966, determined to spend more time in the studio, which they now regarded as their artistic canvas. The result was their landmark 1967 album, *Sgt. Pepper's Lonely Hearts Club Band*, which perfectly captured a moment in popular culture—the psychedelic Summer of Love. TIME's cover story hailed the new album as "a

guaranteed package of psychic shivers … it sizzles with musical montage, tricky electronics and sleight-of-hand lyrics that range between 1920s ricky-tick and 1960s raga."

Other great songs and records—*The White Album, Abbey Road*—followed. But after Brian Epstein's accidental death from an overdose of sleeping pills in 1967, the group's center failed to hold. Once the Beatles had excelled at channeling the cultural upheavals of the decade into their music; now the task seemed to drag them down and polarize them. In particular, John's courtship and marriage to Japanese avant-garde artist Yoko Ono changed the group's chemistry. Paul finally went his own way, breaking up the group in the spring of 1970. The four men, still young, embarked on solo careers that were marked by personal and artistic ups-and-downs. But the Beatles ended where they began, with Lennon. In 1980, one month after he and Yoko emerged from five years of seclusion to release the fine album *Double Fantasy*, John was murdered by a deranged fan outside his home in New York City.

The impact of the Beatles transcended music: they were the heralds of a youth-driven pop culture that would take over the globe. And their music lives on, eternally fresh, seemingly out of time: they sang ballads that could almost be Elizabethan, rock songs that still sound like the distant future. Like Picasso, the Beatles refused to settle into a comfortable creative niche. Like Gershwin, they mixed serious and popular art into a wondrous new alloy. And like Einstein, they bent elementary laws: JohnPaulGeorge&Ringo was one whole that was greater than the sum of its parts. ∎

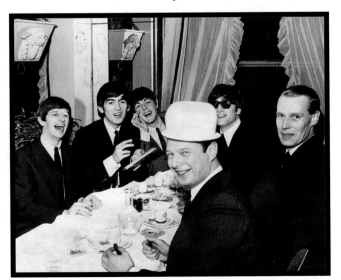

FAB SIX: It's a larf! Celebrating their first No. 1 U.S. hit are, from left, Ringo, George, Paul, manager Brian Epstein (with a chamber-pot crown), John and producer George Martin

JANUARY 17, 1938 From his early "prairie houses" to his influential skyscraper designs and spiraling Guggenheim Museum, Frank Lloyd Wright influenced generations of architects.

MAY 9, 1938 Renaissance show-business man Orson Welles triumphed in a host of forms—in the theater, in live radio drama, and as the director of film classics like *Citizen Kane.*

MARCH 14, 1960 While Hollywood chased the mass market, Sweden's Ingmar Bergman expanded cinema's scope with films that were deeply psychological and highly philosophical.

JULY 17, 1964 Training his eye on a tiny patch of Mississippi, novelist William Faulkner explored the secrets of the heart and the soul of the South in rich prose and modernist forms.

OCTOBER 21, 1946 Son of a famous turn-of-the century actor and at one time a sailor, playwright Eugene O'Neill converted his experiences into searing, poetic dramas.

MARCH 6, 1950 An American who settled in Britain, poet and critic T.S. Eliot captured the shattered consciousness of post–World War I Europe in his seminal poem *The Waste Land*.

JULY 30, 1965 Describing his work as "pictorial arrangements of images that obsess me," Russian-born Marc Chagall crafted richly evocative paintings of folk art and village life.

SEPTEMBER 3, 1979 Visual poet of the wide open spaces, Ansel Adams chronicled America's Western landscapes in photographs of crystal clarity and soaring perspective.

INDEX

CREDITS